N·E·W H·A·M·P·S·H·I·R·E

N·E·W H·A·M·P·S·H·I·R·E

AN ILLUSTRATED HISTORY
OF THE GRANITE STATE

RONALD JAGER AND GRACE JAGER

PICTURE RESEARCH UNDER THE SUPERVISION
OF R. STUART WALLACE
"PARTNERS IN PROGRESS" BY KATHRYN GROVER
PRODUCED IN COOPERATION WITH THE
NEW HAMPSHIRE HISTORICAL SOCIETY

Windsor Publications, Inc.
Woodland Hills, California

Excerpt from "The Gift Outright" from *The Poetry of Robert Frost* edited by Edward Connery Latham. Copyright 1942 by Robert Frost
Copyright ©1969 by Holt, Rinehart and Winston.
Copyright ©1970 by Leslie Frost Ballantine.
Reprinted by permission of Holt, Rinehart and Winston, Publishers

Windsor Publications, Inc.
History Books Division
Publisher: John M. Phillips
Editorial Director: Lissa Sanders
Production Supervisor: Katherine Cooper
Senior Picture Editor: Teri Davis Greenberg
Senior Corporate History Editor: Karen Story
Corporate History Editor: Phyllis Gray
Marketing Director: Ellen Kettenbeil
Production Manager: James Burke
Design Director: Alexander D'Anca
Typesetting Manager: E. Beryl Myers
Proofreading Manager: Doris R. Malkin

Staff for *New Hampshire: An Illustrated History of the Granite State*
Editor: Annette Igra
Picture Editor: Laurel H. Paley
Editorial Assistants: Susan Block, Patricia Buzard, Judith Hunter, Patricia Morris, Pat Pittman
Sales Manager: Michele Sylvestro
Production Artists: Ellen Hazeltine, Chris McKibbin
Proofreaders: Henriette Henderson, Jeff Leckrone, Kaylene Ohman
Typographer: Barbara Neiman

Designer: John Fish

Library of Congress Cataloging in Publication Data

Jager, Ronald.
    New Hampshire, an illustrated history of the Granite State.

    "Produced in cooperation with the New Hampshire Historical Society."
    Bibliography: p.
    Includes index.
    1. New Hampshire—History. 2. New Hampshire—Description and travel. 3. New Hampshire—Industries.
I. Jager, Grace. II. New Hampshire Historical Society.
III. Title.
F34.J33   1983   974.2   83-17117
ISBN 0-89781-069-4

C·O·N·T·E·N·T·S

Frontispiece: Upon its completion in 1870, the China Mill was a major additon to the tiny mill village of Suncook. George McConnell's idyllic painting China Mill *captured the grandeur of the mill in 1871 without reference to the mill's unsightly tenements (built for its workers and known collectively as "China Village"). New York State Historical Association, Cooperstown.*

F·O·R·E·W·O·R·D

In 1823 a group of New Hampshire citizens decided to form an historical society for the purpose of "discovering, procuring, and preserving whatever may relate to the natural, civil, literary, and ecclesiastical history" of the Granite State. After 160 years the New Hampshire Historical Society is proud to be a part of putting New Hampshire's "natural, civil, literary, and ecclesiastical history" between the covers of one book. This has been a cooperative venture from the start, involving two creative authors, various staff members of the Historical Society, and the experienced, professional resources of Windsor Publications. We hope New Hampshire readers will like the result.

The purpose of *New Hampshire: An Illustrated History of the Granite State* is fairly obvious. There has long been a need for a one-volume, current history of New Hampshire that is readable and authoritative, well illustrated, handsomely published, and reasonable in price. The intent here was not simply to *tell* New Hampshire's story, but to *show* it, give it a pulse of its own, and

involve readers in their New Hampshire surroundings.

In this endeavor, the Historical Society and Windsor Publications were fortunate to enlist Ronald and Grace Jager. They have performed the difficult task of squeezing 360 years of New Hampshire history into one, brief volume. By necessity, their text is selective and interpretive; it is also grounded solidly upon the best published and unpublished material available. Better still, it is readable and enjoyable. Good history and good writing belong together.

Anyone perusing this volume and noticing the "Partners in Progress" section will conclude that this book is a form of "subscription" history. In return for its support, the subscribing organization's business history is included in the book. Subscription history was not invented by the New Hampshire Historical Society or Windsor Publications. It has taken various forms and has been the standard means of publishing state, county, and local histories for almost 200 years. New Hamp-

Gosport Village on Star Island is depicted circa 1977—in the white light of the Shoals—by John Hatch of Durham. Courtesy, Amoskeag National Bank & Trust Company

shire's first state historian, Jeremy Belknap, relied upon swelling subscription lists and a modest grant from state government to complete his three-volume *History of New-Hampshire* in 1792. In recent years government subsidies and grants have come to the rescue of some state and local histories; others rely upon support from local businesses, organizations, and individuals. This volume of subscription history follows a similar path to that taken by the state histories of Everett Stackpole, Hobart Pillsbury, and J. Duane Squires. That is pretty good company.

It should also be noted that the "Partners in Progress," whose various stories have been told superbly by Kathryn Grover, do not represent the sum total of New Hampshire's leading corporations and organizations. Obviously these supporters are among New Hampshire's leaders; some of their New Hampshire roots run deep, while others best represent current economic development. Without their support, this volume would not have been possible.

New Hampshire: An Illustrated History of the Granite State is not meant to be *by, of,* or *for* any particular group in New Hampshire. Given the limits of one volume, this book is meant to help us all appreciate the New Hampshire experience. We are all a part of this experience; we all have a vested interest. It is the fervent hope of all of us who teach and publish New Hampshire history that this volume will not only be exciting and rewarding in its own right, but that it will encourage New Hampshire people—natives and newcomers alike—to take an active role in New Hampshire's heritage.

R. Stuart Wallace
Editor
Historical New Hampshire
New Hampshire Historical Society

I·N·T·R·O·D·U·C·T·I·O·N

New Hampshire is a small state, heavy with history. It began life as we know it in the 1620s, that decade of New England beginnings, and grew up to become a vigorous seacoast province and one of the 13 original states. Livelihood for the early settlers lay in lumbering and fishing, and only later in husbandry. In the 19th century the rivers of New Hampshire worked harder than any rivers of record, turning manufacturing wheels and propelling massive textile industries. Late in the 20th century came the high technology businesses.

New Hampshire has an 18-mile coastline, a bright edge of sand between Maine and Massachusetts, with a superb harbor at the outlet of the Piscataqua River, long the center of a maritime culture. Inland the terrain quickly becomes uneven, then rugged, and is eventually crowned in the north by the bold beauty of the White Mountains. In 1850 half the land in the state was cleared for farming, but today 86 percent of it is wooded. However, pastoral landscapes abound, and there is considerable farming still, especially in the southern half, tucked into the spaces between the peremptory suburbs and the equally peremptory woods. In the shades at the edge of live farms are scenic ruins of dead farms: old roads pockmarked with cellar holes and former pastures embraced by stone walls of green and gray, a pain in the back for those who built them then but balm to the eyes of those who view them now. Though some of the memories of the state are maritime and some are industrial, the fondest memories of New Hampshire are rural memories.

The state is somewhat culturally self-conscious, in the manner of New England states generally. Residents suspect that elsewhere in the nation old New England is thought to be something of a national antique—to be kept dusted off and displayed for its authenticity, but a bit too fragile or fussy for the daily grind. Against this is blunt New Hampshire assertiveness: high in electronics, first in mountains, last in taxes, the Presidential primary state, Live Free or Die... uneasy sloganeering. No poise

there. Abetting the self-consciousness is a long, long ambivalence toward Massachusetts, dating as far back as 1640, when New Hampshire towns first joined their governments to the Bay Colony, and continuing through the centuries as Boston capital intermittently funded and drained New Hampshire enterprise. Persistent voices say that New Hampshire is part Vermont, part Maine, part Massachusetts—no center. Such voices are from elsewhere and invite retort in New Hampshire accents that the state has the assets of its neighbors—bucolics, wilderness, coastline—without the liabilities.

The strength of the state, the source of its surprising coherence, may be simply its history—long, complicated, densely packed, and very much present. It is a past unavoidably present in every stone wall and meetinghouse green and in every native disposition to believe that, for almost anything from town meetings to old roads, durability automatically confers distinction. Appropriately, the New Hampshire State Constitution is older even than the U.S. Constitution. A long unity of historical experience, much of it governmental if not political, binds the state top to bottom, just as it had earlier bound the old seacoast towns with the young Connecticut River towns through the political stress of the Revolutionary War, which nearly uncoupled them. The experience has overcome the burdens of major economic shifts and the accidents of location, size, topography, and the arbitrary cut of state boundaries. New Hampshire is a small state, a large community. Any resident can drive to Concord, the capital city, there to look in upon a legislature that has accumulated over 300 years of bent but unbroken legislative history, and still get home in time for dinner.

*   *   *

From the first, the town in New Hampshire was chartered as the locus of government and society: it created schools, hired pastors, elected selectmen, passed ordinances, sent representatives to the General Court, imposed its own taxes, marked its

own bounds, thought its own thoughts. It was New Hampshire towns that recreated the state government when English authority faltered at the outset of the Revolutionary War. In New Hampshire the town possesses a memory; and one of the things it remembers is that it was there before there was a state. Cities came much later: Manchester was first in 1846. Counties are only collections of towns. No wonder it is still widely supposed that the town is the natural instrument of social cohesion and the town meeting the automatic standard of political democracy.

The state itself is the other unit possessing a memory, and one thing it remembers is that its origins and career amount to far more than the sum of town parts. Over time towns and townspeople have come to see, sometimes eagerly, often wearily, that in many areas the state is the unit of significance. This book is a state history. Readers may or may not find here that favorite vignette from a favorite town. We hope they do; but there are too many favorites.

*   *   *

History books are keepers of the public memory and also imaginative creations. Only the inert matters of fact are absolutely given: the rest is endless choice and decision and revision for authors. What data, what context, what meaning? Seen in what light and pattern? Like any book of history this book, too, is full of facts, but it is not meant to be the largest possible pile of information about New Hampshire. History is also color and yarn and connection and drama and nuance—a way of repossessing the past. Sometimes a few big, rough ideas are helpful in nudging the pesky little facts gently into place.

We try to lay out the New Hampshire drama in terms of the four large themes that we think best accommodate the historical experience of the state. These four are: natural history, political-social history, economic history, cultural history. Each dominates one of the four parts of the book. Once the big themes presented themselves, the historical order in which they demanded attention was automatic, for they build upon each other.

The theme of the first part, "Land and Water," is the natural environment, primary encounters with primary things: the terrain the New Hampshire pioneers found, the shores they fished, the boundaries they drew, and the transformation wrought in the land as it evolved from wilderness to farmland to abandonment to a sometimes fragile ecology. That part looks at New Hampshire as possession, commodity; the second part, "Government and People," looks at the state as place, community. What political and social institutions arose upon this land? How did they work and who worked them? What was/is it like to live here? The third part, "Economy and Industry," looks at the Granite State as it became part of an industrial world, through its transportation, manufacturing, textile, granite mining, and lumber enterprises. Though that story pervades the whole life of the state, it focuses on the 19th century and thereafter. We regard the independent contemporary part, "Partners in Progress," as a continuation of it.

The theme of the fourth part, "Mind and Spirit," reaches across the whole spectrum of the state's history to reflect the way religion, learning, and art colored other things, supplied meaning and restated historical experience. Artists of the 19th century made New Hampshire's mountains the symbol of the early American wilderness; likewise, in our own century the poet Robert Frost enlarged New England again and made it, almost, a symbol of America. There have been mythic contours to the New Hampshire landscape ever since the White Mountains were first admired from the sea, and ever since the land was first deplored—and relished—as "this remote and howling wilderness."

Ronald Jager
Grace Jager

I

L·A·N·D
A·N·D W·A·T·E·R

Perhaps more than any other painting, Maxfield Parrish's New Hampshire, *also entitled* Thy Templed Hills, *has been used to extol the state's rural splendor. Parrish, one of America's most popular painters, lived and kept a studio in Plainfield, New Hampshire, from 1898 until his death 68 years later. Painting from the collection of the Vermont National Bank, Windsor Office. Photograph courtesy,* The Magazine Antiques

CHAPTER ONE

N·A·T·U·R·A·L

B·O·U·N·D·A·R·I·E·S

Under the forests of New Hampshire, under the earthy mantle, the texture of the rocky substratum has a certain grain, a grain weathered and worn down by the ages, but yet visible, just as the grain is visible on the old pine boards of a country barn. The grain in the rock of New Hampshire, unimaginably old and going back to the ancient convulsions that broke the crust of this part of the Earth, runs essentially north-south and, like any weathered grain, it is brought out by the wearing away of the softer rock that exposes the harder lines. The Connecticut Valley is a worn-away part, as is the Merrimack Valley and, farther north, the Androscoggin Valley and the great notches, Pinkham, Crawford, and Franconia. Between the notches, accenting the grain, are ranges of mountains and, farther south, there is the long range of hills and highland from Kearsarge to Monadnock. The grain is conspicuous farther west in Vermont, in the wrinkles of the Green Mountains and the worn-away Champlain Valley. In lots of New Hampshire ledges and outcroppings of rock the fine grain appears.

Before man came, before the Ice Age, before the Old Man of the Mountains settled here, before the dinosaurs, millions of years back into the mists of time, there were already hills and high mountains in these parts. The Earth's surface, a layer of ancient rock, surged under the hills. Molten granite was cooking in the bowels of the earth, boiling up, heaving the crust, buckling it, making long tears in it, squeezing granite toward the surface to cool, creating the infrastructure of a future Granite State. That was two or three hundred million years ago. The pressure from below, bending and tearing the surface, also tilted the entire New England landscape southeast toward the Atlantic and poured out the ancestors of the Connecticut and Merrimack rivers toward the sea. The rivers cut down along the grain through northern Massachusetts to the Atlantic. The Connecticut River, too, such was the tilt, might have spilled out eastward but for the heave of the Monadnock and Berkshire ranges. Perhaps already then the ancestral Contoocook River, also spilling eastward because of the tilt, got caught in the lines of the grain and was sent northward—

odd for a New Hampshire river then, and unique now—eventually breaking out and dashing across the grain again to join the Merrimack.

Thereafter, very slowly, through eons and eons of time, New Hampshire settled down in bedrock, gathered vegetation, gathered topsoil, gathered composure. The mountains wore down to stumps during millions of years of calm. Erosion exposed granite that had cooled under the rocky crust. Lakes drained or died. The rivers of the land ran smoothly without waterfalls through long and shallow valleys. Dinosaurs roamed. New Hampshire lay as if it were in the summertime of some grand and transcendent rhythm of the seasons.

Then came the Ice Age. Earth's temperature dropped just enough to affect the snow level in Canada. Each summer as usual the snow melted northward from Pennsylvania to northern Canada; but each fall, when the new snow started, the point of melt-back was a bit farther south. The glacier that, then as now, caps the North Pole was creeping south two steps each winter and retreating one step each summer. No matter if the steps were but a few hundred feet a year. There were thousands and thousands of years for the glacier to grow down out of Canada—thin and benign at the edge in summer, rigid and deep farther back, packed by its own weight into ice. Creeping through the St. Lawrence Valley, up over the ridge, down over the Connecticut Lakes, toward the White Mountains it came, a long white slither, winter by winter, deeper and deeper. Winds scooped up water from the ocean and poured it out on the glacier as snow. As it grew the glacier folded the forests of New Hampshire along its advancing edge into its soft, mushy embrace at first; but inevitably the summer came when it didn't release the trees but froze them rigid in its grip and sheared them off or ground them up.

Maybe a thousand years, maybe two, it took the ice sheet to grow and shove its way from the White Mountains in the north to Mt. Monadnock in the south, then to plow on for ages more. Miles deep it piled up, a frozen flood of Biblical proportions covering the White Mountains, range after range. The sheer weight of the ice turned the bottom of the heap to mush—an ever-shifting, melting, freezing, rocky mass endeavoring to ooze southward from the greater pressure to the north. Walls of rock were torn from the lee side of cliffs—the south or southeast side—or jammed into the ancient channels where they broke up the floors of the old rivers and formed, for future waterpower, the Amoskeag Falls, Bellows Falls, and all the others. As the glacier plowed on like a bulldozer, its force and pressure ground up 10 to 12 feet of bedrock and scooped out lake and river valleys, while rocks, frozen in the slush, sandpapered the surface of the mountains, leaving scours still visible today on top of Mt. Kearsarge and many other places. Altogether it was a mighty drama in white and in slow motion, ghastly, gorgeous, and irresistible—sweeping everything in its path.

Geologists agree that in the Eastern states the glacier reached approximately to Long Island, paused, and then from a slight shift in climate, began slowly to recede, melting back north as deliberately as it had crept south, dropping cargo in its tracks. Then the whole thing, start to finish, happened again. And again. Probably four times. In New Hampshire the Ice Age with its four separate glaciers extended from about a million years ago to what is, in geological terms, only yesterday. As the last glacier melted back, only 12,000 to 15,000 years ago, films of debris accumulated at the edges of temporary lakes, settling down into future farmland. Streams of melt water ran through tunnels in the lower glacier, piling up long veins of sand and gravel, called "eskers." Left in place were large boulders ("erratics") miles from their now-known place of origin. Smaller rocks on the tops of mountains, including Mt. Washington, show by their mineral composition that they came from other mountains. During the sum-

mers of the melting, temporary lakes dropped the sand that washed into them, and when the lakes froze in winter, dropped the clay suspended in the water, dropped sand again the next summer, clay the next winter—thus creating the "varves," the sand/clay layers familiar to every New Hampshire bulldozer operator.

When the last glacier peeled back northward the region lay as if at springtime. And, indeed, behind the retreating ice the New Hampshire landscape would have been as attractive as an abused and muddy driveway on a sullen March day. Moreover, the last glacier that had passed its rough edges against the face of the state and had chiseled away at the rock where its predecessors had chiseled, had finally completed and left there a glacial trademark as if to herald a wholly new era. In that springtime, 15,000 years ago, there peered out from under the masses of rotting ice and rock and mud the Old Man of the Mountains—an eerie human profile glowering upon a scene devoid of vegetation and still intolerable for human life.

All that then remained was to clothe the bony nakedness of Earth with the soft green of virgin forests, the work of just a few centuries. That is when the New Hampshire whose lush and rugged contours we now know and love really began.

The White Mountains

At the basis of history itself is the story of encounters with the land, bringing it into the service of human need; this is especially true of New Hampshire's history, where so much of the terrain, fiercely inhospitable when first found, was developed with such hardihood and patience.

The White Mountains are the centerpiece of the New Hamp-

Pascatway River in New England
by I:S: *is the best map of its time of
the coast of New Hampshire and the
area around the Piscataqua River.
Drawn in London and now owned
by the British Museum, the map is
remarkable in its overall accuracy,
its rich historical detail, its decorative
figures, and even its doggerel verse
dedication to the Duke of York, later
James II. Internal evidence dates
this masterpiece about 1660. Courtesy, the British Museum*

*To artists the light on the Saco River
has often seemed golden, and the
river "sweetly sinuous." In 1899
Benjamin Champney wrote, "if one
was a poet, no more charming
scenes (than the valley of the Saco)
could be found to inspire a pastoral."
Photograph by Bill Finney*

Colonel George Boyd's country seat at Portsmouth, built in the 1740s, served as the country seat of several other owners before Boyd purchased it in 1771. Located on a tidal creek with a wharf and available timber, the estate also included two warehouses, a garden, turning mills, and gristmills. This "South-West Prospect" was painted in 1774, the year Boyd left Portsmouth for England to wait out the Revolution. Returning in 1787, Boyd died on board ship two days before reaching his estate. Courtesy, Lamont Gallery, Phillips Exeter Academy

This William H. Bartlett colored print entitled Mount Washington and the White Hills *was published by S.T. Davies circa 1836. Courtesy, New Hampshire Historical Society (NHHS)*

From earliest times cormorants have been a common sight on the rocky ledges of the New Hampshire coast. Photograph by Timothy Savard. Courtesy, New Hampshire Times

A telephoto lens brings out the Paleozoic wrinkles in the face of the Old Man of the Mountains. Photograph by Dick Smith. Courtesy, State of New Hampshire

shire landscape, and the Reverend Jeremy Belknap of Dover is the dean of New Hampshire historians. These two met just 200 years ago, when Belknap was writing a history of New Hampshire going back to the English settlements of the 1620s. Like any educated man of his age, he regarded history as having two major themes: "natural history," and what was then called "civil history." On both he was eager to examine all the evidence at hand. For the natural history part of his book it was appropriate, therefore, for him to go and study directly the White Mountains. Nobody had ever studied them; few had climbed them, and fewer had written anything about them.

It is likely that Jeremy Belknap had read the first known account of the ascent of Mt. Washington in John Winthrop's famous *History of New England.* Winthrop's journal for the year 1642—which was before white men had even climbed the Berkshires—records that someone named Darby Field of Exeter, New Hampshire, first "went to the top of the white hill." Indian companions accompanied him "within eight miles of the top, but durst go no further, telling him that no Indian ever dared go higher, and that he would die if he went." Perhaps the Indian fear had been originally based upon the solid fact that the weather on Mt. Washington is notoriously treacherous and severe. Sudden storms break, mists and clouds often shroud the top, a world-record wind of 231 miles per hour has been recorded there, and avalanches are common in the winter. It is said that more people have died on its slopes in the last hundred years than on any other American mountain. But Winthrop says that "two Indians took courage by his example and went with him." Field climbed Mt. Washington a second time that same summer and seven years later he died, still a young man. The Indians would not have been surprised.

In Belknap's library there were other tidbits about these mountains. One might have been the Englishman John Josselyn's book *New-England's Rarities,* which describes the outlook from the top of the highest mountain: "the Country beyond the Hills Northward is daunting terrible, being full of rocky Hills, as thick as Mole-hills in a Meadow, and cloathed with infinite thick Woods." The thick woods reach up to about 4,000 to 4,500 feet on the average, leaving nearly two dozen peaks above treeline, like molehills in a meadow.

Fragmentary statements such as these were the main written accounts available to supplement the hearsay and Indian lore of the White Mountains in Belknap's time, more than 150 years

New Hampshire's White Mountains are crowned with the snow-covered peaks of the Presidential Range. Mt. Hancock is in the right foreground, while Webster Cliffs, marking the southern entrance to Crawford Notch, is right of center. Photograph by Dick Smith. Courtesy, Society for the Protection of New Hampshire Forests (SPNHF)

after New Hampshire had been first settled at the coast less than 100 miles away. But if Belknap was to write about New Hampshire, he would have to write about the white hills—"white" because sailors frequently reported seeing the frosted peaks against the blue horizon on clear autumn days. So he organized a scientific expedition to the mountains.

Belknap and six or seven others set out from Dover in July 1784 for the top of the mountain that was later named (by Belknap, most likely) Mt. Washington. They took with them all kinds of clumsy gear: telescopes, compasses, a surveyor's chain, a barometer with a bag of mercury, three muskets, and pistols. It was quite an ordeal for a collection of overloaded scientists, strangers to mountains: a steep and pathless climb led by the rotund and enthusiastic preacher with his notebook. They would have struggled up through the hardwoods and then into the white and black spruces, through stunted evergreens beaten shapeless by the wind and seven months' snow. Finally, breaking into the open they would find themselves climbing up around and over great slabs of rock, seemingly thrown up in heaps. The loose rocks strewn over the peaks are more the result of frost breaks than of glaciers. At the top they could look out upon two dozen neighboring rocky peaks, all kept bare by the cold and incessant wind. Belknap's main party made it all the way, but the leader himself gave out and returned to camp before treeline. "In great enterprises," he said afterward, "to have attempted is enough." The barometer broke on the ascent and the main crew gave a reading at the mountaintop that they knew was inaccurate—9,000 feet. Belknap wrote that an accurate instrument would show that Mt. Washington was more than 10,000 feet high. It is actually 6,288 feet above sea level.

Beneath that summit New Hampshire was spread out before them, an irregular triangle, today comprising 9,282 square miles, 90 miles wide at the base and 120 miles long. From the mountaintop the encircling view, but for the bare peaks, was one of rocky slides and "infinite thick woods." "Nature has, indeed, in that region," wrote Belknap, "formed her works on a large scale."

Why, more than a century earlier, had anyone come at all to this inhospitable terrain? Part of the answer is that the English settlers had not really known what they were getting into.

Jeremy Belknap, Congregational pastor in Dover from 1766 to 1786, was the first historian of New Hampshire, and it is commonly said that he remains the best. He knew firsthand the last years of the colonial era, and he saw the Revolution come and go. Loyal to the American cause, he also retained friendly relations with Royal Governor John Wentworth. Belknap's History of New-Hampshire *was published in three volumes between 1784 and 1792. Its thorough scholarship and literary merit place it among the best historical writing in 18th-century America. Courtesy, Massachusetts Historical Society*

CHAPTER
TWO
P·O·L·I·T·I·C·A·L
B·O·U·N·D·A·R·I·E·S

At the beginning of the 17th century, with the Spanish Armada defeated, the English mind, dreaming of lordship of the seas, turned with fascination toward the strange new continent beyond the ocean to the west. Helping to bend English thoughts toward America was the work of international promoters such as Sir Walter Raleigh and Captain John Smith. There was also Sir Ferdinando Gorges, who by 1615 had three native New Hampshire Indians living on display in his household in England. What stories they told of the riches in the valley of the Piscataqua we do not know. We do know that a few probing voyages and quite a few glowing reports pictured a store of natural resources in New England that could never be used up: fish, furs, timber, perhaps even farmland. Maybe there was gold, too, and possibly still a passage northwest to Asia. By 1620 the King had been persuaded to create a Council for New England, with Gorges as president and with authority to grant land and create trade and settlements in North America between the 40th and 48th parallels—roughly between the present Hudson and St. Lawrence rivers. The wealth of the New World was to be tapped.

The Council for New England

Retrospectively, the Council for New England seems to be the spiritual ancestor of that legendary Yankee who inherited a hundred measured acres and later sold them as three lots, each of "40 acres more or less." One thing to be said for the council is that under its aegis New Hampshire got started. On the other hand, the council didn't always know what it was doing. Within little more than a decade (1622-1635) the council's grants created boundary and ownership confusion that 150 years of litigation, and the fattening of teams of lawyers, politicians, and developers, could never sort out. Bounds of council grants were vague and sometimes overlapped; some lands were granted several times. True, they had only very poor maps and scant knowledge of the land; but this seems to have enforced no discretion. Their grantees, who included members of the council, fully expected to make money off developments, and that didn't work out either. New Hampshire was born struggling for life: a collection of rather poorly conceived settlement efforts that cen-

tered around the Piscataqua River and didn't do very well.

It started out directly enough with David Thomson of Plymouth, England, a clerk for the Council for New England, who was paid for his services with 6,000 acres and an island in the New World—somewhere in the council's territory. Accordingly, his ship *Jonathan,* having followed the *Mayflower* out of Plymouth by a bit over two years, eventually arrived at what the Indians called Pannaway—now Odiorne's Point in Rye—on April 16, 1623. Claiming this land as his own, he and his wife and their small company built a house and set about planning a trading post and a fishing operation. Though still without its name, New Hampshire was on its way. Within three years, however, Thomson moved away to Boston and took up life on an island in the harbor; and his little settlement, the first in the state, is presumed to have passed to the brothers Hilton who were supervising the activities.

Meanwhile, back in England the Council for New England had been giving away this very land to others: once to John Mason and Sir Ferdinando Gorges in 1622, next to John Mason alone in 1629. Also in 1629 the council granted several other "patents" (land grants) of uncertain location; and in 1631 John Mason and eight others were granted yet another, called the Piscataqua patent. It included, sure enough, much of the same territory. Then the council collapsed, a disaster; no one at the time realized the extent of the mischief.

John Mason, who probably never set foot on New Hampshire shores, named "his" land, wherever it was exactly, New Hampshire, after his native county in England. He at least had the broadest and most complicated claims to the largest grants. An adventurer by nature, he was also a man who ardently wanted to see this part of the world settled—preferably by Anglicans, not Puritans. It was to be for him both a business and an extension of the Church of England, and he hoped to achieve the development of colonies as an absentee landlord by maneuvers from London.

Under the grants by the council before 1635 there were, besides Thomson's beginnings, a number of other meager efforts directly under John Mason's supervison: a fur trade on the Piscataqua (the natives, however, couldn't supply enough furs), a fishing base, a saltworks (it didn't pay), a lumber mill, and some farms. The records of the time, thin and fragmentary as they are, make it clear that before 1640 most of these scattered efforts struggled more than thrived. Fishing near the Isles of Shoals was immediately successful, but the station there was more a base of commercial operations than a settled colony. By the mid-1630s the community in the Piscataqua Harbor at Strawbery Banke seems to have made some progress at farming—it was recorded in 1632 that 16 hogsheads of corn were being sent from there to Charlestown for grinding. Cattle, horses, and hogs arrived from England, and a few ships returned to England with lumber that found a ready market there.

The harsh truth of the first two decades was that the New World resources were much harder to tap than the early entrepreneurs had expected. A visitor to the Thomson settlement in 1624, Christopher Levett, had summed the matter up in a letter that the next decades could only confirm. "There is fowl, deer, and fish enough for the taking if men be diligent," he wrote of early New Hampshire; but he added, "I will not tell you that you may smell the corn fields before you see the land, neither must men think that corn doth grow naturally (or on trees), nor will the deer come when they are called . . . nor the fish leap into the kettle."

Partly because the settlement was such a struggle to maintain, the question of the ultimate ownership of these large tracts of land could often be ignored by most of the settlers. The uncertain boundaries of the council grants were like time bombs shallowly buried when John Mason died conveniently just as the council itself was killed by internal English politics in 1635. Mason's grandson dug up the claims a generation later and triggered a century of litigation. Considered as real estate, the province of New Hampshire had a curious parentage in John Mason and the Council for New England—fathered by adventure and mothered by indiscretion. Politically, the infant province was an orphan from birth. Granting land was one thing; granting governmental authority was another.

Masons and the Masonian Proprietors

One of the council grants to John Mason put a western limit of 60 miles on the grant. To this day, two-thirds of the residents of New Hampshire live within that 60-mile arc from Portsmouth, and every piece of land owned there has in its legal ancestry the weirdly tangled tale of Masonian claims.

Captain John Mason, who had a strong though questionable claim to New Hampshire up to the 60-mile limit, died in 1635, leaving his New Hampshire claim to a grandson, Robert Tufton Mason. Robert started litigation to recover the land, protesting the "unjust encroachments" of Massachusetts upon his property and trying to collect rent from the residents. His efforts got confused in the political shuffle whereby New Hampshire was established as a Crown Colony in 1680. When Robert Tufton Mason died in 1685, he left his claim to his sons John and Robert, who, as Londoners, found the New Hampshire problem tedious and in 1691 sold the claim—through a London court transaction—to Samuel Allen. Allen got himself appointed lieutenant-governor

Captain John Smith helped to popularize the New England coast with the publication of his book A Description of New England *in 1616. Unfortunately, while helpful with most of the area, Smith's account had little to say about the portion of New England that was to become New Hampshire. He visited the Isles of Shoals, immodestly naming them after himself, and virtually ignored New Hampshire's Great Bay area. In preparing an otherwise excellent map of New England, Smith compensated for ignorance of the region by placing this engraving of himself over present-day New Hampshire. NHHS*

If Captain John Mason and Sir Ferdinando Gorges had had access to accurate maps of the New England coast, perhaps some of the overlapping and otherwise conflicting land grants for "New Hampshire" would have been avoided. Unfortunately, they did not. Pictured is a rather fanciful illustration of "Gorges and Mason naming their provinces." NHHS

of New Hampshire and made a number of moves to take possession of the lands that he now governed. This made him few friends in New Hampshire. Eventually a bargain was struck that would give him all "the waste and unimproved lands" up to 60 miles west in return for his not pushing claim to settled towns in the east. The document was drawn up, and on the day before it was to be signed, Allen died. His son inherited the claim, discovered that there was a mortgage on it, sold half of what remained to a Boston man in August 1706, and then he died. *His* son, then an infant, having inherited the claim or problem, whatever it was, ignored it for 40 years.

Enter another Mason. In the 1740s a great-great-grandson of the original Mason appeared in court claiming that since his grandfather's sale to Allen had been transacted in London and not in New Hampshire, it was invalid, and that therefore *he* had inherited New Hampshire. There was some slim legal basis for this and a lot of smoke in it too; and before the claim was vindicated or the smoke had fully cleared, Mr. Mason shrewdly sold his alleged inheritance to a new corporation of 12 prominent Portsmouth businessmen—friends and relatives of New Hampshire Governor Benning Wentworth.

Calling themselves the "Masonian Proprietors," the new "owners" quickly offered quitclaim deeds to their somewhat nonplussed neighbors in the settled towns and started speedily surveying, mapping, and granting dozens of townships in the "waste and unimproved lands" to the west—Hopkinton, Hillsborough, New London—the boondocks of the day. It was a smooth professional and profitable operation by the Portsmouth aristocracy. Who was to say them nay?

In these transactions—first to last, 1620s to 1740s—it is impossible to sort out exactly what was legal from what was bluff, what was merely complex from what was entirely confused. Obscure inheritance laws and blatant politics colored nearly every move in a game wherein many a reputation and career was made, and many lost. For intricacy and duration as well as for the extent of the stakes, the Masonian controversy set the colonial record in North America. Eventually it was just easier to let the Masonian Proprietors boldly pretend that their title was clear right back to the Indian chiefs and the English kings. The controversy was never resolved; it was dropped.

Land ownership disputes may be dropped for good, but land boundary disputes are often only shelved—to be dusted off again in troublous times. Moreover, boundaries of states are often arbitrary, unnatural, indifferent to ownership of the land and to the grain of the landscape itself. Politics, not nature, determines state boundaries. Or so it seems. Yet there is a complex reciprocity between the claims of the land and the claims of the politicians in the three major boundary controversies that determined the main outline of New Hampshire. In the controversies with Massachusetts and with Vermont, both land and the future of the state itself were very much at issue.

The Massachusetts Boundary Controversy

The northern reach of the Massachusetts Bay Colony had originally been set as "all those lands . . . which lie and be within the space of three English miles to the northward of the . . . Merrimack River *or to the northward of any and every part thereof"* (italics added). The Englishmen who penned those words in the 1620s thought that the entire Merrimack flowed easterly as it does at its outlet. By the time it was common knowledge that it flows south and then cuts sharply east 30 miles to the ocean, there was no one to care, for the settled New Hampshire towns along the coast were part of Massachusetts anyway. Even when the New Hampshire colony was separated off in 1680, the boundary, yonder in the wilderness, didn't much matter. Indeed, when the 10 italicized words were left off the newly chartered description of Massachusetts in 1691, it also concerned few people. Though they had separate assemblies, Massachusetts and New Hampshire shared a governor, and they had common worries about very practical problems such as Indians and Masons. The conveniently vague assumption grew that for some distance, the Merrimack was three miles inside Massachusetts; west of the Merrimack was only wilderness anyway.

About 1720, between Indian wars, Massachusetts opened the dispute with a trivial question—three miles from the *center,* or from the *bank* of the river? A much bigger issue promptly took over and dominated politics for two decades: (a) three miles north of the Merrimack outlet and then on a line straight west? (New Hampshire's claim); or (b) three miles north of "any and every part" of the river? (Massachusetts' claim). Moreover the north-south line that now divides New Hampshire and Maine was also in dispute. Massachusetts, which then "owned" Maine, drew that line so as to put much of upper New Hampshire into Massachusetts (Maine) as well. In Massachusetts' eyes, New Hampshire was just a little coastal enclave like Rhode Island. At issue was more than three-quarters of what is now New Hampshire.

Lieutenant-Governor John Wentworth led the maneuvering for New Hampshire. Local commissions having failed, he managed to present the case in London as the latest version of the Crown's problems with Massachusetts—with New Hampshire loyal to royal interests. Back on the frontiers the legislative assemblies of Massachusetts and New Hampshire were poised like boys drawing a line in the gravel between them, daring the other to cross. Both dared.

First, in the 1720s, there was only pushing: Massachusetts reached up and granted the township of Pennycook (today's Concord); New Hampshire reached over and granted the township of Bow on much the same land; Massachusetts retaliated by granting Suncook on top of parts of Bow and dividing the township into lots; New Hampshire responded by superimposing Bow lots on top of Massachusetts' Suncook lots.

This was confusing, so they started shoving: Massachusetts chartered the whole line of towns straight across the southern edge of present-day New Hampshire. New Hampshire sent distress signals to the King about Massachusetts imposing taxes on New Hampshire citizens and bullying "this poor little province." New Hampshire then boldly raised the ante by entering pleas for a separate governor. The common governor of the two provinces, Jonathan Belcher, wrote to London that the unfortunate inhabitants within these disputed and shifting boundaries had to "live like toads under a barrow," yanked now into the jurisdic-

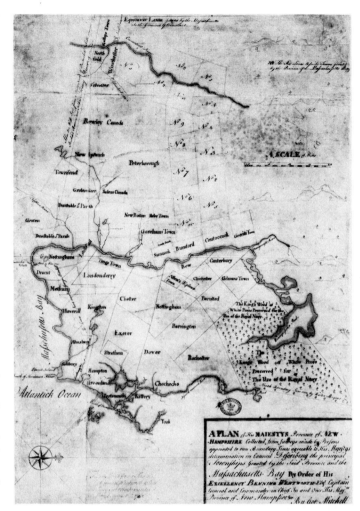

When the New Hampshire/Massachusetts boundary controversy was settled in 1740, authorities in victorious New Hampshire were quick to prepare an accurate map of their enlarged province. As George Mitchell's 1745 map indicates, however, a number of smaller boundary disputes remained to be settled, particularly Kingston's and Londonderry's. Courtesy, Public Record Office, London

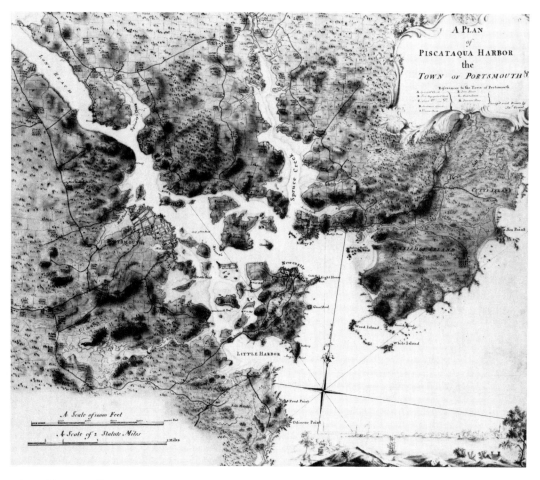

tion of one state, now into another. To complicate matters further, at this time, after nearly a century's lapse, Anglicanism was being carefully revived in Portsmouth. Dr. Arthur Browne, a distinguished Rhode Island cleric, arrived in 1732 to head the new Queen's Chapel in the capital. John Thomlinson had arranged this as the London agent for the New Hampshire colony—explaining carefully, no doubt, the attractive prospects of a compliant "Anglican" New Hampshire colony next to the perpetually troublesome Puritan Massachusetts. Thus the plot thickened.

In London the Privy Council investigated the boundary dispute and made a recommendation to King George II, which he then decreed on March 5, 1740. His decree settled 20 years of contention with a victory for New Hampshire that outreached anyone's wildest dreams. The north-south line with Maine on the east was set where New Hampshire had claimed it and essentially where it is now, securing the North Country for New Hampshire. The south line cut deeply into the traditional claims of Massachusetts: three miles north of the "Course of Merrimack River" to a point north of "Pawtucket Falls and a strait line drawn from there due West cross the said River *till it meets with his Majesty's other Governments"* (italics added).

That fixed the boundary officially, though a satisfactory survey of it was not achieved until 1901. The King's decree clearly put 28 former "Massachusetts towns," hundreds of square miles, into New Hampshire. Many of these towns immediately petitioned Boston and London pleading for readmission to Massa-

chusetts. They got no hearing. The petitioners, wrote New Hampshire's London agent, were "full of false facts, false geography, false reasoning—a most weak but wicked attempt of the unruly province of the Massachusetts Bay." For good measure, Governor Belcher of Massachusetts was fired and replaced by a new governor for that state; and a separate governor, Benning Wentworth, an ardent Anglican, was appointed to the now vastly enlarged province of New Hampshire.

Enlarged to the west, "till it meets with his Majesty's other Governments." Where was that? Of course His Majesty had no idea at all. Presumably, it was wherever New York was bounded on its east—which was very unclear. Thus the explicit solution of the boundary dispute with Massachusetts on the south just as explicitly created—with those eight inexact words—a boundary dispute with New York on the west. Out of the resulting affair between New Hampshire and New York, Vermont was born.

The Vermont Boundary Dispute
Governor Benning Wentworth made the opening move, casually telling Governor Clinton of New York in 1749 that he was about to start making grants "in the unimproved lands within my government" to the west. He then reached far across the Connecticut River and granted a new township to a group of friends who promptly named it Bennington (now Bennington, Vermont; *then* Bennington, New Hampshire). New York's Governor Clinton complained, cited some century-old docu-

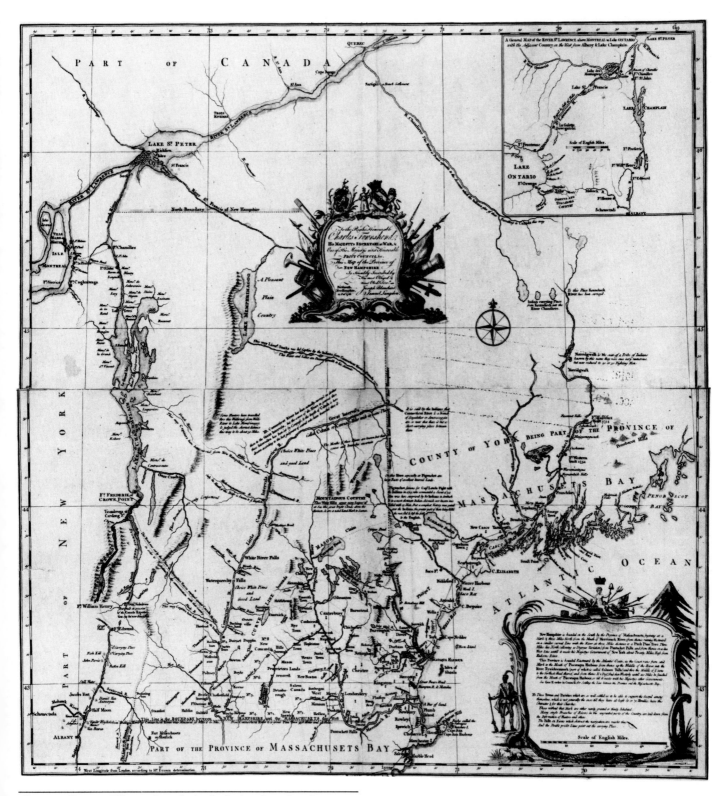

Governor Benning Wentworth undoubtedly had nothing but the greatest admiration for the cartographic skills of Colonel Joseph Blanchard and the Reverend Samuel Langdon when they completed this map of New Hampshire in 1761. The boundaries were somewhat generous. Not only does "New Hampshire" seem to extend well beyond the Connecticut River, but the province's northern boundary lies well north of Lake Memphremagog. NHHS

ments, and let the matter be referred to the Crown. Governor Wentworth simply went on chartering towns, dozens of them, all across the southern part of present-day Vermont. These territories beyond the river came to be called the "New Hampshire grants;" "iniquitous grants" was what the New York governor called them. Well before the Revolutionary War they were populated with a class of stalwart pioneers who, having carved their homes out of the remote wilderness, were serenely defiant of *all* distant governments, whether in Portsmouth or Albany, let alone London.

The problem as it developed was not only that the boundaries were uncertain, but also that the residents of the towns along both sides of the Connecticut increasingly felt an economic and social cohesion among themselves which they shared with neither New York nor the New Hampshire coastal towns.

Though King George tried to clarify matters in 1764 by decreeing the western shore of the Connecticut River as the eastern boundary of New York, this turned out to be just one round in a complicated skirmish that echoed the "line in the dirt" game New Hampshire had played earlier with Massachusetts on the Merrimack. Now the line was the Connecticut River and the adversary was New York. Now the "toads under a barrow" were the New Hampshire grants in "Vermont" as well as a row of New Hampshire towns on the eastern bank who felt akin to them. An association of river towns, first called New Connecticut and then Vermont, appeared and thumbed its nose east and west. By the time the Revolutionary War was well under way Vermonters had a government of sorts, authorized by themselves. Eventually two rows of Connecticut River towns in New Hampshire, long dissatisfied with that state's government, were leaning toward affiliation with Vermont. Dartmouth pamphleteering, arguing that there is "no legal power subsisting in the [NH] colony," and that the future lay with Vermont, encouraged the rebellion against the wartime New Hampshire government. All kinds of jurisdictional claims flared on both sides of the river. Who owed taxes to whom? Which courts had what jurisdictions? The old boundary dispute showed signs of becoming a full-scale civil war. In 1781 Vermont boldly asserted jurisdiction over not only the New Hampshire grants but also over all the dissident towns in New Hampshire and began dropping broad hints of direct negotiations with England. "Unless Congress interferes," wrote President Meshech Weare of the New Hampshire Council, "very probably the sword will decide it." But Vermont was not listening to Congress.

Forty years earlier the King had simply settled matters concerning the Massachusetts border. One longed for a King George again; but this was 1781 and the country was at war with the King. A novel tactic suggested itself, and it turned out to be a masterstroke, namely, to appeal to George Washington. The Commander in Chief of the American army was in Philadelphia with a war on his hands, and he needed to be brought into a turf fight in New England about as much as he needed another Benedict Arnold. But Washington was deeply wise, knowing full well the force of his authority and how to use it with casual grace. The letter he struck off to Governor Chittenton of Vermont pulled everybody up short, and changed the course of New En-gland history.

Chittenton had written to enlist Washington's sympathy for Vermont's ambition, which was essentially this: admission to the Union for Vermont with territories extending into New York on the west and across the Connecticut to the east, including the string of 16 rebellious New Hampshire river towns. Washington replied on January 1, 1782, saying that he could not of course respond in any official capacity, but the request "gives me an opportunity of offering you my sentiments, as an individual," suggesting that this was also "the prevailing opinion of congress." The message was: let Vermont be content, as Congress had earlier proposed, with a western boundary on a line southerly from Lake Champlain to the corner of Massachusetts, and an eastern boundary at the western bank of the Connecticut River, and on that basis apply for admission to the Union as the first new state. The letter went on about how Washington dreaded the thought of restraining territorial claims by "coercion on the part of congress," which in Vermont's case would lead to the "ruin of that state"; how talk of Vermont joining Great Britain had sown "seeds of distrust" and must have been intended only as a clever ploy to deceive the enemy. The letter was shrewd, respectful, conciliatory—and very threatening.

No king could have acted so effectively, for this voice spoke with accents of native authority, earned and conferred in the course of a democratic revolution. The Vermont Assembly, with the New Hampshire delegation temporarily absent, accepted the proposal in principle; and the New Hampshire towns, cast adrift at the river's edge, eventually came back to New Hampshire. The borders of Vermont were essentially set as proposed by Washington and from that time the general territorial and political integrity of both New Hampshire and Vermont were assured. (The definitive resolution of the New Hampshire-Vermont boundary came only with a 1934 U.S. Supreme Court decision that set the boundary at the low-water mark on the western bank of the Connecticut River.)

The natural social and political unity among the Connecticut River towns on both sides of the river was self-evident to everyone: the lines of nature itself provided on the west the Green Mountains and on the east the Kearsarge-Sunapee-Monadnock range, with the river between. As a political idea, centering the new state of Vermont athwart the river reflected the patterns of development and historic experience of the people and it was true to the run of the ancient grain of the rocky substratum. However, Washington's proposal, though it did not originate with him, turned out to be decisive for subsequent history, and it involved for New England an explicit political self-assertion against the shape of the land. Politics conquered the landscape.

The Indian Stream Republic

The Treaty of Paris of 1783, which concluded the Revolutionary War and, incidentally, paved the way for New Hampshire to unite under a new constitution and for Vermont to be admitted to the Union as the 14th state, also planted the seeds of a new boundary dispute to the north. This dispute was with Great Britain, and the entire U.S./Canada line from New Brunswick to New York was at issue. Once more the language that had fixed

Between Walpole on the New Hampshire side and Bellows Falls in Vermont, the waters of the Connecticut roll around "two shelving mountains of rock." In 1784 Enoch Hale of Rindge constructed a bridge there, acclaimed "to exceed any ever built in America in strength, elegance and public utility. . . ." In 1840 the frame of the bridge was found to be weakened from decay. When a new bridge was built upriver, Hale's bridge was cut down and thrown into the Connecticut. This sketch of the original bridge was made by John Trumbull in 1791. Painting from the Charles Allen Munn Collection of Fordham University Library. Photograph courtesy, Frick Art Reference Library

the New Hampshire part of the boundary was ill-chosen. The Treaty of Paris described a part of the new line as running from the source of the St. Croix River to "the northwesternmost head of the Connecticut River." A few words had done it again. Three tributaries might claim the honor of being the "northwesternmost": Halls Stream on the west, Indian Stream in the center, and Perry Stream to the east. Depending upon the choice, about 100,000 acres of excellent, reasonably accessible timberland belonged either to one country or to the other. Many a fine tree went from seedling to sawmill during the 60-year boundary dispute. Indeed, commissions and committees formed to solve the problem came and went, resolutions multiplied and gathered dust, and a whole series of United States Secretaries of State, preeminently John Quincy Adams, wasted their diplomatic skills on non-solutions. While diplomats dithered and quibbled over big issues, a little independent republic grew up in the New Hampshire part of the disputed territory.

The saga of the Indian Stream Republic is a droll bit of history, charming to distant viewers, but far more earnest than charming to the participants. The contest over political authority within the region that is now the town of Pittsburg was more than a generation old when in June 1832, a committee of five Indian Stream residents was appointed by their fellow citizens to draft a constitution for an independent republic. Their document had a preamble and a bill of rights, and laid out the several branches of government, including an assembly composed of all men over 21. In July the constitution was ratified by a 56-3 vote and the new country, the United Inhabitants of Indian Stream Republic,

was in business. They created a militia of 41 men, and one supposes—without direct evidence—that they may even have planned a birchbark navy. However, there quickly developed two political factions in this remote nation; one faction inclined toward annexing Canada, and the other leaned toward an international merger with the United States. In 1835 unrest was so severe among the Republic's inhabitants that civil war seemed likely, and 50 New Hampshire militiamen were sent abroad to restore order. Rocks were thrown. The next year the New Hampshire legislature sent up another commission—which duly recommended, to no one's surprise, that the nation become a part of New Hampshire. The Assembly of the Indian Stream Republic contemplated this for a few years and then agreed. In 1840 the area was incorporated as the town of Pittsburg.

None of these goings on, however, helped anyone to locate the northwesternmost head of the Connecticut River, or to solve the initial boundary question. Eventually the true head of the Connecticut River was located by Lord Ashburton of Great Britain and Daniel Webster, native of New Hampshire and U.S. Secretary of State. Over dinner in Washington, D.C., and no doubt over a map and port that Webster supplied for the occasion, they easily agreed that Halls Stream on the west was indeed the "northwesternmost head" of the river; this "discovery" was incorporated into the larger border resolution. Accordingly, on August 20, 1842, the United States Senate formally ratified a major document, the Webster-Ashburton Treaty, which established the entire northern New England boundary and incidentally defined the boundary of New Hampshire and of Pittsburg.

C·H·A·P·T·E·R
T·H·R·E·E

T·H·E U·S·E A·N·D
R·O·M·A·N·C·E O·F
T·H·E L·A·N·D

In the London of the 1620s they told tall tales of New Hampshire lakes bubbling with beavers. Captain John Mason would have heard the tales and he hoped to develop a major fur trade in his colony. Three years of effort by his agents in the early 1630s produced just 500 pounds of furs, mostly beaver traded from the Indians. The frail project collapsed when Mason died in 1635. Others continued the trade in increasing competition with the more aggressive traders and trappers who came north from Massachusetts. In 1640 Dover tried to regulate activity by encouraging trade with the Indians but forbidding sale of "arms" and "strong water." After 1641 the Massachusetts General Court asserted a monopoly on the New Hampshire fur trade and enforced it by licensing fur traders and forbidding unlicensed trading. Nevertheless, fur trading remained a small-time business in New Hampshire, profitable for only a few. The custom records for 1692 show 54 pounds of beaver and 130 small "fur-skins" sent from New Hampshire to London that year. After that, fur exports from New Hampshire virtually stopped, though local furriers and hatmakers continued using local furs for the next 200 years.

Fishing was another story. Throughout New Hampshire's first century, it was a major enterprise, though it suffered several ups and downs. The 1660s were a high point, the 1690s and the 30 years thereafter were a low point, and the 1720s were another high point.

Already in the 1640s, when the young colony was barely established on the mainland, the Isles of Shoals—some eight miles out from the Piscataqua Harbor—had become a well-known spot for processing fish, and by the 1660s there were as many as 1,500 men working there. Mackerel were salted and cod were dried and both were sent all over Europe, especially Portugal and Spain, as well as to England, the West Indies, and the wine

islands off the African coast. The palate of Catholic Europe became addicted to Isles of Shoals "dun fish," dried cod.

The fishing business broke down drastically in the 1690s. Along the coast severe Indian troubles, including several massacres, demoralized the communities, often bringing enterprise to a standstill. A tax imposed by Massachusetts on its section of the Isles of Shoals so annoyed the fishermen that hundreds of them left Appledore (then called Hog Island), many moving across the bay to Star Island in tax-free New Hampshire. At sea, vessels were being harassed by the French around Nova Scotia. The Shoals population had dropped to about 100 by the end of the decade.

But by the 1720s fishing was back in high gear. The Shoals were booming, New Castle was almost completely a fisherman's town, and fish were used as currency in Portsmouth. One hundred fishing vessels were based in Piscataqua River in 1720, and many of them were owned by merchants who systematically fished off Newfoundland as well as the Shoals regions.

However, after the first dramatic spurt in the 1660s, New Hampshire was always far overshadowed in its fisheries by Massachusetts Bay. Ultimately, fishing was to be Massachusetts' speciality as lumbering was to be New Hampshire's. Indeed, in April 1770 Governor Bellomont of Massachusetts complained to the London Board of Trade that New Hampshire fishing had fallen off because the people there were too preoccupied with lumbering.

Lumber and the Broad Arrow

"Lumber" is an American word, invented in colonial New England. For years the English avoided it in official documents, preferring "timber." New Hampshire was clear on this from the beginning: timber goes into a mill, lumber comes out. There

---

were 20 sawmills in New Hampshire in 1665, 50 by 1700. Most of the lumber that came out of the earliest ones and was not used locally went to Boston. Already by 1680 more than 50 vessels carried New Hampshire lumber to Boston, and in the year 1695 alone more than 100 vessels carried nearly two million board feet of lumber from Portsmouth to Massachusetts.

The building of Boston provided one market, the rebuilding of London after the Great Fire of 1666 provided another. Then there was the barrel-stave business for trading rum and molasses with the West Indies and wine with the islands off the coasts of Africa and Spain. But something bigger still was in the air: England's wars with Spain, then with the Dutch, then with France, decimated the Royal naval stores. Trade problems with Sweden threatened to close off the Baltic Sea area, which for centuries had supplied the British navy with planking, masts, and naval stores. New England pine, oak, and pitch were discovered just in time to keep Europe supplied for its traditional pursuits of mercantilism and warfare.

Since the 1630s entrepreneurs looking for return cargo had bought and taken to England shiploads of lumber, including pine masts, but it was in 1652 that the British Admiralty itself began annual purchases at Portsmouth. Soon thereafter the mast trade came to be the dominant area of the New World timber industry, and for more than 100 years—long enough for a second generation of masts to grow—it continued with little interruption. Portsmouth was the New England center of the trade. Initially, the Admiralty purchased at the dock the lumber, masts, and spars that had been cut, hauled, sawed, and finished to specifications by the New Hampshire loggers. Very soon everybody involved was making money at the business, and the pine and oak forests along the New Hampshire coast were being harvested with a cheerful abandon from the common lands of the four towns and from the no-man's-land up the river. One reason that farming developed so slowly in New Hampshire was that timbering developed so rapidly. So efficient was the Piscataqua River in

draining the pine from its slopes that the British Parliament began to take steps.

A broad arrow was the longstanding insignia of the Royal Navy. A kind of three-toed turkey track, it had for years been branded on cannon, ships, and slaves; and in America after 1685 it was regularly cut into the bark of a pine tree by six blows with a hatchet. That was the year the office of Surveyor of the King's Woods was created for New England and was charged with identifying and branding the trees to be reserved for masts.

The vital question was "Who owned these trees?" Was it those who owned the land on which they grew? By 1699 the Crown, going as far as it dared, officially laid claim (first only in Massachusetts and then, through the legislative Assembly, in New Hampshire as well) to all trees of 24 inches in diameter and upward on land not previously granted to a private person. Inevitably, this opened a blast of disputes about land ownership, to say nothing about the precise meaning of the laws. But the Royal intent was clear and increasingly effective: the Crown was bent on claiming all the large trees in all the future land grants in townships of New Hampshire. (Royal ownership of large trees on private estates had been standard policy in Old England, abolished by the Civil War in 1647, to be reasserted 50 years later in New England.)

Top: Stone walls give definition to the Charles French farm in Washington, New Hampshire, circa 1880. Courtesy, Ronald and Grace Jager

Left: Exactly what use these women will make of their day's catch of kelp is impossible to determine. The year is roughly 1905, and the place is Little Boar's Head. NHHS

Rural New Hampshire is portrayed in this circa 1836 lithograph, View of Meredith, *by William Bartlett. NHHS*

The policy was enforced by stiff penalties for unauthorized cutting, and by the high price offered for finished masts: usually it paid to be legal. Although the government controlled the business through the appointed surveyor, his licensed mast agents, and the network of subcontracting tied to it, such was the demand for lumber in general and masts in particular, and such was the extent of the resources, that it was still a profitable business to be in. It was profitable also for those who ignored the law or who continued to sell masts and lumber to Spain and France after it was made illegal in 1740.

Exact shipping records before 1695 are scarce, but in that year 56 masts of record went to England and an unknown number elsewhere. In 1718, two hundred went to England. In 1742 more than 500 masts of record were exported from the Piscataqua, nearly a fourth of them to the Caribbean and other North American colonies. In 1752 alone, the record year, 554 masts were sent to England.

Too soon, however, the profits were being siphoned off from the choppers and sawyers to the merchants and politicians. Understandably, enormous numbers of the King's mast trees simply disappeared at night and there was, coincidentally, everywhere in the lumberyards an endless supply of boards 23 inches wide. By the middle of the 18th century, New Hampshire Governor Benning Wentworth, who was also Surveyor General of the King's Woods, and whose brother, Hunking, was mast agent for

New Hampshire, was well aware that there was far more profit in controlling the market for himself than in enforcing the law for the King. He kept to appearances, though: every charter the governor authorized for a hill town, no matter how remote from the sea or from any plausible masting route, dutifully carried a clause that reserved all the white pines for His Majesty. When "His Majesty" was George III and the New Hampshire yeoman felt aggrieved against His Majesty's government, he could vent his feelings by going out and chopping down a big pine tree on his own land—if there were any left.

Nearer the coast, the woodcutters in the sawmills and logging crews developed into a class by themselves, hardworking, hard drinking, hard up. Belknap wrote, "The too free indulgence of spiritous liquor, to which this class of people are much addicted, hurts their health, their morals and their interest. They are always in debt, and frequently at law." Casting an eye back from the 1780s over the long New Hampshire experience at thinning its thick woods, Belknap opted for "husbandry; which, after all, is much preferable to the lumber business, both in point of gain, contentment and morals."

Husbandry

Contrasting the life and character of the lumberman with that of the farmer, a contrast still common today, was already a cliché 200 years ago. Farming always gets a better press than lumbering, and it is the "family farm" that has long been a staple in the nation's mythology. "Those who labor in the earth are the chosen people of God," wrote Thomas Jefferson, and many a contemporary who followed a plow wrote in the same vein. The romance of lumbering lies not in the humdrum of labor with the ax but in the great dramas of the business: the spring river runs of the logs, the mast trees, the logging railroads. No one ever wrote, "Those who chop down trees are the chosen people of God."

The New Hampshire "yeoman" settled into "husbandry" (standard colonial terms for "worker" and "farming") with an industry and optimism that compels admiration even at a distance. Incredible natural obstacles were simply taken for granted: they would yield to labor and patience. Hardly any reports come down to us suggesting that New Hampshire was thought inhospitable to farming. An exception occurred in 1738 when the grantees of what is now Bradford lost heart and sought a refund. To the Massachusetts General Court they sent a petition:

> ... shewing that the lands in said township are so rocky and mountainous on a View thereof that renders the settlement impracticable; praying they may be allowed to take up a Tract of Land in lieu of the aforesaid Township, lying West...

Shortly thereafter the King took all this territory from Massachusetts and put it in New Hampshire, and the Masonian Proprietors regranted the township to settlers undeterred by things "rocky and mountainous." Bradford thrived as did all its neighbors. So it went throughout the 18th century and into the 19th.

Moving inland, the pioneers shaved the hills to make way for cornfields, hewed the logs, and built sturdy post-and-beam

buildings. Land too steep or rocky to cultivate was grazed. Buildings and fences they constructed as if to last forever, as if every farm established would be a farm forever, as if they had no inkling at all that the land was perverse and resilient enough to retrieve these fields from their grandchildren and restore them to forests again. From one end of the state to the other the development of New Hampshire farming shows a remarkably similar, repetitious pattern for 200 years—starting in 1650, when development was very slow, and ending in 1850, when it had virtually stopped. The pattern had certain stages.

First a group of perhaps two dozen adventurers would secure a grant of a township, lying 20 or 50 or more miles away, beyond roads, perhaps six miles square, roughly surveyed and laid out on a very imperfect map of the state. Little or no money was involved, but choice lands in the township were reserved by the grantor and conditions were attached to the grants depending on local circumstances and grantor's aims and shrewdness. If the date was 1750, the grantor was likely to be either Governor Benning Wentworth, acting ostensibly for the King of England, but pretty much for himself and his friends; or the Masonian Proprietors, acting for themselves. The governor and the Masonians "owned" New Hampshire, so to speak, and both were ambitious. Conditions normally attached by the Masonian Proprietors included: development to a certain point within a specified time (for example, 20 families settled and 200 acres cleared within eight years); 200 acres reserved for a minister; 200 free acres for whoever put up the first mill; 200 to be sold to finance a school; and things of that kind. When conditions were not met, the grant was forfeited, and in some cases the township was then regranted to others. Nevertheless, between 1750 and 1775 more than 100 successful townships were planted in New Hampshire.

Having secured the township, the grantees engaged a surveyor to measure and divide the land into lots of several hundred acres, which they then divided among themselves. Each got 1,000 acres or more, which he then further divided and offered for sale. Many surveyors' maps are still extant: they look more impressive than they are, for they were often made up in a Portsmouth office and show little knowledge of the actual terrain. Broadsides, word of mouth, and, after 1756, advertisement in the *New-Hampshire Gazette* publicized the availabilty of land. Here was opportunity undreamed of in Europe: hard work virtually guaranteed security on land of one's own. Settlers poured in from Massachusetts, Connecticut, and England. In the 40-year period 1790-1830, New Hampshire's population nearly doubled, going from 141,885 to 269,328.

Every lot partially cleared and built upon enhanced the value of the remaining ones: land development, whether by the Council for New England in 1625 or by Benning Wentworth in 1755 or by Samuel Tamposi in 1975, is a very stereotyped operation. In the colonial period many grantees never saw their land, but stayed at home in Dover or Portsmouth to speculate on land in other towns. Others went to their lots, cleared the land, settled down, and sold other lots to new neighbors. Many cleared and developed a lot, built on it and cultivated it, then sold out at a profit after a few years and took a wagonload of goods over the hills to the next town. Then they did the same thing over again, sometimes a third and fourth time, restlessly preferring the ax to the plow. Pioneers.

A township had reached the next stage in its life when sawmills and grist mills were running, a few dozen farms were cleared, and permanent houses had been built to replace the log houses that were often erected as temporary quarters for the first few years, when a meetinghouse was planned or being built and when starting schools and getting a pastor were being actively discussed. A township might then reasonably petition the legislature for incorporation as a town. If successful, its town meetings and board of selectmen and other officers (hog reeves, surveyors of timber, pound keepers, and the like) were thereby invested with the authority of the province or state, a representative could perhaps be sent to the legislature, and taxes could be collected and expended for public necessities such as road agents, schoolteachers, and a minister.

If the town was along the Merrimack or the Connecticut river, the first few dozen farms might be near the riverbank, the broad prehistoric flood plain. If the town was in the hill country between these rivers or to the north, the first farms of the town were usually on the highest elevations. This land was drier, more easily cleared because less brushy, freer of late and early frosts. A century or more later these same highlands were also the first areas to be abandoned to the forest; for by that time the lower lands, which had deeper, better soil and were more accessible to roads and buildings, were under control.

Having achieved a name and a political identity, the town was now a healthy adolescent, swiftly growing into a nearly self-sustaining and almost prosperous community wherein everything and everyone was closely connected with agriculture. Here, hard work, optimism, and self-reliance joined hands. Cities were necessary for some things—iron, salt, tea, schoolbooks, glass—and desirable for other things, such as markets for surpluses, but the key to the scheme was that the farm should supply raw materials for most of what was needed, the rest to be bartered in the village or in the local mill. There was little difference between the life and work of those who settled in, for example, Northwood at the beginning of the 18th century and those who settled 80 miles west in Goshen 80 years later. A letter written from Merrimack, New Hampshire, and published in the September 1821 *Monthly Magazine* in London said: "We have now a comfortable dwelling and 2 acres of ground planted with potatoes, Indian corn, melons, etc. I have 2 hogs, one ewe and a lamb. . . . I can assure you I have made every possible inquiry and can safely invite you to this happy country . . ." Prosperity was not at all unknown, a fact evidenced today in the many surviving specimens of "colonial" homes built around 1800 in hundreds of villages. In an essentially barter economy any cash crop—maple sugar, land, lumber, surplus livestock—was money in the bank. The town of Lyme may have been a bit unusual, but this is what the *Farmers' Monthly Visitor* said of it in 1839:

The almost universal condition of the inhabitants of Lyme is the possession of abundance of good things of life. The difficulty is there that most of the farmers have money to let and there are few speculators anywhere with credit sufficient to hire it.

The basic frame of reference within which the farm communities developed and thrived was simply nature itself, not an economic system. The price of wool in New York or of rum in Boston simply did not matter. What mattered was that the millpond was full, that there was still more land and water in the hills, and still demand for it. Nature was the ally and the adversary. In 1792 Jeremy Belknap penned an eloquent summary of this sort of New Hampshire life. His idea of the happy society—and he spoke for his age—is entirely pastoral: man and nature in harmony, without alien intrusion. His sketch of New Hampshire husbandry is expressive of an image that has passed straight from the New England landscape into the American imagination, to become a permanent social and aesthetic resource.

Were I to form a picture of happy society, it would be a town consisting of a due mixture of hills, valleys and streams of water: The land well fenced and cultivated; the roads and bridges in good repair; a decent inn for the refreshment of travellers, and for public entertainments: The inhabitants mostly husbandmen; their wives and daughters domestic manufacturers; a suitable proportion of handicraft workmen, and

At the turn of the century the New Hampshire College of Agriculture and the Mechanic Arts practiced what it preached. It was a working farm. The dairy barn is on the left; the unmistakable profile of the towered Thompson Hall rises in the background. From the University Collection (UC). Courtesy, UNH Department of Media Services (UNH)

Opposite page: Temple has always been one of the smallest of the New Hampshire hill towns. In 1810 its population peaked at 941, plummeting by the turn of the century to one-third of that figure. Most of the cleared slopes depicted in this lithograph have since reverted to forest. Yet Temple had regular stage service throughout the 19th century, and the state gazetteer of 1856 listed "two stores, two sawmills, one gristmill, one tannery, and one hotel" in town. NHHS

two or three traders; a physician and lawyer, each of whom should have a farm for his support. A clergyman of any denomination, which should be agreeable to the majority, a man of good understanding, of a candid disposition and exemplary morals; not a metaphysical, nor a polemic, but a serious and practical preacher. A school master who should understand his business and teach his people to govern themselves. A social library, annually increasing, and under good regulation. A club of sensible men, seeking mutual improvement. A decent musical society. No intriguing politician, horse jockey, gambler or sot; but all such characters treated with contempt. Such a situation may be considered as the most favourable to social happiness of any which this world can afford.

By the next generation New Hampshire Governor Benjamin Pierce saw a cloud on the horizon. In his 1829 speech to the legislature Pierce worried about the growing dependence upon factory products, and he spoke of the dangers of trying "to support the style of modern days." He foresaw the old self-sufficiency beleaguered by the press of the industrial world, but he could not then foresee the competition to come from the American West. Hardly anyone foresaw what was to be: that every step away from self-sustaining husbandry and a barter economy toward commercial agriculture and a cash economy, and every step toward dependence upon manufactured merchandise and railroad transportation, was a stage in the slow disintegration of an entire social system. By the 1830s a garden of sorts had indeed been created within the wilderness. And the wilderness was hunkered down beside the garden—waiting.

Saving Wilderness

From the viewpoint of husbandry the forests of New Hampshire have usually been a problem—especially in the northern portions of the state. John Josselyn in 1672 had described Mt. Washington as encircled by "the infinite thick woods," and declared that the high country northward to the far horizon was "daunting terrible." When later loggers and farmers peered beneath those trees, the murmuring pines and the hemlock, they found a terrain likewise daunting terrible. Throughout most of the first two centuries of settlement the northern areas of New Hampshire stood as a physical and romantic challenge, more suitable for wonder and adventure than for agriculture. The mountains themselves—depending on whether one's perspective was aesthetic or mercantile—were either invaluable or

This "farmer" is wearing a tie because he is an agriculture student at New Hampshire College of Agriculture and the Mechanic Arts. He is doing his homework on the college farm in Durham. The year is 1919, and the modern equipment is a double-disc harrow and a Fordson tractor. UC, UNH

When Roswell C. Osgood of Sullivan brought his "champion load of wood" through Keene's City Square on February 6, 1875, local photographer J.A. French wasted no time capturing the event. The ordeal for Osgood's oxen ended when they reached the nearby Cheshire Railroad Company. NHHS

In 1877 the Saunders Company laid rails to bring lumber out from the sawmills at Livermore. Lumbering made Livermore a boom town, and changes in the town's population reflect changes in the mills' productivity. The 1890 census counted 155 inhabitants (not including the transient population from the camps). In 1920 there were 98; in 1930, 23; and in 1940, only 4. Today Livermore has been reclaimed by the forest that was its genesis. From The Enterprise of the North Country of New Hampshire, *1983*

worthless. Adventurers and artists resorted to the White Hills, but the captains of enterprise went elsewhere. In retrospect, it appears that the most important of those who labored in the North Country in the early 19th century were the poets and artists. They went to work on the unconscious sensibility of the state, with effects that surfaced at the end of that century.

Husbandry was at its peak in 1831, though several hundred thousand acres of North Country land had never been granted in townships. The legislature that year, meaning to strike a blow for both farming and forestry, decided to sell all remaining state-owned lands. Up for sale went most of the White Mountains. Sargeant's Purchase, 25,000 acres near Mt. Washington, was sold in 1832 for $300; soon thereafter Chandler's Purchase, 10,000 acres nearby, went for the same amount. And so on. In 1867, 172,000 acres that included Mt. Washington were sold for $25,000—not quite 15 cents per acre. By 1876 all public lands had been sold.

There soon emerged throughout the state a kind of numbed puzzlement: Why on earth did we do *that?* By now railroads and pulp industries had penetrated the mountains, and the logger's ax, like a terrible swift sword, had struck even the remotest mountainsides. Across the White Mountains lay a depressing trail of erosion, forest fire, sawdust-clogged rivers, and general waste—sufficient to trigger a reaction on behalf of the land and the water. Having promoted northern timber cutting for half a century, the legislature in 1881 appointed a commission to inquire into "the extent to which the forests of New Hampshire are being destroyed by indiscriminate cuttings..." To a very large extent, the Commission Report stated in 1885. The report also stressed the interdependence of the transportation industry, the general economy, and the conditions of the forests.

Shortly, a conviction took hold in New Hampshire that certain traditional attitudes ought to be stopped cold and put into reverse gear. Fruits of this conviction were the Society for the Protection of New Hampshire Forests (SPNHF), founded in 1901, and the Weeks Act, passed by Congress in 1911, which initiated funding for the White Mountain National Forest. Since its inception the SPNHF, or the Forest Society, has been the leading conservation organization in the state. Saving the White Mountains was its initial crusade.

Founders of the Forest Society were among the political and financial heavyweights of the East Coast, and included New Hampshire Governor Frank Rollins (its first president), several soon-to-be U.S. Senators, the attorney general of Massachusetts, a bishop, and prominent newspapermen. Soon membership included other governors, senators, the president of the state university, the dean of the Yale School of Forestry, past and future U.S. cabinet secretaries, and the president of the Brown Paper Company. Theodore Roosevelt was the U.S. President; "conservation" (the famous ancestor of "environmentalism") was in the air and forestry was its major impulse. In New Hampshire books were written, commissions made ecological studies, committees made economic reports, corresponding committees of the Forest Society sprouted in towns, posters and editorials kept up a steady blast. Bills were drafted. The aim was to rewrite forestry law and provide a rationale for creating a White Moun-

In a state that is 86 percent forest, forest fires periodically take on catastrophic proportions. The fires of the summer of 1953 were among the worst in memory, forcing Governor Hugh Gregg to apply for federal relief. The men above are building a fire line at the Grantham Mountain fire of that summer. SPNHF

tain Forest Reservation. Despite all the high-powered activity, progress was very slow. Many a politician dismissed the White Mountains project as sentimentalism: railroad and lumber interests were deeply entrenched. Eventually the Weeks Act of 1911 passed, and shortly thereafter the first national purchases were made in the White Mountains. By 1912 over 72,000 acres had been purchased at a cost of a bit more than $6 per acre. Sold as surplus wild land by one generation, they were bought back by the next generation as a natural resource, to become a national treasure. Late in 1914 Mt. Washington was purchased by the national government. Since that time New Hampshire lands owned by the national and state governments and by the Forest Society have grown to more than 750,000 acres.

The Forest Society was followed in 1914 by the Audubon Society and accompanied by the longer-standing interstate Appalachian Mountain Club. These were the conservation forerunners in the early 20th century. They remain the most influential conservation groups in New Hampshire today. In their wake have come dozens of similarly motivated local and statewide organizations, ranging from the Loon Preservation Committee (1979) and the Seacoast Anti-Pollution League (1969) to various kinds of environmental coalitions.

Lincoln was a tiny farming village when timber baron J.E. Henry moved his lumber company into town in 1892. By the time this photograph was taken in 1906, logs, shown filling the East Branch of the Pemigewasset River, were carried into Lincoln by Henry's East Branch & Lincoln Railroad. The White Mountain forests were accessible to major logging operations only by such logging railroads. NHHS

Once upon a time the King of England had simply said of New Hampshire: "This is my land; I give it to whom I will, to do with as he wills. These are my pine trees; I choose to keep them for myself." That was a long time ago. In the late 20th century, whenever the fate of the land or water is seriously at issue, three kinds of contenders are present. One is the array of various independent environmental organizations and ad hoc groups, ranging from the Forest and Audubon societies to the town conservation commissions authorized under a 1965 state law. A second is the cluster of governmental bureaus and officials charged with administering the laws. The third is the restless dynamic of economic interests, often driven to override public and long-term interests. In such a matrix laws must now be made and unmade.

Two major laws of recent decades illustrate that the kind of work initiated a hundred years ago by the first forest study commission continues and sometimes bears fruit: they concern "timber yield" and "current use." Until 1949 New Hampshire imposed an inventory tax on growing timber, thus encouraging owners to market even immature timber to avoid taxes. Efforts by the Forest Society and some legislators to change this began before 1920, and a Timber Yield tax—on harvested timber only—was eventually signed into law by Governor Sherman Adams in 1949. It has been a saving grace for the forests. A similar problem beset land taxes. For years tax assessments were legally bound to reflect the market value of the land, and though the law was widely ignored, the effect was to force some owners to sell land for development that was better left in field or forest.

The Current Use law passed in 1973 permits assessment of land based upon the purpose for which it is used (be it bird watching or cutting cordwood) rather than the price for which it could be sold.

An example of a contemporary portrait of rural New Hampshire is this 1982 photograph of a West Lebanon cornfield. Photograph by Tom Wolfe.

* * *

On January 20, 1961, Robert Frost, by then America's unofficial poet laureate, participated in President Kennedy's inauguration. He stood there on the platform, a venerable figure leaning against the breeze, speaking lines, slightly obscure, that yet touched the heart of the national experience and of New Hampshire's experience:

The land was ours before we were the land's.
She was our land more than a hundred years
Before we were her people.

New Hampshire settlers bought land, or got it as a gift out-right, or somehow came to own it—to clear it, conquer it, ravish it, harvest it, have it. The land was ours. But *owning* it was chastened by time and the discipline of experience so as to become something more, something akin to *preserving*. So diverse were the forms of possession, and so open to predation and destruction were the natural resources, that defenses were necessary. There grew up a system of institutions, laws, and societies forming a zig-zag line of restraint against the worst assaults on the land. We became her people.

Opposite page: In late 1973 and early 1974 Governor Meldrim Thomson (left) promoted a plan whereby Aristotle Onassis (right) would build the largest oil refinery on the East Coast in Durham, with a tanker station at the Isles of Shoals. Local citizens rose in vigorous protest, and the project became a cause celebre. The issue was "home rule"—the authority of local munici-palities. In the end home rule carried the day: when the citizens of Durham voted against the project at town meeting, the plan was dead. Photograph by Bob LaPree. Courtesy, New Hampshire Times

II

G·O·V·E·R·N·M·E·N·T
A·N·D P·E·O·P·L·E

It took Franklin Pierce 49 ballots at the Democratic Convention of 1852 to win the honor of having his likeness placed on this Nathaniel Currier campaign poster. Oddly enough, he knew his opponents better than he knew his running mate. Whig Presidential candidate Winfield Scott had been Pierce's commanding officer in Mexico, and Free Soil candidate John Parker Hale was an old New Hampshire friend and political adversary. NHHS

T·H·E
D·E·V·E·L·O·P·M·E·N·T O·F
G·O·V·E·R·N·M·E·N·T

B·E·F·O·R·E 1·7·8·4

A tale related by several early historians, beginning with Cotton Mather, tells of a Boston preacher who came to Dover and urged his hearers to be faithful to "the divine purpose for which this colony was planted," only to be interrupted by a New Hampshire voice, which declared: "Parson, we came hither to fish." At any rate, the earliest settlements around the mouth of the Piscataqua River were not parts of a religious movement or of a chartered colony. The King of England, through the Council for New England, had granted *land* to developers—Thomson, Mason, Gorges, Hilton, and others—while retaining political *authority*. The settlers were not expected to set up government: their mission in English eyes was not political or religious, but economic. From the King's point of view, early New Hampshire was just another piece of England, a remote province.

The First Four Towns
A little bit of England—that was the circumstance in the 1620s and 1630s for Dover and Strawbery Banke, two of the first four towns of New Hampshire. The other two original towns, Exeter and Hampton, lying to the south, had been primarily settled from Massachusetts, partially under religious impulses. John Wheelwright, a religious dissenter banished from the Bay Colony, had started Exeter by purchasing land from the Indians in 1638. Hampton, a Puritan political outpost in the wilderness, was a creation of the Massachusetts General Court between 1636 and 1639. During the same period, while England was distracted by civil war, Strawbery Banke had devised a government for itself and elected a governor; and Dover, just up the river, had put

together a three-paragraph compact (the 1640 Dover Combination) in which the inhabitants pledged loyalty to the laws of England "together with all such orders as shal bee concluded by a major part of the free men of our Society."

The Reverend John Wheelwright, who founded the town of Exeter in the 17th century, looked something like this in 1677 when he was 84 years old. Commissioned in 1947, this portrait is probably a copy of the John Wheelwright portrait in the Massachusetts State House. The original portrait showed a man with less hair and a trimmer mustache. Privately owned

It was a somewhat confused beginning for New Hampshire—in its land grants, in its religious assumptions, and in its political structure. By 1643 these four towns, awkward political orphans as they were, with a population of somewhere near one thousand, had come, one by one, under the political wing of the swiftly developing Massachusetts Bay Colony. Bringing this about involved considerable tugging and hauling. But the arrangement with Massachusetts gave to these four towns a focus of government closer to home than England, and it authorized their makeshift town governments.

Though the liaison with Massachusetts lasted nearly 40 years, until 1680, it was never a legal marriage from the mother country's point of view. But England was riven by civil wars and general upheaval, and too distracted to care. The tie with Puritan Massachusetts came to seem almost natural and, to all but the scattered Anglicans left in Portsmouth, it seemed permanent. But viewed from London, the expansion of Massachusetts' political influence was worrisome, as were the claims to ownership of New Hampshire by Robert Mason. Under pressure of an official inquiry by the Lords Chief Justice, Mason was bought off and Massachusetts backed off and "disavowed any right either in the soil or government thereof." This cleared the way for the King to establish New Hampshire as a Royal colony with a new government separate from Massachusetts. It went into effect on January 1, 1680.

A Crown Colony

This new "constitution" structured the New Hampshire government until the Revolutionary War. It called for an executive consisting of an appointed Council of nine men with a president, as well as an Assembly of representatives from the towns. In time, the Council presidency evolved into the role of Royal governor—sometimes called lieutenant-governor, sometimes governor-general. This Council, appointed by the English Board of Trade, is the historical antecedent of the present-day Executive Council.

The Council was designed to be far more powerful than the elected Assembly. The Council determined that voting rights for Assemblymen be restricted to Protestant males aged 24 and older with an estate of £20 or more. The Council and its president, or governor, at first initiated important legislation—tax levies, for example. The Assembly was invited to "concur." The governor called the Assembly into session and could dismiss it; he could veto its laws in the King's name, and he could determine its membership by controlling the process ("writs of election") whereby towns were invited to send representatives. The writs were issued in accordance with the political winds. Why invite representatives from troublesome towns? The governor also controlled major appointments to office—judges, justices, and administrators of shipping and masting contracts. In short, it was the governor and not the Assembly that became the locus of political authority in New Hampshire, though the "power of the purse" remained with the Assembly—and they used it.

These arrangements were not lost to the memories of those who forged new and very different governments for New Hampshire in a later generation. The little New Hampshire Assembly of 1680 and beyond, though politically weak, was symbolically mighty; it was a tiny democratic hairline fracture in the solid wall of monarchy, a crack that grew inexorably for 100 years, until finally the wall came tumbling down.

On the other hand, being governor of New Hampshire was not easy, and there were rival factions everywhere. Some cabal was usually ready to undermine the governor's authority, or to dispatch an informer to London to discredit somebody, or to rebut the normally self-serving reports the governor sent to the home office. A governor learned to pull strings all across the board, from town meeting to English court. Frequently, one tugged too hard or pulled rank too often and got into trouble. In 1717 Lieutenant-Governor Vaughan lectured the Council about "the arrogance and pride of those who do not consider I am a superior match, as being armed with power from my Prince, who doth execution at the utterance of the word." For this he was fired by his then superior, the governor of Massachusetts. To the degree that a governor was successful, it was perhaps because he was conciliatory, ruthless, personally ambitious, and public spirited all at the same time. It helped if he was also intelligent, well-born, religious, and had a sense of style. Even knowledge of government could be useful.

The Wentworth Dynasty

Between 1680 and 1741 sixteen governors served New Hampshire, under different kinds of political protocols, not easily summarized. For reasons of empire, the British government arranged for New Hampshire, Massachusetts, and sometimes New York to be nominally governed by the same person, while each province retained its legislative assembly and in some cases a local lieutenant-governor. This system, which lasted until 1741, enabled the Crown to coordinate both defenses and aggressions against the Indians.

But well before that, 18th-century New Hampshire was developing a gubernatorial dynasty that was to be unmatched in any of the American colonies. It consisted of three native American Wentworths, father, son, and nephew, and it lasted nearly six decades, from 1717 to 1775. John Wentworth was governor (technically, lieutenant-governor) from 1717 until his death in 1730; after a decade's interruption, he was succeeded by his son, Benning Wentworth, the most formidable of the three; and Benning was succeeded in 1767 by his nephew, John Wentworth II, who stayed until 1775. The Wentworths genuinely cared about New Hampshire—or at least managed to merge their own political ambitions with the ambition that the colony should prosper. Natives of the state, they understood local concerns; educated men, they were worldly enough to know they had to please the Crown without alarming the natives, and vice versa.

John Wentworth I, appointed as New Hampshire's lieutenant-governor when Vaughan was fired, a grandson of one of the earliest settlers of Exeter, New Hampshire, had risen through the ranks by serving a number of terms in the Council. A successful merchant and mast trader, he knew that as chief of state he would face border disputes in the south with Massachusetts as well as Indian raids on the north and east and financial problems in every section. But he had asked for the job. At that time, Massachusetts claimed everything west of the Merrimack River, and he instigated the opening moves against that colony by informing the Board of Trade in London that Massachusetts was both unneighborly and "strangers to all Kingly power." Manipulating kings of England became a Wentworth specialty.

Benning Wentworth

The central figure of the Wentworth establishment, Benning

ment." It worked better than one might have expected, and historians generally credit his "machine" with having established reasonably good, though imperialistic, government. His colony had to cope with extremely difficult terrain and climate, it had to accommodate a great deal of religious diversity, and it served as a battleground for the New World conflict between France and England.

One mark of his success as governor can be read today in the streets of Portsmouth. The port city with "safe harbor and rocky shore" was becoming a stylish provincial capital. There was wealth in masting, lumber, fishing, and land; and Portsmouth merchants and Wentworth relatives cornered enough of it to begin cultivating the tastes of those who, then and later, erected some of the finest Georgian and Federal homes in America. Nevertheless, Benning Wentworth's sumptuous and increasingly high-handed style triggered so much public disapproval, complaint, and conniving that he was in effect forced to retire in 1767, to be replaced by his nephew, John Wentworth II.

The Last Wentworth

Though he was run over by the revolution that he tried to slow down and was in some sense a failure, historians have given John Wentworth II a very good press. As much as any British official in America in the turbulent decade before the Revolution, he was ground up between the British Parliament and the American populace.

Returning to his native New Hampshire in 1767 as governor, John Wentworth was accepted with great enthusiasm, and for some time he maintained popularity with all levels of society. He took special interest in the interior of the state and in the conditions of the forests. He hiked to the hills, climbed one of the higher peaks in the White Mountains, visited logging camps, and promoted road building. In 1771, over the objections of many aristocrats in Portsmouth, he instituted the organization of the state into five counties and pushed the development of county government. He enthusiastically supported the founding of Dartmouth College in 1769. He liked New Hampshire's people and thought of them in heroic terms. Before becoming governor he had written: "At great expense of their whole fortunes . . . [the New Englanders] transported themselves to and purchased the country of the natives [this was largely a myth], cultivated with incredible labor, defended and extended it with their lives, entirely unassisted and for many years unknown." Especially at first, he was perceived as one who genuinely wanted to be a good governor.

But, of course, like his Uncle Benning before him, and his grandfather John before that, he ruled as a family oligarch. The relationship between the people of New Hampshire and the Royal governor, any Royal governor, was always an uneasy one—religiously, politically, and economically. On Sunday, the governor occupied an island of Anglicanism in a sea of Yankee Congregationalism. On Monday, the governor—through family, lackeys, and Council—controlled political patronage. On Tuesday, the governor—through the lumber and masting trade and town chartering—controlled the economy. But on Wednesday the governor could not control the sentiment of the people. Ten-

Wentworth, was an amiably conservative aristocrat. He became governor in 1741 of a province much enlarged by the settlement of the boundary dispute with Massachusetts, and he also managed to get appointed Surveyor General of the King's Woods. His 26 years at the helm are unmatched by any American colonial governor. He grew wealthy by chartering scores of towns and reserving some of the best acres for himself, to be sold at a profit when the town was developed. As the most powerful and resourceful New Hampshire governor up to that time, he also managed to intensify some of the inherent problems of the political system. Like his father, he was good at playing off the appointed Council against the elected Assembly. Indeed, for a governor who preferred to rule by decree, a legislative Assembly was something of a nuisance: legislators could decline to grant funds, and they could lapse into the habit of initiating their own laws. Part of the time he dealt successfully with this kind of independence by giving Assemblymen huge chunks of land in newly chartered towns. He could also be liberal with military commissions, since he fell heir to the last and most bitter of the guerilla wars with the original Americans—the French and Indian War.

In fact, Benning Wentworth knew all the arts and wiles of patronage and practiced them to the hilt, sprinkling his tracks with Royal appointments, judicial offices, land grants, military commissions, and commercial preferments. His father, founder of the dynasty, had sired 14 children, and during Benning's years in power he arranged what his opponents called "family govern-

sions in the system came to the breaking point in the years 1774-1776, two years of stress that undid the assumptions of nearly a century. In all the 13 colonies, Royal government collapsed completely during these years, and every colony had its characteristic mode of creative disintegration according to its own traditions and grievances. One major grievance in New Hampshire was summed up by Jeremy Belknap a few years after the Revolution as "the unequal representation of the people in the General Assembly."

As late as the year 1773, of 147 towns, 46 only were represented.... The towns of Nottingham and Concord, though full of people... had not once been admitted to the privilege of representation; and this was the case with many other towns;... No uniform system of representation had been adopted.

The governor wanted to broaden the legislative base, and feared what would happen if he did. In particular, he feared the influence of Massachusetts firebrands such as Sam Adams and Paul Revere. Of course, he had personal motives for blaming outside influence for internal troubles, but he also had good reason for writing to England that he did not expect to see law and order in the province "until they are effectually restored in the Massachusetts Bay." While he hesitated, local resentment grew: resentment of his manipulation of the Assembly; of patronage and nepotism in his "court"; of British authority.

Above: New Hampshire native John Wentworth was in many ways the most able of the Wentworth "dynasty," but his term as royal governor of New Hampshire (1767-1775) was cut short by the events of the Revolution. Wentworth was forced to flee his native province in September 1775, never to return. John Singleton Copley painted this portrait in 1769. Privately owned

Left: Mrs. Theodore Atkinson was portrayed by John Singleton Copley in 1765. Four years later, following the death of her first husband, Frances Deering Wentworth became the wife of John Wentworth, the last royal governor of New Hampshire. As such she became a Loyalist in the American Revolution. In August 1775, a month before her 30th birthday, she, her husband, and their infant son were forced to flee their Portsmouth home. From the Lenox Collection. Courtesy, New York Public Library

Opposite page: Theodore Atkinson, Jr., was prominent among the aristocratic Harvard-educated young men of Portsmouth before the American Revolution. Like his politically powerful father, he was closely allied to the Wentworth families and married a relative, Frances Wentworth. Atkinson became collector of customs at Portsmouth, secretary of the province, and a member of the Governor's Council. His career was cut short when he died of consumption at age 32. This circa 1757 portrait, long attributed to Joseph Blackburn, is now recognized as the work of John Singleton Copley. Courtesy, Museum of Art, Rhode Island School of Design

Province of NEW-HAMPSHIRE,
BY HIS EXCELLENCY

JOHN WENTWORTH, Esq;

Captain-General, Governor, and Commander in Chief, in and over His Majesty's Province aforesaid, and Vice-Admiral of the same.

A PROCLAMATION,

For a public FAST.

IT being our Duty humbly to acknowledge our Dependance upon the Mercies of Almighty GOD, with penitent and contrite Hearts to confefs and repent of our manifold Sins, which render us unworthy of the divine Favor, and by fervent Prayer to fupplicate Forgivenefs and Grace to amend our Lives.

I HAVE therefore thought fit to order and appoint, and I do, by the Advice and Confent of his Majefty's Council, order and appoint Thurfday the Fifteenth Day of April next, to be folemnly kept as a Day of general Fafting and Prayer throughout this Province, hereby calling upon all Minifters and People, ferioufly to devote the faid Day to public Worfhip, in their feveral religious Affemblies, devoutly praying that the Life of his moft facred Majefty King GEORGE may be long preferved, and bleffed with the divine Favor. That the Lives of our moft gracious Queen CHARLOTTE ; His royal Highnefs GEORGE Prince of Wales and all the royal Family may be under the fpecial Care of Heaven. That GOD would fmile upon and profper the Adminiftration of Government, in all it's Branches in this Province. That our civil and religious Privileges may be continued. That the various Employments of our Lives may be profpered. That the Voice of Health be long heard in our Habitations. That Wifdom and Piety may fpread over this Land. That the faving Power of the Redeemer may be acknowleged through the whole World ; and that fincerely repenting, by the Grace of GOD, we may be made Partakers of his Kingdom.

And all Servile LABOR and RECREATION are ftrictly forbidden on faid Day.

GIVEN at the Council-Chamber in Portfmouth, the 19th Day of March, in the 13th Year of the Reign of our Sovereign Lord GEORGE the Third, by the Grace of GOD, of Great-Britain, France and Ireland, KING, Defender of the Faith, &c. And in the Year of our Lord CHRIST, One Thousand Seven Hundred and Seventy Three.

By His EXCELLENCY's Command, with Advice of COUNCIL, **J. WENTWORTH.**

Theodore Atkinfon, Sec'y.
GOD SAVE THE KING.

Above: New Hampshire residents commonly took part in public fasts to celebrate military victories, commemorate special events (particularly those pertaining to the royal family), or pray for deliverance from disease, famine, or oppression. One fast was and still is observed annually in April. The tradition began in 1680 with a fast for the good health of council President John Cutt (who died shortly afterwards), and evolved into a general day of thanks and school vacations. NHHS

Opposite page: From New Hampshire's earliest days the Piscataqua Harbor was protected by the strategically located Fort William and Mary, shown in this view from 1705. During the Revolution the fort was the scene, on December 14, 1774, of New Hampshire's first systematic act of aggression against British authority. Under the protection of Captain J. Cochran and only five men, the fort and its stores of gunpowder fell easy prey to an organized force of several hundred New Hampshiremen who, having been warned by Paul Revere that a British ship was coming to remove the fort's gunpowder, gathered to take the powder for their own use. After firing on the "attackers," the six men were captured and "kept prisoners about one hour and a half," Cochran wrote, "during which time they broke open the powderhouse, and took all the powder away. . . . And having put it into boats and sent it off, they released me from confinement." Courtesy, the British Museum

Lady Wentworth, in a private letter to an English friend, happened to sum it all up: "They love The Governor as Mr. Wentworth, tho' they dislike him as Servant to the Crown."

During the year 1774, there were several turning points—and no turning back. In January Governor Wentworth asked the Assembly to combat the "infectious & pestilential disorders being spread among the inhabitants," but the Assembly just couldn't see the problem. In June, and again in July, he dismissed the Assembly shortly after it had convened in Portsmouth. The second time the Assemblymen promptly gathered at a nearby tavern and planned for a new "congress" to meet the next week in Exeter. At that gathering they appointed Colonel Nathaniel Folsom and Major John Sullivan as delegates to the Continental Congress in Philadelphia, and agreed to meet themselves again at Exeter. In December the New Hampshire patriots, prompted by rumors delivered from Boston to Portsmouth by Paul Revere, forcibly removed a store of guns and powder from Fort William and Mary. The governor called out the militia, but the militia pretended to be busy elsewhere. The governor wrote dolefully to his English patrons that of those who had led this attack "no jail would hold them long and no jury would find them guilty."

In the course of a year, the politicians and the citizen-soldiers of New Hampshire, acting separately, had developed together a devastating defense against British authority. They ignored it.

Seventeen Seventy-Five

After the battles at Lexington and Concord in April, revolutionary fever rose dramatically in New Hampshire. After the battle of Bunker Hill in June, there was no stopping it. Inevitably, much of the turmoil in New Hampshire swirled around the Royal governor, a symbol of wounded authority—forced out of his Portsmouth home and living under military protection at Fort William and Mary, unwilling to let the regular Assembly meet in Portsmouth, unable to stop the irregular Provincial Congress from meeting in Exeter. Stalemate, at a high level of chaos.

Then, on August 23, 1775, something stunning and unprecedented happened that baffled the entire colony. His Excellency, John Wentworth, Esquire, His Majesty's Captain General and Governor of New Hampshire, Surveyor of the King's Woods, not a rich man but the presumed owner of 27,000 acres of New Hampshire land, born and reared in New Hampshire, Harvard friend and classmate (1755) of John Adams, a New Englander to his fingertips, but alas, in the service of the King of England, packed his bags, climbed aboard the British man-o'-war *Scarborough,* and sailed out of Portsmouth Harbor toward Boston. It was really wonderfully simple and simplifying: the end forever of British rule in New Hampshire. Where once all political authority had been focused, was now—nothing. Of that vacuum, Belknap wrote: "All commissions under the former authority being annulled, the courts of justice were shut and the sword of magistracy was sheathed."

What to do? There was nothing to do—except devise a government and run it, raise a militia and support it, fight a war and pay for it, consolidate efforts with a dozen other disorderly colonies, and deal with pockets of perplexed Tories in scores of

scattered towns. It was the worst of times. True, the British governor was gone, but the situation was now more confusing than anything anyone had contemplated. It was also the best of times. For in fact, there in the autumn of 1775, New Hampshire stood alone of all the colonies, with no resident British authority. Without declaring it, without seeking it, and without fully realizing it, she was free and independent.

Of course New Hampshire was not really without government. The province, colony, or state—whatever it was to be called at this awkward moment—was really a collection of towns, and in the towns, officers and selectmen maintained authority by force of tradition, or exhortation. And town government itself rested on social bedrock: Belknap tells us that "habits of decency, family government, and the good examples of influential persons contributed more to maintain order than any other authority."

In the background, the Provincial Congress, which had started unauthorized meetings in Exeter the year before, had been constantly assuming more authority. Indeed, even before Wentworth's departure this Congress, ignoring the governor, had organized from its militia a New Hampshire "army" at Cambridge, Massachusetts, had sent delegates to the Continental Congress in Philadelphia, and had created a small executive group, the Committee of Safety, to act for the Provincial Congress between sessions. Then, in a meeting just after the battles in Lexington and Concord, it had petitioned the Continental Congress in Philadelphia for "explicit advice respecting the taking up, and exercising, the Powers of Civil Government." That fall (1775), still awaiting an answer, but now with all British authority gone, the New Hampshire patriots were far, far out on a political limb. They urgently pressed the Continental Congress again for "advice and direction . . . with respect to a method for our administering justice, and regulating our civil police."

Until this time the Continental Congress had had no occasion at all to tell a colony how to organize a government, or whether to do so. Pressured by New Hampshire, the Continental Congress did the normal thing: it formed a committee. Wisely, it put John Adams of Massachusetts on the committee, and Adams, sensing as usual the historic significance of an issue, grabbed the assignment. He had already made a speech on the need for setting up "state" governments. "State" was the Adams word of the hour; he taught a generation to dislike the words "province" and "colony." He had just urged "Congress to resolve on a general recommendation to all the States to call conventions and institute regular governments." Within a week the Adams committee reported and soon got the Continental Congress to pass the resolution that would lay open a new page in American political history:

> . . . that it be recommended to the provincial Convention of New Hampshire, to call a full and free representation of the people . . . [to] establish such a form of government as . . . will best produce the happiness of the people, and most effectively secure peace and good order . . .

The resolution was just what was wanted. Very general, but very definite: set up a form of government in New Hampshire. It was destined to be a beginning for America of *state* government—government to be based upon the will of a people and not upon the will of a king. And the transaction itself anticipated the intricate reciprocity that is now the heart of the federal/state system: New Hampshire's letters to Philadelphia had carefully deferred to the authority of the Continental Congress, and in the resolution of reply, the Congress had carefully validated the relative autonomy of New Hampshire.

Seventeen Seventy-Six

Immediately, a new Provincial Congress was called for and gathered at Exeter, nervous and exhilarated. No one dared call it a "state congress." Within little more than a week after getting the endorsement from Philadelphia and then voting solemnly "to take up Civil Government," the Exeter Provincial Congress had written and adopted a short state constitution, which specified the main elements of government. January 5, 1776—the day the positive vote was taken on the document—is the date that marks the real beginning of written constitutional government, not only in New Hampshire but in America. This constitution served the new state throughout the Revolutionary War. Like the old system it provided for an elected Assembly and also for a Council—not appointed but elected by the Assembly members. *This* Council is the ancestor of the present-day Senate, the "upper chamber." In this wartime constitution there was no provision for a governor. Of governors they had had enough.

Did the representatives fully know what they were doing? Yes and no. They were experienced sailors sailing political seas

Kingston's Josiah Bartlett was a physician, legislator, chief justice of the New Hampshire Superior Court, president and later governor of New Hampshire, and signer of the Declaration of Independence. Along with Matthew Thornton and Meshech Weare, Bartlett gave the state unspectacular but steady leadership during the American Revolution. His efforts delivered postwar New Hampshire from political and economic hardship. This 1790 drawing is the work of John Trumbull, who sketched the various signers' likenesses for his painting The Declaration of Independence. *It is believed to be the only life portrait of Bartlett. NHHS*

New Hampshire revenue and currency problems during the Revolutionary War were horrendous. Inflation was often rampant. The paper money shown here was issued in 1780 in many denominations and for a time was much in demand. But within a few months Meshech Weare, president of the Provincial Council, wrote: "The present situation of our currency makes me shudder." Shortly thereafter this paper money was withdrawn from circulation and punched to invalidate it. New Hampshire reverted to barter, to silver and gold, and to European currency. NHHS

uncharted. Many New Hampshire citizens were alarmed at the audacity of the venture. Ten towns sent protests to the Exeter Assembly almost immediately. A particularly impressive letter came from Portsmouth citizens: a New Hampshire constitution with no reference to Great Britain was going too far too fast, they said; it sounded dangerously like a claim to "independency" (i.e. treason); it was presumptuous to go far beyond what the other colonies had done, and also beyond what had been asked for by the New Hampshire citizens; moreover, it would cost money. Such protests were prompted by a thought too demoralizing to state: what if we Americans should lose this confusing war? New Hampshire will then be in terrible trouble; in English eyes it will be the worst province of the lot.

But the stronger arguments were on the other side. During the spring of 1776, all the frozen reluctance of the conservatives melted like snow, and by June it had evaporated completely. A New Hampshire constitution of sorts was in place. But the political air was now thoroughly heated by a new idea as bold as "constitution," and bigger. "Independency" was its name—only yesterday a cautious whisper and now the talk of the town. Why brood and bicker in Portsmouth about that makeshift government in Exeter when something so electrifying as Thomas Paine's *Common Sense* is in the wind? A drama far beyond Exeter was abroad, and like jagged lightning it was flashing up and down the Atlantic seaboard. New Hampshire, through a quirk of history, seemed to be out in front of it all—perhaps, for all anyone could tell at the moment, even leading it.

New Hampshire was not exactly leading, for it was independent in fact only, not theory. So on June 11, 1776, a committee of the Assembly was appointed to draft a resolution for "independence of the united colonies on Great Britain." Unknown to the New Hampshire Assembly, it was on that very day that the Continental Congress appointed a committee to draft a Declaration of Independence—just in case one would be needed. The New Hampshire declaration adopted in Exeter on June 15, a one-sentence masterpiece of 332 words with an array of rotund and eloquent "whereas" clauses, protested that New Hampshire was impelled to independence "by the most violent and

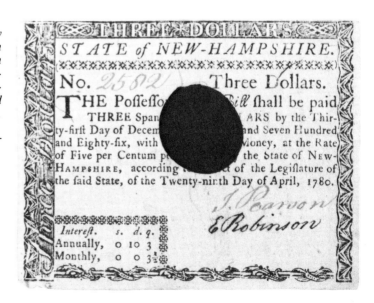

injurious treatment.'' The declaration was in the form of instructions to the New Hampshire delegation and included also a pledge of support for independence with "our lives and fortunes." The pivotal clause reads: "We do hereby declare that it is the opinion of this assembly that our delegates at the continental congress should be instructed, and they are hereby instructed, to join with the other colonies in declaring the thirteen united colonies a free and independent state." Josiah Bartlett and William Whipple cast the New Hampshire vote for independence along with the rest of the colonies' delegates on July 2, and also for the Jefferson committee draft of a declaration on July 4.

Writing a dozen years later, Jeremy Belknap said of New Hampshire's action at this time, "it relieved us from a state of embarassment. We then knew the ground on which we stood, and from that time everything assumed a new appearance."

Wartime Government

Throughout the Revolutionary War the legislature, elected annually under the new constitution, met in Exeter rather infrequently. It set general policy, or tried to, on matters concerning imports and exports, taxes, minting money, raising troops, handling deserters, appointing military officers, dealing with Tories, incorporating towns, corresponding with the Continental Congress, and the like. The legislators had to improvise every step of the way. But it was the Committee of Safety, which met frequently, that carried out the legislature's policies, and also a good many policies of its own. No such committee was provided for by the constitution. It was provided for by necessity: somebody had to be in charge. The Committee of Safety was a small group, usually less than a dozen, and it always included some of the ablest men in the state. Chief among them, both president of the Council (and thus sometimes referred to as the "President of New Hampshire") and chairman of the Committee of Safety throughout the war, was Meshech Weare of Hampton Falls, a pillar of strength in his own right. Weare is the unassuming and unsung hero of this difficult period. He was not theatrical like a Webster, or overpowering like a Washington, or flamboyant like a John Langdon or John Stark. No painting of him exists; his biography remains to be written. Yet during this entire time, as historian Frank B. Sanborn writes, "his hand is seen, energetic and unshaken by danger and difficulty, in all the measures of government."

Periodically the Committee of Safety called the legislature into session and gave it an agenda, such as raising troops and sending food in response to the urgent pleas of General Washington. The Committee also bought and deployed supplies on behalf of the state, punished Tories, and generally ran the war effort. It fell to the Committee, too, to administer the loyalty oath in the spring of 1776 as suggested by the Continental Congress. The Association Test, as it was called, required all adult males to sign a pledge to "oppose the Hostile Proceedings of the British Fleet and Armies." More than 90 percent of them signed.

But the New Hampshire Constitution of 1776 was a frail reed and it had a mortal weakness: there was no amending process. There was no way to deal constructively with such old sore spots as the question of representation in the Assembly. True, as soon

A physician by trade, Matthew Thornton had represented his town of Londonderry in the Provincial Assembly before the Revolution. As royal government collapsed in New Hampshire, Thornton was vaulted to statewide leadership, serving as president of the fourth Provincial Congress, chairman of the state Committee of Safety, associate justice of the state superior court, and delegate to the Continental Congress where he signed the Declaration of Independence. NHHS

as the governor had left, the Provincial Assembly had promptly given the vote to all adult male taxpayers, eliminating a property qualification. But that did not resolve the problem of apportioning representation to the towns, and neither did the constitution resolve it. Western New Hampshire towns especially felt discriminated against. The state fathers were obliged to consider redrawing their form of government from the ground up.

A New Constitution

Throughout these turbulent years, the state's leaders had to run the war and the state with one hand, and give to themselves constitutional sanction with the other. The United States Declaration of Independence in July, the official name change of New Hampshire from "province" to "state" in September, the Association Tests, gallantry on the battlefield—while all these rallied the people to sacrifices for the war effort, to loyalty to the Continental Congress, and to all the heady uncertainties of independence, they did little or nothing to bolster commitment to the state's own fragile constitution. Editorializing and pamphleteering against the government as unrepresentative and allowing too much power to too few—in particular, the Committee of Safety, mounted throughout 1776 and 1777, much of it emanating from Dartmouth College and surrounding western New Hampshire towns. The "college party" the critics were called. There was also sometimes an anti-Committee of Safety faction within the Assembly led by Representative John Langdon. In such a climate the authority of the Assembly itself inevitably eroded.

John Langdon, wealthy Portsmouth shipbuilder and successful privateer, later a delegate to the national Constitutional Convention, was Speaker of the House. Meshech Weare, Harvard class of 1735, lawyer, farmer, merchant, and jurist with legislative experience in the colonial Assembly going all the way back to 1745, was President of the Council, the upper legislative chamber, Chairman of the Committee of Safety, and the Chief Justice of the Superior Court. The New Hampshire legislative leadership was thus fortunately in superb hands. One or both of these men commanded the respect of nearly everyone in the state, sometimes even of each other. Together they piloted a resolution through both houses on February 26, 1778, calling for "full and free representation . . . in convention for the sole purpose of framing and laying a permanent plan or system of government. . . ."

Though the convention was held at Concord, a more central location than Exeter, the college party did not show up. A year's intermittent work under the presidency of Meshech Weare produced a new constitution—which was voted down by the towns in the summer of 1779. Weare continued as President of the Council, Chairman of the Committee, and Chief Justice, and John Langdon was renamed Speaker. Another Constitutional Convention was called in 1781 and instructed by the "legislature" (as the Assembly was now coming to be called) not to disband until a new constitution had been accepted by the towns.

The college party argued that every inhabited town, no matter if it were remote or small or unincorporated, should have at least one delegate to the House of Representatives. (As an indirect consequence of this view the New Hampshire House even today has 400 members, far more than that of any other state.) Ironically, when the new convention assembled on June 5, 1781, to draft a constitution, it was found that fewer than half the towns had bothered to send delegates. Clearly, New Hampshire was a politically distracted state. Small wonder. There was a war on. Inflation was rampant. Filling the ranks of the Continental Army was a terrible drain—economically, emotionally. The rural towns were made up of farmers still trying to subdue a wilderness, and roads to Concord from the interior were only trails. The war was always elsewhere. Would it soon be over? Would it soon be here? It was hard to get accurate news, hard to keep track of what was really going on.

Yet a constitutional draft emerged from Concord the next year and, like its failed 1779 predecessor, it proposed to put sharp curbs on the legislators' practice of appointing themselves to most of the civil offices. The draft was sent out to referendum in the towns borne on the wings of an eloquently argued letter signed by George Atkinson, president of the convention. The present legislators (meaning in particular the Committee of Safety) will not like this constitution, said the letter, for they have vested interest in all the powers and privileges they have accrued. "The love of Power is so alluring, we had almost said infatuating, that few have ever been able to resist its bewitching influence." In solemn irony, the letter added a thought for all ages: "A perfect system of Government is not to be expected in the present imperfect state of humanity. But could a faultless one be framed, it would not be universally approved unless its Judges were all equally perfect."

This version failed too. The proposed House of 50 representatives was not sufficiently representative, said the towns that had not troubled to send representatives to the convention. Each proposed version was dissected and debated in the pages of the Portsmouth *New-Hampshire Gazette*. A new version, submitted to referendum the next year, 1782, was also defeated—the word from the towns being that this one proposed too strong a chief executive. Even friends of the effort couldn't resist a jeer. Belknap wrote: "The hen has laid again. We have a Constitution as often as we have an almanac, and the more we have the worse." Indeed, it was a tiresome, exasperating, almost hopeless process upon which the delegates had embarked. In New Hampshire, which saw no bloodshed or battles on its own soil during the Revolutionary War, *these* were the times that tried men's souls—by trying their patience.

And yet. Through this very process, through referenda and revisions and decisions, through factions and compromises and blizzards of broadsides, New Hampshire was finding its own mind, forging in the midst of a disquieting, wearying war a political self-image that was to endure. Among its emerging features were: a larger, more widely representative legislature (officially styled the "General Court"); focus upon the town as the political unit in state government, and upon the people as the source of authority; a clear separation of judicial, legislative, and executive powers; prohibitions on office monopolies and conflicts of interest; a forthright and extensive bill of rights; and a rather weak and carefully circumscribed chief executive office. The next version, the fourth try, hit upon the combination of these

Merchant and ship captain, member of the Continental Congress, speaker of the New Hampshire House of Representatives, president and later governor of New Hampshire, delegate to the Constitutional Convention, and U.S. Senator, John Langdon was one of the most prominent figures in Portsmouth at the end of the 18th century. His house, built between 1784-1785, enjoyed similar status. When George Washington visited Portsmouth in 1789, he observed that there were "some good houses . . . among which Colonel Langdon's may be esteemed the first." The property is currently maintained by the Society for the Preservation of New England Antiquities. Photograph by J. David Bohl. Courtesy, the Society for the Preservation of New England Antiquities

features that, whether out of wisdom or weariness or wariness of alternatives, proved acceptable to the towns. In the autumn of 1783, shortly after the Revolutionary War officially ended with the Treaty of Paris, the local political war in New Hampshire also ended. On October 31 the announcement came that the draft had been accepted by the required two-thirds of the towns, and that the new constitution would go into effect on June 2, 1784.

Under the new constitution the principal appointive powers went to the chief executive, not to the legislature as before, and legislators were also excluded from holding most of the paid offices. It blithely thumbed its nose at the "college party" by barring from the General Court "any present professor or instructor in any college"—a prohibition since removed. Fortunately, it also built into the document a provison for amendment by giving the people, at least once every seven (now ten) years, a chance to call a convention "to revise the Constitution" if they so desire. Fourteen times during the last two centuries they have so desired.

In his introductory letter to an earlier, rejected, constitution, President George Atkinson had written eloquently about the need for a constitution more lasting than the one adopted in 1776: "When the people of this state first thought proper to assume government for themselves, it was a time of difficulty and peril. That form which was the simplest, and first presented itself to their view, in the perturbation of spirits that then prevailed, they adopted without that thorough discussion and calm deliberation which so important an object required. It was not intended to be lasting."

The 1784 constitution *was* intended to be lasting, and it has lasted.

C H A P T E R
F I V E

N·E·W H·A·M·P·S·H·I·R·E
P·E·O·P·L·E A·T P·E·A·C·E
A·N·D W·A·R

B·E·F·O·R·E 1·7·8·4

In his 1628 report on a tour of the New England coast, Christopher Levett wrote that he reproached an Indian chief for having several wives, saying that even the King of England had but one, "at which he wondered, and asked me then who did all the king's work."

Most American Indians appear intermittently on the edges of recorded history, usually only as shadowy figures and not always in favorable light. In New Hampshire a few individuals stand out rather clearly from the shadows, and among these are Passaconaway (ca. 1575-1665), his son Wonalancet, and his grandson Kancamagus.

Passaconaway ("Child of the Bear") is a legendary personage; this has obscured the fact that he is also an important historical person. He was chief among Penacook tribes for at least a half-century and creator of the Penacook Confederacy against the Mohawks. When New Hampshire was first settled in the 1620s, his people were much diminished by a mysterious disease that had wiped out thousands of New England Indians before 1618 and by wars with the Mohawks. Passaconaway was greatly skilled in physical feats, juggling, swimming, handling the bow, sleight-of-hand, and the like; among both followers and enemies he was credited with supernatural powers. The personage overshadowed the person. One English observer, Thomas Morton, speculated in 1632 that his tricks were "done by the agility of Satan, his consort." Passaconaway said in later years that he had at first been unhappy with the Englishmen and had tried to relieve his land of them through sorcery. It hadn't worked.

Toward the English Passaconaway was always peaceful: in the 1620s, with an estimated 500 warriors at his command, he could have wiped out the frail and scattered Piscataqua settlements, but he chose peace. From the Indians the English acquired the seeds and the techniques of New World farming—squash, pumpkins, cucumbers, beans, and especially Indian corn, which soon became English staples as well. The next decades record fleeting glimpses of Passaconaway struggling to help his people come to terms with the intruders: . . . handing over to Massachusetts authorities an Indian who had murdered an English trader (1632) . . . negotiating his son's release from Boston officials who had taken him hostage . . . acquiring English arms, later agreeing to give them up . . . officially submitting to the authority of the Massachusetts General Court (1644) . . . farming and fishing with his people along the Merrimack . . . petitioning the General Court for permanent land . . . meeting the Reverend John Eliot, "Apostle to the Indians" (1648) . . . being impressed with the Christian gospel. Eliot says that Passaconaway "purposed in his heart from henceforth to pray unto God, and . . . would perswade all his sonnes to do the same."

There is reliable evidence that about 1660, at a great gathering of Penacooks at Pawtucket Falls, Passaconaway, aged and beloved and venerated as near divine by his people, said his farewell. In the version reported secondhand from an Englishman present there, Passaconaway tells his people "never to contend with the English nor make war with them. . . . you will all be destroyed and rooted off this earth, if you do." By 1669 his son Wonalancet was sachem and living by his father's counsel.

Legend has it that the great Passaconaway did not die. He mounted a sled drawn by 24 prancing wolves, drew his bearskin about him, and then sped to the north. Over the treetops, over the lakes and rivers, up the slopes of Mt. Washington he rode at a furious pace, finally speeding up through the clouds and disappearing from sight. During his lifetime there had been peace between the Native Americans and the European intruders, and the Child of the Bear more than anyone had been responsible for it.

Wonalancet ("Fair Breather"), son of Passaconaway, had the pacific temper of his father, but was tragically caught in a clash of cultures. The Massachusetts General Court granted him a hundred acres "on a great hill about twelve miles west of Chelmsford, because he had a great many children and no planting grounds." Wonalancet and his tribe built forts near Pawtucket and in present-day Penacook for protection from the Mohawks. Like his father, he fished and planted along the Merrimack between these points, a man of peace. In May 1674, in response to a sermon by Eliot, he formally accepted the Christian faith, testifying that he had spent all his days in an old canoe "and now you exhort me to change. . . . I yield up myself to your advice, and enter into a new canoe, and do engage to pray to God hereafter."

The next year, when King Philip's War against the English began, all Indians became suspect to all the English. Philip, son of Massasoit, tried to draw Wonalancet, son of Passaconaway, into his plan to kill off the English. Wonalancet was trapped between his race and his religion. Desiring neutrality, he withdrew into the woods of New Hampshire to maintain it, and he spent some time with his followers far to the north in the Connecticut Lakes region. In 1676 he appeared at Dover to add his signature to a peace treaty.

Major Richard Waldron, the captain of the Dover militia who had helped arrange the treaty, was a man of few scruples. Having gained the Indians' confidence but wanting to punish some of the warmakers, he devised an elaborate farce whereby he took hundreds of Indians captive. Wonalancet and his people were released but others were sent to Massachusetts, where a few were tried and hanged, some escaped to return to New Hampshire, and dozens of others were sold into slavery in the West Indies. This betrayal the surviving Penacooks did not forget. For years after this Wonalancet was a vagabond leader: now and again back in Chelmsford . . . intervening to bury hatchets . . . withdrawing to the northern hills . . . residing in the upper Merrimack . . . back on the river island near his English protectors.

By 1685 Wonalancet was sachem of only the peaceful Penacooks, totaling perhaps a few dozen families, and his nephew Kancamagus ("Fearless One") was sachem of the war party of the Penacooks, a larger group. Kancamagus and his band conducted a savage raid on Dover in June 1689, burning houses and mills, killing 23 persons, and taking 29 captives to Canada. Settling an old score with Major Waldron, the Indians cut him to pieces on his own table. Kancamagus retreated north as Massachusetts put a price on his head. He continued raids and skirmishes in northern New Hampshire for several years and was presumably killed in battle about 1692. His uncle, Wonalancet, apparently spent most of his latter days among Christian Indians near the English settlements along the lower Merrimack, still referred to as "chief sachem on Merrimack river." He fades from record still faithful to his father's final counsel: "Never be enemies to the English but love them and love their God also."

Indian Wars

New Hampshire, located between the French in Canada and the English on the Atlantic coast, became one of the bloodiest battlegrounds in what was ultimately a struggle for control of North America. The French proved to be infinitely resourceful in exploiting the standing hostility between Mohawks and Penacooks. Thus, large international enmities and vague local terrors hovered over the New England landscape—under which conditions the daily life of ordinary people had to make its way. For nearly a hundred years, 1675 to 1763, there was intermittent random bloodshed and cruel guerilla raiding between English and Indians in New Hampshire. Periods of worst carnage, times when English settlers often feared for their lives whenever they were outside their garrisoned villages and when few Indians were safe at large, have been named: King Philip's War (1675-1678), King William's War (1689-1697), Queen Anne's War (1703-1713), Dummer's or Lovewell's War (1720-1725), King George's War (1745-1748), French and Indian War (1756-1763). The last of these proved in retrospect to be superb training ground for future officers of the Revolutionary War. In each war, hundreds died on each side. Time and again the astonishing human capacities for both savagery and gallantry were raised to a high pitch in all parts of New Hampshire.

One of the worst attacks of the early period occurred in July 1694, a few years after the Dover assault. Two hundred and fifty French and Indian attackers fell upon the Oyster River settlement (Durham), destroyed the buildings with fire, and killed and captured a hundred people. The survivors were dragged to Canada for slavery and ransom, in what became thereafter a regular pattern.

Massachusetts had put a bounty on Indian scalps in the 1690s. In 1711 New Hampshire followed with a bounty for one year only: £50 for a man, £30 for a woman, £15 for a child. When a new bounty law in 1722 offered £100 for an adult, Captain John Lovewell of Dunstable, Massachusetts, and others began hunting Indians for recreation and money. At first there was little money to be made, for most of the hostile Indians had left the eastern part of the state for the northern wilderness. One day in February 1725, near what is now Lovewell's Pond, Lovewell and his men came upon 10 Indians sleeping around a fire, and were soon £1,000 richer. Having turned in his trophies, Lovewell returned with his men to the north woods for more, and was promptly waylaid by Indians who put a violent end to his violent career.

After a truce was put together in 1725, settlers moved into the Merrimack Valley, lands claimed by both Massachusetts and New Hampshire, and new towns were started, literally on top of each other, at the site of present-day Concord. Free of Indian worries for a time, the settlers of the contended lands of Bow, Rumford (Concord), and Pennycook were, as an early historian remarked, at peace to fight amongst themselves.

In the 1740s at the instigation of the French in Canada, the entire Connecticut River Valley was beleaguered anew. Surprise

The Reverend Arthur Browne was for 37 years rector of Anglican Queen's Chapel (called St. John's Church after 1791) in Portsmouth. His parishioners there included the families of the Wentworth governors and many seacoast merchants. Robert Rogers, of Indian-fighting fame, and Samuel Livermore, a leading New Hampshire senator and jurist after the Revolutionary War, were Browne's sons-in-law. This somewhat routine, stylized portrait was done by John Singleton Copley around 1757. Courtesy, Historic Deerfield, Inc., Deerfield, Massachusetts

Indian attacks, massacres, and scalpings were frequent: on both sides it was capture or kill on sight. The New Hampshire bounty was now £50 per scalp; Massachusetts paid £75. Since English captives were taken to Canada to be ransomed by the French, Indians had a motive to take victims alive, the English to take victims dead. Raids continued around Keene, farther north around Fort Number Four in Charlestown, and then spread inland to Hopkinton and Rumford (Concord). In one incident in August 1746 nine militiamen were ambushed near where the Concord Hospital now stands. Five were killed, stripped, scalped, and mangled; two were captured and taken to Canada. These were the days when the Reverend Timothy Walker of Rumford, the town's leading citizen, preached each Lord's Day with his musket in his pulpit. Such was the land where Passaconaway and Wonalancet had quietly walked.

Robert Rogers: Faded Laurels

Much of the agony and tainted glory of the Indian Wars is writ large in the life of Robert Rogers. At the time of the raid in August 1746, Rogers was a 15-year-old Rumford farm boy already studying the arts of wilderness hunting and survival. Ten years later he was captain of an elite scouting corps that roamed the frontiers in the service of the British army: Rogers' Rangers. Indian warfare was his natural medium but French adversaries served him well as relief. He had a knack for spectacular exploits and for initiating and surviving bloody raids. Fearlessness, cruelty, and generosity were dramatically compounded in his nature, and for a time all North America was his stage: he fought in Nova Scotia, Michigan, and South Carolina, but was usually in and around New Hampshire. Before the French and Indian War had reached its peak, word of his dash and daring had spread to England and fear of him to France. In one familiar exploit he led his men far to the north where at daybreak, on October 4, 1759, he fell upon St. Francis, the key Indian village of the region, destroyed its buildings with fire, and wasted its inhabitants—200 of them, he said in his journal. Other estimates put the number killed nearer 50; but in any case, this raid was the force that broke the French and Indian power in the Connecticut Valley. Final peace came at last in 1763 with the Treaty of Paris, and Rogers was sent to Michigan to receive the surrender of the French posts there. He then married the belle of Portsmouth, daughter of the Reverend Arthur Browne, rector of Queen's Chapel.

Peace was Rogers' undoing. At age 34 and out of wars he went to England, where he published his journals and a play, both to critical acclaim. Though he held several military posts in the colonies thereafter, he never oriented himself to American civilized life sufficiently to face the next crisis, the American struggle for independence. He was often deeply in debt. At the outbreak of hostilities with England, his actions were erratic and his position ambivalent. George Washington regarded him as a spy for the British and had him imprisoned. Upon his release the British gave him a command but relieved him almost immediately. His wife divorced him. Back in England before the war was over, he faded from view and died there years later in relative obscurity. So romantic and melancholy a career seems born of fiction more than life, and one part of it, the suffering and hardihood of his return to New Hampshire from the St. Francis raid, has been unforgettably rendered into fiction in Kenneth Roberts' *Northwest Passage*.

John Stark: "Unfaded Laurels"

Another scion of the Merrimack Valley, tempered in the fires of the very same wars, was John Stark of Derryfield. Stark and Rogers were two of about 5,000 New Hampshire foot soldiers who joined the 10 regiments of the colony between the years 1755 and 1763. Late in life it was still the French and Indian Wars about which John Stark reminisced—his capture by Indians in 1752 and his trip through wilderness to Quebec, his ransom and return—but all New England remembers him better as a hero of the Revolutionary War, and of two battles in particular, Bunker Hill and Bennington. Stark and Rogers grew up in the same region and served side by side in 1756 as captains of the Rangers. Parallel paths diverged in 1759 when, the southern Indian wars over, Rogers went north to attack St. Francis and Stark went home to farm.

It was from his Derryfield farm, more than 15 years later, that Stark answered the alarm from Lexington and Concord in April 1775. Arriving near Boston on April 20, he was appointed colonel of a group of New Hampshire volunteers. That June at the Battle of Bunker Hill, Stark and his New Hampshire troops brilliantly defended the rail fence on the American left. In the next two years Stark saw distinguished service in a number of operations in New Jersey and also in Canada, but he abruptly resigned his commission and returned to farming in March 1777, when Congress promoted a junior officer over him.

That same spring the British had worked out a definitive plan for winning the war before autumn. General Burgoyne was to land at Quebec, sweep south through the Champlain Valley, rallying the Loyalists, and take Albany, thus cutting off New England, consolidating the inland, and quelling the northern part of "the Rebellion."

On schedule, Burgoyne headed south from Quebec in June with 3,700 British regulars, 3,000 German mercenaries, and a large assortment of Indians, Canadians, and American Loyalists. Northern New England had never seen anything like this, nor would again: a ponderous advance of color and power—English red, German blue, American homespun—sweeping out of the north and down the valley, gathering strength as it went, apparently as irresistible as a glacier. Indian scouts kept New Hampshire informed. Burgoyne's American recruiters fanned out into the countryside, enlisting hundreds of Loyalists to the cause. The descent from the north was like a refiner's fire, for suddenly Vermont farmers found the Loyalist/Patriot issue translated from ideas to actions, and neighbors were choosing sides against neighbors. Hundreds enlisted under Burgoyne's banner.

Sporadic groups of Patriots from New Hampshire and Massachusetts headed for Ticonderoga to lend assistance to the American forces, but it was too little too late. The American commander at Ticonderoga, with over 3,000 men, worried through July 4 and then evacuated in terror on July 5, some of his men

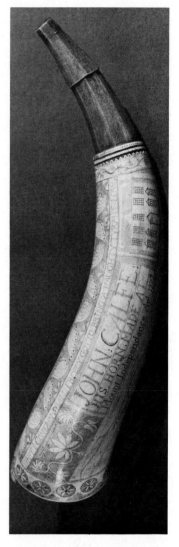

While stationed in the general vicinity of Fort Ticonderoga in April 1777, Hampstead's John Calfe exhibited both artistic flair and patriotic zeal upon his powder horn with the threat to the British "What I contain shall freely go: to bring a haughty tyrant low." In spite of such boasts, however, Calfe and his regiment were forced to retreat soon afterward. NHHS

being overtaken and attacked from the rear by Burgoyne's advancing troops. Dismay and alarm spread afar as the British laid seige upon the will of New England, just as they had planned. Burgoyne would need supplies for the final move upon Albany and would sidestep through New York and into Vermont for that detail: conscripting a few hundred oxen and horses and enough beef and cereal for the men would be fairly routine. The Vermont Council of Safety called to Boston and Exeter for help.

In immediate response, the New Hampshire Assembly met at Exeter on July 17, called John Stark from his farm at Derryfield, gave him the invented title "Brigadier-General of State Militia," and authorized him to raise and command an expedition to Vermont. The operation was to be executed in such manner "as shall appear expedient to you." But how would such an emergency action be financed? It was a state venture unauthorized by the Continental Congress and unknown even to General Washington. John Langdon, Speaker of the New Hampshire House of Representatives, is reported to have rallied his colleagues by pledging his own fortune:

I have three thousand dollars in hard money. I will pledge the plate in my house for three thousand more, and I have seventy

Brigadier General John Stark rallies his troops before the Battle of Bennington, August 16, 1777. NHHS

hogsheads of Tobago rum which shall be disposed of for what it will bring. These and the avails of these are at the service of the State. If we defend our homes and our firesides, I may get my pay; if we do not defend them, the property will be of no value to me.

In the atmosphere of general alarm over the Ticonderoga disaster and the emergency meeting of the Assembly, the appointment of Stark to lead the forces of rescue electrified the New Hampshire countryside. There was haying to be finished and the rye was ripe. No matter. Farmers dropped their scythes, picked up their muskets as if addressed by a supernatural command, and headed for Charlestown and the rendezvous at Fort Number Four. One hundred and sixty-five were veterans of Stark's command at Bunker Hill. Within a week nearly 1,500 had volunteered and were ready to follow their leader into Vermont, into battle, and into history.

By Sunday, August 3, Stark had winnowed his troops, organized and equipped them, and pulled out of Fort Number Four. A week later he had crossed the mountains, turned south, and was encamped at Bennington. It was not entirely clear just what this band of a thousand New Hampshire farmers stamping about in western Vermont was going to do that 3,000 American regulars entrenched at Ticonderoga had not even dared to attempt.

The issue, however, proved to be morale and strategy, not numbers or fire power. Burgoyne had sent a 600-man detachment, including many Vermont Loyalists, under Lieutenant Colonel Frederick Baum toward Bennington to seek out supplies. Meeting Stark's scouts, they encamped on a hill, built breastworks, waited out a day of rain, and then on August 16 had no choice but to face the New Hampshire musketeers, now strengthened by added forces from other New England states. Pointing to the camps across the valley, Stark is reported to have roused his men: "Yonder are your enemies, the redcoats and tories; if you cannot prove yourselves better men than they, let Molly Stark sleep a widow tonight."

The Battle of Bennington on August 16, 1777, was two battles, each brief and bloody: one from 3 to 5 p.m., in which Stark's troops stormed the hill from three sides and completely overwhelmed the foe, and the second when a surprise reinforcement of British troops arrived at 6 p.m., with the same outcome.

American losses were about 30 killed and 40 wounded. British losses were summarized in Stark's report:

We obtained four pieces of brass cannon, one thousand stand of arms, several Hessian swords, eight brass drums, and seven hundred and fifty prisoners. Two hundred were killed on the spot; wounded unknown. The enemy effected his escape by marching all night, and we returned to camp.

One hundred and fifty-five of the captives were American Tories, many from nearby Vermont towns; many of the others were Germans. These all, together with wounded captives, were sent to Boston for Boston to handle as best it could. The total rout shattered Burgoyne's confidence, demoralized his troops, and effectively cut off his supplies. "The most active and rebellious race on the continent . . . hangs like a gathering storm on my left," wrote Burgoyne as he prepared for Saratoga. Stark could scarcely have known what a mortal blow he had inflicted. On October 17, instead of taking Albany and finishing the war, General Burgoyne, with Stark blocking his retreat across the Hudson, surrendered his entire army to the Americans at Saratoga. Two weeks earlier the Continental Congress had made the Derryfield farmer a brigadier general in the army of the United States. Some years afterward Thomas Jefferson put the victory at Bennington into the perspective it has since retained.

This success was the first link in the chain of events which opened a new scene to America. It raised her from the depths of despair to the summit of hope, and added unfaded laurels to the veteran who commanded.

Life on the Farm

Lives of high drama becloud the fact that for most people most of the time life is more humdrum than heroic. It was for most early residents of New Hampshire. Matthew Patten was born in Ireland and came to Londonderry, New Hampshire, as a young boy in 1728. He later married and settled in the neighboring town of Bedford. Here he and his sons farmed along the same river plains where Passaconaway and his sons had farmed, and fished at weirs at the same Amoskeag Falls where they had fished. Besides farming and fathering 11 children, Patten worked as carpenter and cooper, surveyed land, lumbered, trapped for furs, fished, and was a judge of probate, a delegate to the New Hampshire Provincial Assembly in the crucial years 1776-1777,

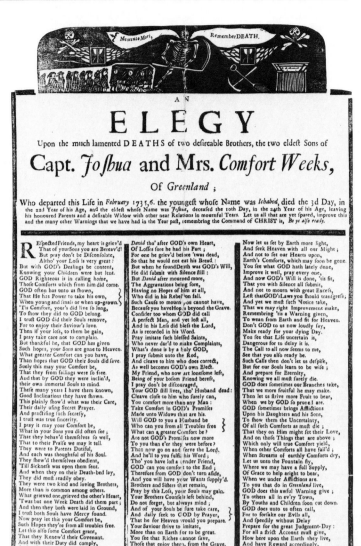

A cartoon of "Death" heads this broadside of an elegy, occasioned by the passing of two brothers in Greenland in 1735. "A warning given to wean from earth and fit for Heaven," the labored verse admonished: "Be ye also ready." NHHS

Thursday, October 7. 1756. · THE · NUMB. 1.

New Hampshire GAZETTE,

With the Freſheſt Advices *Foreign and Domeſtick.*

The Printer to the PUBLIC.

UPON the Encouragement given by a Number of Subſcribers agreable to printed Propoſals, I now publiſh the firſt WEEKLY GAZETTE, for the Province of NEW-HAMPSHIRE; depending upon the Favour of all Gentlemen who are Friends to *Learning, Religion* and *Liberty* to countenance my Undertaking, as this is the beginning of Printing in this Province, ſo that I may go on cheerfully, and continue this Paper in a uſeful and entertaining Manner.

Fondneſs of News may be carried to an extreme; but every Lover of Mankind muſt feel a ſtrong Deſire to know what paſſes in the World, as well as within his own private Sphere; and particularly to be acquainted with the Affairs of his own Nation and Country—Eſpecially at ſuch a Time as this, when the *Britiſh* Nation is engag'd in a juſt and neceſſary War, with a powerful Enemy, the *French*, a War in which the *American* Colonies are moſt nearly intereſted, the Event of which muſt be of the utmoſt Importance both to us and all the *Britiſh* Dominions, every true Engliſhman muſt be anxious to know from Time to Time the State of our Affairs, at Home and in the Colonies.

I ſhall therefore take Pains to furniſh my Readers with the moſt material News which can be collected from every Part of the World, particularly from *Great-Britain*, and its Dependencies: And great Care will be taken that no Facts of Importance ſhall be publiſhed but ſuch as are well atteſted, and theſe ſhall be as particular as may be neceſſary.

But beſides the common News, whenever there ſhall be Room, and as there may be Occaſion, this Paper will contain Extracts from the beſt Authors on Points of the moſt uſeful Knowledge, moral, religious or political Eſſays, and other ſuch Speculations as may have a Tendency to improve the Mind, afford any Help to Trade, Manufactures, Huſbandry, and other uſeful Arts, and promote the public Welfare in any Reſpect.

As the Preſs always claims Liberty in free Countries, it is preſumed that none will be offended if this Paper diſcovers that Spirit of Freedom which ſo remarkably prevails in the *Engliſh* Nation: But as Liberty ought not to be abus'd, no Encouragement will be given by the Publiſher to any Thing which is apparently deſign'd to foment Diviſions in Church or State, nor to any Thing profane, obſcene, or tending to encourage Immorality, nor to ſuch Writings as are produced by private Pique, and fill'd with perſonal Reflections and inſolent ſcurrilous Language. It is a great Abuſe of good Senſe as well as good Manners to employ thoſe Means which may be ſerviceable to the beſt Purpoſes, in the ſervice of Vice or any thing Indecent, or which may give juſt Occaſion of Offence to any perſons of true Taſte and Judgment. And therefore proper Caution will be always us'd to avoid all reaſonable Grounds of Complaint on that Score. **The**

Printer Daniel Fowle gave New Hampshire its first newspaper in 1756. Before then news came largely from the Massachusetts press. Fowle promised that the New Hampshire Gazette *would carry not only the news, but "useful Knowledge, moral, religious or political Essays," and just about anything else of interest to readers in the Portsmouth area. NHHS*

Opposite page: Portsmouth remained New Hampshire's chief commercial port in the years after the Revolution, even though it relinquished its role as the provincial capital and center of government. In this circa 1778 view of Portsmouth from Badger's Island, the spire of Queen's Chapel (center) is flanked by that of North Church (right) and, at some distance, South Church (far left). NHHS

and a frequent member of its Committee of Safety. None of this was the least bit unusual. Somewhat unusual, however, was the fact that he kept a daily diary for over 30 years—basically a record book, noting most of his activities, travels, business transactions, but only rarely his thoughts. Two of the Patten sons, John and Bob, figure in the following passages.

In April 1775 the news from Lexington and Concord intruded upon the family springtime routines in the Pattens' Bedford household, but did not completely stop the normal activities.

[April] *20th I Recd the Melancholy news in the morning that General Gages troops had fired on our Contrymen at Concord yesterday . . . We Generay met at the meeting house about 9 of the Clock and the Number of twenty or more went Directly off from the Meeting house to assist them . . . james Orr made me a great wheel Spindle of my Steel and he mended the Ear of a little kittle and finished the chain for my cannoe . . . And our john came home . . . and intended to Sett off for our army to morrow morning and our Girls sit up all night bakeing bread and fitting things for him and john Dobbin*

21st our john and john Dobbin and my bror Samuell two oldest sons sett off and joyned Derryfield men and about six from Goffestown . . . there was nine more went along after them belonging to Pennykook or thereabouts and I went to McGregores and I got a pound of Coffie on Credit

There was probably but one musket in the family so there was no way to send the second son, Bob, to Massachusetts; anyway he was needed at home since on April 22 Matthew Patten "was wakened in the morning by Mrs. Chandlers comeing with a letter from the Comitee of the Provincial Congress for calling another Congress of the Province immeadeately and I went with it as fast as could to john Bells but he was gone to our army . . . " At this meeting the Provincial Congress voted, according to its records, to ask the Continental Congress meeting in Philadelphia for "explicit advice, respecting the taking up . . . of Civil Government." Back home on April 26, Patten went "at the desire of the town to Col Goffes and Merrils and MacGregores and Cautioned them to take Special care of Strangers and persons Suspected of being Torys Crossing the River to Examin and Search if they judge it needful and I got a pound of Coffie and nine flints from MacGregore . . . " A pound or two of "Tobacca" and a jug of rum were other staples frequently noted.

On April 28 Patten "began to Stock Capt Blairs Gun and I went and got jamey Orr to forge me a Screw nail for the breach of the Gun and I fitted it and cut the screws . . . " Any old gun barrel lying around was invaluable now. A 1773 census of New Hampshire shows that there were nearly twice as many adult males between 16 and 60 as there were muskets, and there were no gunsmiths in New Hampshire at the time. (Later, in 1775, when a town muster turned out 12 men and only 5 guns, Patten was put on a committee "to procure Guns for the men that goes out of this town but got none.") Again, on April 29, Patten "worked some at Stocking the Gun and the boys planted Potatoes." But things were not quite normal in May 1775 in

Bedford:

From the 15th to the 20th Inclusive I fished at the falls I got 106 Ells and how many shad I cant Remember on the 19th we finished planting corn on the 16th we had a town meeting in Bedford at which we Voted to Shut the meeting house against Mr Houston [their minister, who was suspected of Tory sympathies].

In early January 1776 the Provincial Congress was meeting to adopt a temporary constitution for New Hampshire, but Matthew Patten was in Cambridge, Massachusetts, with his second son: "I went out with a Slay to go to the army and Bob went with me to tarry a year . . . 3rd we arrived at the Camp and went and viewed the encampment at Cambridge and Prospect Hill and I lodged at Col Starkes Barracks in his bed."

That summer in early July, when the Declaration of Independence was adopted, the Provincial Congress and the Committee of Safety were meeting in Exeter, and Patten was with them. He started home on July 20 with "2£ of tobacca a rub ball for my breeches and a Declaration for Independance."

Matthew Patten arrived home with a copy of the Declaration to show his wife, and his wife had a document to show to him. Independence had been dearly bought. On the way home on July 21:

I got an account of my johns Death of the Smal Pox at Canada and when I came home my wife had got a letter from Bob which gave us a particular account it informed us that he was sick of them at Chambike and that they moved him to Saint johns where they tarried but one night when they moved him to Isle of Moix where he died on the 20th day of June the Reason of moveing him was the Retreat of the army which was very preceipitate and he must either be moved or be left behind whether the moveing hurt him he does not inform us but it seems probable to me that it did He was shot through his left arm at Bunker Hill fight and now was lead after suffering much fategue to the place where he now lyes in defending the just Rights of America to whose end he came in the prime of life by means of that wicked Tyranical Brute (Nea worse than Brute) of Great Britain he was 24 years and 31 days old

Three weeks later word came that son Bob was sick near Ticonderoga. On August 6, "my bror borrowed ten Dollars for me and lent me four himself and we had sixteen dollars and 2/6 among us in the famely and I set out for Fort George to see Bob." On August 16, "I arrived at Tyconderoga and tarried at Col Starke and his other field officers untill the 22d in the morning which time I set off for fort George and Bob [who had recovered] with me on Furlow We were two days comeing over Lake George and September first we arrived home I was 27 days from home." During Patten's absence the family and neighbors had harvested the "Rie." On October 15 Bob returned to the army so "our women folks all helped us husk" the corn and later dig the potatoes—"we have 165 bushell in the wholl this year." Potatoes at this time were no longer simply an Irish crop, for English Americans had now accepted this once-curious ethnic food.

Life went on, the banal and the dramatic, the trivial and the sublime, side by side throughout the long years of the Revolutionary War. The year 1778 closed out thus:

[Dec.] *30th WAS A CONTINENTAL THANKSGIVING BY ORDER OF CONGRESS and I got a copy of the plan of government from my bror and I copyd a considerable part of it*

31st I finished Copying the Plan of Government and Shed made nails to set the shoes on my horse

CHAPTER SIX

T·H·E R·O·L·E O·F
G·O·V·E·R·N·M·E·N·T

A·F·T·E·R 1·7·8·4

The New Hampshire Constitution does not envision political parties. Framers of constitutions in the early American states feared the party spirit, as did the framers of the U.S. Constitution, and would do nothing to encourage it. The rift during the Revolutionary War between the Dartmouth-based "college party" and the rest of New Hampshire had been a cultural and regional squabble that came within inches of destroying the state as a political entity.

Party Politics

There were good reasons to worry about party politics. The New Hampshire Constitution of 1784 emphasized that the three branches, legislative, executive, judicial, "ought to be kept . . . independent," but it failed to assure this independence. It did not define the jurisdiction of the higher courts, and did not even expressly create a "supreme court." As a result, throughout the 19th century the courts were periodically "reorganized"—sometimes by a wholesale dismissal of judges—by the legislature on partisan grounds. The solution to this problem was a long time coming and lay not in squelching political parties, but in adopting constitutional amendments (1966, 1978) to protect the courts.

Generally speaking, it has turned out that political parties are very natural and usually valuable instruments of political expression. A bare-bones sketch of party life for 19th-century New Hampshire is this: the first half of the century belonged essentially to the Democrats, who did very well both in New Hampshire and beyond; the last half-century belonged essentially to the Republicans, who did less well both in New Hampshire and beyond. That skeleton needs to be fleshed out a bit on both sides and then made more complicated.

The Democratic Party

The heirs of Thomas Jefferson largely dominated New Hamp-

shire politics almost up to the Civil War. They were the Democratic-Republican party, after 1830 called simply the Democratic party. The opposing Federalists, the party of Washington and Adams, prevailed early in the century: John Taylor Gilman was the Federalist governor from 1794 to 1804, the only person to serve in that role for 10 years. The Democratic party (sometimes also called "Jeffersonian Republicans" at the time) took its rise from John Langdon's election as governor in 1805, though he was elected by personal popularity more than party politics. Langdon had been the chief executive also in the 1780s, before the advent of parties. Generally, the Democratic party stood for the common man, for curbing vested money interests, and for progressive social action on a wide range of issues: stopping the slave trade; building a state prison (1812) and a State House (1816); revising the criminal code and expunging the whipping post and the pillory (1812); separating church and state (1819); abolishing debtors' prisons in principle (1820) and totally (1840); and developing a hospital for the insane (1840).

From the Democratic party came outstanding leaders, many of them distinguished far beyond New Hampshire. Even a short roll call is long on achievement. Governor John Langdon was a leader from the earliest Revolutionary days, eight times chief executive between 1785 and 1812, delegate to the national constitutional convention, many times Speaker of the New Hampshire House, and for 10 years a U.S. Senator. William Plumer had dominated the 1791 convention, had then been a leading Federalist, joined the Democrats in 1808, and was subsequently elected U.S. Senator and three times governor during the next decade, after which he retired to write biographies of several score of his contemporaries and to help found the New Hampshire Historical Society, becoming its first president. Isaac Hill was editor, after 1809, of the *New-Hampshire Patriot,* and turned it into an eloquent and powerful voice of the Democratic party, after which he went on to become a U.S. Senator and governor, and also to edit the *Farmers' Monthly Visitor,* the paper that kept the entire New England countryside in touch with the social mainstream. Levi Woodbury moved with ease from governor to U.S. Senator, to Secretary of the Navy, then of the U.S. Treasury, and finally to the U.S. Supreme Court. A onetime law student of Woodbury, Franklin Pierce of Hillsborough and Concord was U.S. Senator, Mexican War general, astute party organizer and spokesman, and in 1852 was elected President of the United States.

These were men of stature. Through them, and others like them, New Hampshire continued to be a vigorous participant in the national dialogue up to the eve of the Civil War. Through them the validity of New Hampshire rural impulses—dedicated, independent, righteous—and the success of its institutions as expressed through the Democratic party, were vindicated and thoroughly woven into the larger national fabric. The election of President Pierce in 1852 appeared to consolidate and confirm all this. The one worrisome cloud on the horizon, at first no bigger than a man's hand, was the inability of the Democratic party to face the issue of slavery without ambivalence.

The Republican Party
New Hampshire Republicans of the Civil War time were a gathering of remnants of the dying Whig party (which, after the Federalists disappeared, had been the main alternative to the Democrats), of the anti-slavery Free Soilers, of the Know Nothing party, of rebellious Democrats, and miscellaneous others. New Hampshire Republicans, legislators especially, became closely allied to the booming affairs of capitalist adventure in textiles, lumber, and railroads. They were usually more in tune with business entrepreneurs than with common farmers, who were leaving their hillside farms in droves. Democrats inherited the thinning countryside and Republicans dominated the growing cities—except for the immigrant ghettos, which tended to be Democratic. For nearly two generations after the Civil War, Republicans called the shots and Democrats tried to imitate them. Meanwhile, New Hampshire seemed to withdraw from the great national conversation: in contrast to the Democratic heyday, almost no distinguished national leaders went forth from the state. In the last half of the century William E. Chandler, Secretary of the Navy and then U.S. Senator from 1887 to 1901, stands out almost alone as a national voice with a clear New Hampshire accent. On the slavery issue, the Democrats in their day had lived under a cloud, not of their own making, which eventually broke on their heads; the Republicans in their day, half a century later, had in the railroad monopolies a serious canker of their own making.

The Dartmouth College Case
The summary of party affairs just given needs to be complicated by facts that blur its simple symmetry. One of these facts is the career of Daniel Webster, New Hampshire's greatest gift to the nation during this era, ever a man apart. Like England's Winston Churchill, whom he most resembles, Webster greatly complicates any picture he enters. Among other things he turned par-

In the 19th century Concord took advantage of its central location and its role as state capital by building some of New Hampshire's finest hotels. Abel Hutchins opened the first Phoenix (or Phenix) Hotel, built on the site of his burned house, with this announcement in the New-Hampshire Patriot *of January 19, 1819. Before it burned in 1856, the Phoenix had been a "pleasant asylum" for such visitors as Abraham Lincoln, Daniel Webster, Horace Greeley, and actor Edwin Booth. In 1857 a new Phoenix Hotel rose from the ashes. NHHS*

tisan oratory from mere politics into theater and literature. His political roots lay in the New Hampshire countryside, and he entered national life as a Federalist congressman from Portsmouth in 1812. For 40 years he was the pride of New England before the world, though he was not an intrinsic part of New Hampshire's party politics. Webster moved his base of operations to Boston in 1816, and though he kept a home in New Hampshire, it was as a lawyer, Whig Senator, Secretary of State, and force of nature from Massachusetts that he was known across the world.

The "Dartmouth College Case" cast Webster in his most characteristic role and demonstrated how difficulties nurtured in the spirit of partisan politics sometimes mature into genuine achievements of state.

In 1815, for a variety of reasons, the Trustees of Dartmouth College (mostly Federalists) replaced President John Wheelock, son of the founder. In June 1816 the New Hampshire legislature, controlled by Democrats and led by Democrat Governor Plumer, passed a law that revised the college charter of 1769 and created around the college an additional entity, Dartmouth University, with a governor-appointed Board of Overseers with veto power over the college trustees. The legislature then named college ex-President Wheelock as president of the university. Many Democrats had wanted a state university anyway, and now they had one, acquired by a novel process of creative theft. However, having done the deed, party leaders Plumer and Hill conducted a brilliant justification for it through pamphlets and the pages of the *New-Hampshire Patriot,* arguing that Dartmouth was, after all, chartered by and for the people of New Hampshire and that its trustees had been turning it into a sectarian preserve for the wealthy.

Affairs in Hanover were a little odd for the next two years. Though it was a bizarre nuisance, the university didn't amount to much educationally, and the college trustees, though threatened with fines by the legislature, did not cooperate with the university overseers (all Democrats). Amid the confusion

After Dartmouth College's 1773 commencement and trustees' meeting, President Wheelock apologized to his guests about the unfinished condition of his house, about his lack of table linen, and about the cook's getting drunk again. Nevertheless, at that meeting the college got its seal, a gift from Trustee George Jaffrey. The seal showed American Indians responding to a "voice calling in the wilderness" and striding upward toward the halls of learning. In the 18th century most people who saw the seal probably knew that "Hant" is the abbreviation for the Latin translation of the Old English word that in modern English became "Hampshire" (simple for scholars, but it drives cooks to drink). Courtesy, Dartmouth College Archives (DCA)

John Wheelock, president of the alleged university, made a clarifying contribution by dying in April 1817. The college trustees brought suit against the offending law of 1816, lost in the New Hampshire Supreme Court (all of whose members were Democratic appointees as a result of a recent legislative "reorganization"), and appealed to the U.S. Supreme Court with Daniel Webster as their chief advocate. There, history and histrionics converged.

The basic question as to the meaning of the growing clamor must be answered from at least three points of view. Viewed from Hanover, the issue was whether the president or the trustees should administer the college. (A valid question: the college had had just two presidents, the Wheelocks, father and son, who tended to regard the college they had created as property they owned.) Viewed from Concord, the question turned on the rights and prerogatives held by the people of New Hampshire in their only chartered institution of higher learning. (A valid question: this was a time when the distinctions between public and private education had not yet been historically expressed.) Viewed from Washington, D.C., the issue turned on the question of the constitutional powers of a legislature over a corporation it had created. (A valid question: in days when towns ran the churches they had organized, it might naturally be supposed that the state should run the college it had chartered.)

Thus, crucial collegiate, state, and constitutional issues surfaced one after the other, and as they did the heat of partisan politics melded them together. The case was made for Daniel Webster, a Dartmouth alumnus who was handed the opportunity of a lifetime to make of it what he could—which, being Daniel Webster, is what he did. The rather slim legal basis of the appeal was the U.S. Constitutional clause forbidding states to pass laws "impairing the obligation of contracts."

The case, which opened before the U.S. Supreme Court in March 1818, ultimately brought the rights of state-created corporate entities under the protective wing of the U.S. Constitution, and it was a major instrument of judicial self-assertion for the Supreme Court of Chief Justice John Marshall. It became the landmark case throughout the United States in the freeing of education from party politics, and after more than 150 years, it still has enough potency left to launch a flock of legal footnotes every year. Not incidentally, the case also etched into New England memories the phrase that still raises warm smiles—"It is, sir, as I have said, a small college, —and yet there are those that love it"—the words with which Webster began the climax of his four-hour spellbinding presentation before the U.S. Supreme Court judges.

Webster's logic and rhetoric swept the day. The court voided the action of New Hampshire's legislature as unconstitutional. At age two Dartmouth University folded up in March 1819, Dartmouth College thrived, and party politics in New Hampshire turned from education to other turf. Other kinds of corporations—railroad companies, with powers then undreamed of—would haunt the politics of the state at a much later date.

Democrats and Slavery

In 1800 there were but eight slaves in New Hampshire. The

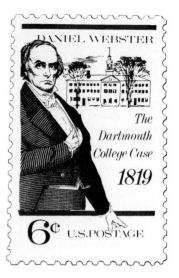

In 1969 a U.S. postage stamp commemorated the sesquicentennial of the celebrated Dartmouth College Case, in the course of which Daniel Webster (then age 36) became a national figure. An alumnus of Dartmouth's class of 1801, Webster represented the trustees of the college in the power play between the New Hampshire legislature and the school. DCA

Daniel Webster's later career tends to eclipse his New Hampshire beginnings. Born in Salisbury in 1782, he graduated from Dartmouth in 1801. After studying law in Salisbury for several years, Webster was admitted to the Boston bar in 1805. Shortly afterward, however, he was recalled to New Hampshire by family matters, "dropping from the firmament of Boston gayety and pleasure, to the level of a rustic village, of silence and obscurity." In 1807 Webster settled in Portsmouth, where he launched his national political career. In 1817 he returned to Boston, after which point he belongs to Massachusetts history. Webster's 1824 portrait was painted by Joseph Wood. NHHS

Above: This William H. Kimball daguerreotype of Franklin Pierce shows the future President as a Mexican War general. Pierce's superior officer was General Winfield Scott, his unsuccessful Whig opponent in the 1852 Presidential election. NHHS

Opposite page: An 1853 view of Concord included the State House, the opera house, mercantile blocks, banks, and homes. Lyford's 1903 History of Concord *acknowledged that Concord "may not equal Portsmouth and Exeter and other coast towns in aristocratic traditions and old memories of foreign trade, and . . . may have a less exclusively intellectual tone than a village dominated by a college." However, the work asserted that "there are probably few places . . . where the general social life is so agreeable . . . due, in a measure, to the large proportion of official society." NHHS*

institution was being denounced from many pulpits—following the example of Jeremy Belknap, who strongly condemned slavery in the last chapter of his *History of New Hampshire* in 1792. The 1820 census indicated there were "786 free persons of color" and no slaves in New Hampshire. In that year the legislature, led by Portsmouth Federalist Jeremiah Mason, declared unequivocally that slavery was "morally wrong" and that nothing could justify the "extension of this great evil to newly formed States." But after that, resolutions of the Democratic legislature were bland, as were speeches on the subject by a string of Democratic governors unbroken until 1846, when Whig Anthony Colby of New London was elected. Colby promptly denounced slavery in his inaugural address, stating flatly that it was "at variance with our declaration of liberty and equal rights, and repugnant to our moral sense"—sentiments Democratic party leaders would neither disavow nor declare. In 1834 a chapter of the new American Anti-Slavery Society was formed in Concord, one in Dover the next year, and within a decade many others in other towns.

John P. Hale, a faithful party organizer and New Hampshire Congressman, came to fame in mid-career through his courageous opposition to slavery. As a Democratic Congressman, he wrote an anti-slavery letter to his constituents in 1845. In response, the Democrats, led by Franklin Pierce and his clear vision of a national, unified Democratic party, promptly dealt Hale out of the party by removing his name from the party ticket. The next year Hale was elected to the U.S. Senate by a coalition of Whigs and anti-slavery Democrats, and became then the most outspoken opponent of slavery in the U.S. Senate. After that, it took all of Franklin Pierce's very great talents as state party leader to keep the Democrats together. Hale and his cause were too deeply rooted in morality and principle to be held comfortably within the accommodating mentality of the Democratic party. Of course, the whole tangled tragic fact of slavery and the national agony it generated from plantation to battlefield went beyond all party, but in New Hampshire it was scattered Whigs, Free Soilers, and assorted splinter parties of abolitionists whose moral outrage raised the anti-slavery standard. The Democratic position was essentially the states' rights position: let the states and territories themselves decide. Democrat Franklin Pierce disliked slavery intensely and disliked unctuous abolitionists too, but he was an acceptable Presidential candidate in 1852 partly because he had made few enemies in the South. Copious evidence can be marshalled for each of two opposing verdicts: either the Pierce Democrats rightly helped to hold off the war to a time when the Union but not slavery would survive it; or the Pierce Democrats were too acquiescent for too long with an institution they knew to be evil.

"Young Hickory of the Granite State" was elected as the United States President in 1852: a good man in the wrong place. Historians have not considered Pierce notably successful as President, but the whole period between Andrew Jackson and the Civil War is occupied by forgettable presidents. Pierce's management of complex foreign affairs was adequate and, in the Perry mission to Japan, outstanding. Domestically, the slavery problem stained every issue, and with the Kansas-Nebraska Bill in 1854 the Great Compromise of 1850 seemed to be coming apart.

It is unlikely that anyone could have been a great President in these years. The trick was to avert calamity, and Pierce did that. Personally, the Pierce family had suffered the agony of seeing their only surviving child killed in a train accident just after Pierce's election. They went to Washington in 1853 without joy, managed four years without disaster, and returned to Concord without triumph.

Republicans and Railroads

Early in the 19th century the decline of the Federalist party and the rise of the Democrats corresponded with the rise of a statewide agricultural society. Later in the century the decline of the Democratic party and the rise of the Republicans corresponded with the decline of agriculture and the rise of industry. The Republican party, though born in Wisconsin, was conceived and named at a meeting in Exeter, New Hampshire, called by Amos Tuck in 1853. In 1857, with the Industrial Revolution going full blast, the new Republican party elected its first New Hampshire governor, and for a hundred years thereafter only three Democrats were permitted to occupy the chief executive's chair.

Ichabod Goodwin, the second Republican governor, typifies the new Republican era: he had once been a Whig; he was a bank president and for 24 years president of two railroads; he was a forthright opponent of what he called in his inaugural address "the curse of slavery." In March 1860 former Illinois Congressman Abraham Lincoln visited New Hampshire, made four triumphant speeches (Concord, Manchester, Dover, Exeter), and suddenly became a leading candidate for the Presidency. Nevertheless, under Republicans after the Civil War, New Hampshire political life tended inward. Industrial development was the consuming passion, and Republican legislators were very compliant. Railroads reached in every direction, and state forest land was sold for change to lumber companies. Before the Civil War national issues had been common currency in New Hampshire, and Democrats sometimes left office in Washington, D.C., to assume office in Concord, leavening the local discourse with national concerns. Republican governors usually came from the business community and returned to it. However, one, Charles Bell (1881-1883), was a scholar and historian, and 18 years president, not of a railroad but of the New Hampshire

Historical Society; another, Moody Currier (1885-1887), wrote poetry which, said historian Everett Stackpole, "lacks fire, inspiration and moral vigor." So did most of the governors.

The governorship was something of an honorary office, probably unavailable to anyone with real pretension to govern. But bland and honest governors were providing a face of decency for a pattern of corruption that was getting harder and harder to hide. By 1907 critic Frank Putnam would write: "The true capital of New Hampshire is the North Union Railroad Station in the city of Boston," adding that no matter who sat in the governor's chair, the man who really governed New Hampshire was "the president of the Boston & Maine Railroad."

William Chandler, later a U.S. Senator, owner of *The New Hampshire Statesman* and the *Concord Evening Monitor,* had predicted it in the early 1880s. Enough was shady in the system then for a wise man to draw a dark conclusion: free railroad passes for the chosen; low tax assessment for the railroads; heavily lobbied legislators; evidence of votes being bought in statewide elections. Chandler warned that if too much economic power flowed to too few railroad corporations, then they

will rule New Hampshire with a rod of iron. They will debauch and control both political parties, subsidize and destroy every newspaper, retain every lawyer, nominate every legislator and fill his pockets with free passes of mileage books, select the presiding officers of both Houses; name the Committees and secure the legislative action or non-action needed.

Matters did go almost that far: the free pass and retainership for lawyers became open bribery.

For a time Chandler, who enjoyed a fight (they called him "the stormy petrel"), battled the interests of the railroads almost single-handedly, much in the way his father-in-law Senator John Parker Hale, who did not enjoy a fight, had battled the interests of the slaveholders in an earlier day. In one memorable case in the early 1890s, Chandler published a brilliantly devastating analysis of the state supreme court's conclusion that the state had no equity in the Concord Railroad. Chandler argued that this "morally dishonest" decision, supported by "irrelevant and unintelligible verbiage," cost the state's people $2 million, and made likely a complete Boston & Maine monopoly. He was

right; the Concord/Boston & Maine merger was railroaded through.

In 1887 the New Hampshire House Judiciary Committee investigated Democrat Frank Jones, a Portsmouth brewer and railroad man, on charges of attempted bribery of legislators. His testimony, published by Chandler, included this revealing statement:

> *I say I could take a hundred Republicans tomorrow and in two years 90 of them will vote just about as I do. That has been my experience. . . .* Men are a good deal like hogs; *they don't like to be driven, but you* throw them down a little corn *and you can call them most anywhere.*

Progressivism in New Hampshire

The wan smile and the bright remark that after all "the Boston & Maine gave New Hampshire pretty good government" were wearing thin by 1905. There was truth in the remark, bitter though it be, but reform was overdue. It came from within the the Republican party, though it soon caught the political winds coming from Robert LaFollette's Wisconsin and Teddy Roosevelt's Washington.

A young writer named Winston Churchill, at the time America's best-known novelist and least-known politician, first mobilized the citizenry against the "corporation," as the Boston & Maine Railroad and its political machine were known. He had served two terms in the legislature and poured his observations into a 1906 novel, *Coniston,* which brilliantly depicted the power and manipulations of a political machine. A citizen's group persuaded Churchill to run for governor as a reform candidate. Such a thing was unheard of—but not for long. With help from wise old ex-Senator Chandler, the reform group put together a program of specific proposals: laws against free railroad passes to government officials; public election of railroad commissioners; reassessment of the property of railroads and other public-service companies; a corrupt practices law to deal with corporate campaign funding; public registration of lobbyists and their fees; direct primary election of party candidates; general tax reform; enforcement of liquor and anti-gambling laws; and the like. The New Hampshire group called themselves Lincoln Republicans, but the collection of ideals and attitudes that linked proposals such as these came to be known nationally as Progressivism. It was the time, shortly before World War I, when New Hampshire seemed to rejoin the national political conversation. A main theme of that conversation was retrieving political leverage from corporate and party machines and restoring it to the people.

Churchill was attractive, sincere, and certainly seemed to know what he was talking about. Thousands were persuaded that David had a chance against Goliath. The September 1906 Republican convention was a brawl: Churchill led in the eighth ballot, then lost when the other candidates united against him. His dramatic campaign clearly indicated that reform was in the air, and new legislators soon responded. Indeed, the very next year, 1907, the first legislative curbs were put upon the free railroad pass.

One of the new legislators was Robert Bass, a wealthy, upper-class Peterborough farmer and forester who had come to the state from Chicago through Harvard. His own interest in conservation and his work on the State Forestry Commission, which was then working on rescuing the White Mountains, helped to add a new theme to New Hampshire Progressivism. In 1909 he sponsored legislation creating the direct primary system for the selection of candidates for state office—hitherto the party convention had selected candidates. The next year the Republican party nominated Bass for governor and he was subsequently elected. Thus by 1910 the movement, started long before by Senator Chandler, focused and made popular by Churchill, and consolidated and deepened by Bass' experience as forester and legislator, was in ascendancy.

Under Bass there was soon a new regulatory body for utilities and monopolies (now the Public Utilities Commission), and new laws covering campaign contributions, workmen's compensation, child labor, corporate tax assessments, factory inspections, forest protection, and the like. Historians Elizabeth and Elting Morrison summarize thus:

Between 1910 and 1912, New Hampshire achieved a place in the national consciousness that it had not held since the great days of Jacksonian Democracy.... New Hampshire in two years more nearly fulfilled the stated and promised objectives [of Progressivism] than any other state in the Union, with the probable exception of Wisconsin. And what in 1910 seemed radical in New Hampshire became, in not so many years, commonplace throughout the nation.

The Winant Years

William Chandler, who had long warred against the railroads and a host of other vested interests in Concord and Washington, died in 1917, and his Concord funeral was appropriately graced by a roaring snowstorm—nature itself saying farewell to a long, tempestuous career. That same year a young history teacher from St. Paul's School in Concord had spent his first term in the New Hampshire legislature, a man of utterly different temper, quiet and unassuming, but destined to become the heir of New Hampshire Progressivism. He was John G. Winant, three times elected governor (1924, 1930, 1932), at 35 the youngest man to serve in that office and the first since John Langdon to serve in it for six years.

No New Hampshire public servant of modern times has so sure and favorable a grip on the imagination of the citizenry as John Winant. One attributes this in part to his personality, a compound of ambition, utter sincerity, and a humility unknown in politicians—stuff of which martyrs are sometimes made; in part to the fact that he was New Hampshire's Depression governor, heir to the tangled emotions that attach to ennobling leadership in dark times; in part to his later distinguished wartime role as Ambassador to Great Britain, beloved and admired by all of Europe, an intimate of Churchill and Roosevelt; in part to the fact that he died tragically by his own hand (1947) after his wartime service was over. Those who knew Winant were constantly put in mind of Lincoln, whom he uncannily resembled in more than one respect.

In 1924, with considerable help from a powerful ally, former Governor Robert Bass, John Winant was elected governor, and did a novel thing: he laid out a specific and detailed legislative program and got much of it passed (though two of his favorite measures—a better workmen's compensation law and a 48-hour week—failed). In an ironic twist for Progressivism, he successfully opposed efforts of the Boston & Maine Railroad to drop one-third of its trackage. In 1930 Winant was elected again, and reelected once more two years later, running against the Democratic Roosevelt tide. Remarkably, he led the state along two parallel paths at once. One involved increasing the efficiency, administration, and organization of state government, a course based upon an extensive 1932 Brookings Institution study of New Hampshire, which he had initiated. The other path involved relief efforts to lift the burden of the Depression: food, housing, and work projects, such as the State Unemployment Committee, the National Civilian Conservation Corps, and even the League of New Hampshire Craftsmen. These activities were spearheaded by the most activist, accessible, and visibly involved governor the state had known. Here was a man devoted to the common weal. In his State House office he often ran an open-door policy, admitting all who wished to see the governor. To some, Winant seemed to be New Hampshire's Republican Roosevelt; indeed, by 1935 he was familiar and sympathetic enough with the New Deal to be appointed by President Roosevelt as head of the International Workers Organization in Geneva, Switzerland.

Winant replaced Joseph P. Kennedy in 1941 as Ambassador to Great Britain—to international sighs of relief—and came in remarkable degree to symbolize in his own person and action the supporting American presence to the beleaguered nation. His unusual resources of benevolence and fellow-feeling surfaced in wartime England as they had in Depression New Hampshire. The Prime Minister and the Ambassador often toured England together, a memorably reassuring combination of resoluton and compassion amid the storms of war. At a farewell dinner for Ambassador Winant, Churchill spoke of him as "always giving us that feeling, impossible to resist, how gladly he would give his life to see the good cause triumph. He is a friend of Britain, but he is more than a friend of Britain—he is a friend of justice, freedom, and truth."

Returning from England in late spring 1946, Winant gave the

New Hampshire Governor John Gilbert Winant is also remembered as the U.S. Ambassador to Great Britain during the Second World War. Seen here in 1943, Winant managed to squeeze his lanky frame onto a light railway car with British Prime Minister Winston Churchill in order to inspect coastal defenses in Sussex. Courtesy, Wide World Photos

President Dwight D. Eisenhower received a hero's welcome when he visited New Hampshire in 1955, the state that launched his 1952 campaign with its primary, traditionally the first in the nation. Sitting next to him as the car swings through downtown Concord is New Hampshire Senator Styles Bridges—a Taft supporter in 1952. NHHS

main eulogy at the belated Joint Congressional Memorial Service for President Roosevelt. Then, freed of the pressure of the public's distresses for the first time in 15 years and cast back upon himself, he set about to write his memoirs—but found the reflective effort excruciating and emotionally disastrous. His was a public life of strangely compelling impulses, gifts, historical moments, and quietly magnificent achievement.

The Primary State

In the early 20th century New Hampshire shook its political insularity and, through the Progressive movement, rejoined the national political discourse. How much that spirit of adventure prevailed after World War II is difficult to measure. Politically, it appears that the state's major engagement with issues of national concern is not through ideas or powerful figures or progressive institutions but through something more exotic—the "first in the nation" Presidential preference primary, held in New Hampshire every four years since 1952.

Like many political institutions, the primary came to significance more by inadvertence than by design. There had been a direct primary vote for Presidential convention delegates in New Hampshire since 1913, and few realized in 1949, when the primary law was sponsored by Speaker of the House Richard Upton, how drastic was the meaning of the switch to voting directly for the candidates. Whether or not it now represents the best way for the nation to conduct its political business, it is one of the best ways now available for New Hampshire to draw attention to itself. The state has found the national spotlight thoroughly addictive, and the primary has become a national institution—a circumstance enhanced by the fact that since 1952 no one has been elected President without first winning his party's primary election in the Granite State. The primary enhances tourism, and it has also become the pliant instrument of considerable political patronage from the party in power in Washington. The eventual significance of the patronage factor was not foreseen in 1952. It was, however, in that year that Sherman Adams, a popular and effective governor of New Hampshire, joined the campaign of General Dwight D. Eisenhower and went on to become an extremely powerful chief-of-staff in the Eisenhower White House.

Curtailing Authority

In the late 20th century two conspicuous features of New Hampshire government are its enormous House of Representatives (400 members versus 24 Senators) and its weak chief-executive office. Written into the New Hampshire Constitution and attested in popular attitudes, both of these bespeak a long, deep distrust of strong central authority—a distrust extending back to the Wentworth governors of colonial days. The House, for example, has been bloated for a century: in 1876 it had 391 members, was then cut to 280, but blew up again by 1942 to 443, and was then constitutionally restricted to a maximum of 400. The salary of legislators has been fixed by the same constitution for more than a hundred years as $200 per term. A "citizens legislature" is the favorite self-description of the House of Representatives.

The New Hampshire Constitution gives the governor but a two-year term, just as it did a hundred years ago; and it surrounds him with an Executive Council, just as it did two hundred years ago. Traditionally, the Council approves all major appointments and expenditures. Many appointments extend years beyond a governor's term; so each governor inherits a "team." In colonial days the governor also had to barter with a Council, but usually he controlled appointments to it, thus selecting his own adversaries. In early New Hampshire the Council was elected from the legislature, but today's Councilors are independently elected and have formidable constituencies of their own. Attempts through constitutional conventions from 1850 onward to restrict the Council's essentially negative authority (as in Maine and Massachusetts, the only other states with this colonial leftover) or to abolish it completely, have uniformly failed. The sheer force of the impulse to baffle central authority, force of tradition more than of thought, is felt on every hand. For example, in 1982 the voters rejected a legislature-proposed constitutional amendment to give the governor a four-year term. Another example is older and subtler: many New Hampshire statutes that establish an executive office vest its authority in the "Governor and Council," even though the constitution would not require the Council's participation.

Inevitably these attitudes and arrangements affect the course of New Hampshire's political history, and affect too its idea of political leadership. Tepid leaders have been more common than forcefully effective ones. While bluster, veto, and threat of veto can produce a kind of negative strength, positive strength requires a rare combination: a cooperative Executive Council, persistent diplomacy, imaginative staff work, legislative initiative, and considerable personal prestige. New Hampshire traditions and institutions make it difficult for the democratic process to cast up a John Langdon or a John Winant.

The New England institution of the town meeting has continued in New Hampshire. Traditionally held on the second Tuesday in March, it is the annual occasion when the affairs of the town are deliberated—at length. A farmer wrote in his diary on March 13, 1860, "Went Town Meeting some in wagons, some in sleighs." On March 16 he continued: "went Town Meeting haint got through yet." Pictured are the citizens of Webster meeting in 1979. Courtesy, New Hampshire Times

CHAPTER SEVEN

P·E·O·P·L·E O·F P·L·A·C·E, P·E·O·P·L·E O·F M·O·V·E·M·E·N·T

A·F·T·E·R 1·7·8·4

At home in Concord, the family of the Reverend John Atwood sit for their portrait in 1845. Having served 18 years as minister of the Baptist church in New Boston, Atwood was appointed chaplain of the state prison at Concord in 1843. In 1850 he ran unsuccessfully for governor, returning afterward to New Boston with his family. This portrait is the work of artist Henry F. Darby, then only 16. In later years Darby recalled that he spent three months in Concord "to paint the Atwoods all on one canvas. The father was represented . . . expounding his Bible." From the M. and M. Karolik Collection. Courtesy, Museum of Fine Arts, Boston

Many a New Hampshire family occupies an ancestral home or farms land farmed by generations of forebears; yet already in 1830 Alexis de Tocqueville, visiting from France, found Americans to be a restless people. New England, famous for images summoned by the phrase "sense of place," was settled, and nearly unsettled, by people who moved from place to place to an extent unknown to European contemporaries. The Fogg *Gazetteer* of New Hampshire said that in 1870, when the resident population was 318,000, there were 125,000 natives of New Hampshire living outside the state. Something similar holds true today: one-half of the nearly one million residents of New Hampshire were born elsewhere.

This chapter highlights the vision of those who tended to stay put, those who focused upon the recurring and enduring things, be they as banal as the ever-returning mud season or as sublime as the hills: people of place. The chapter then turns to reports of comings and goings, of nomads and tourists, of soldiers of fortune and soldiers of war: people of movement. This chapter sticks close to the people by sticking close to their own words. Their words extend from the homes and hearths of the 18th century to the United Nations of the 20th century.

Interior Places

The domestic hearth—whether fact, symbol, or cliché—remains a vivid image. By means of it, two diarists, widely separated in time, temperament, and outlook, unintentionally sum up more than a century of New Hampshire experience. Francis Parkman, a young Harvard student, later a famous Harvard historian, tramped through the Granite State in 1842 and jotted into his journal a classic description—the hearth as locale. "We spent that evening about their enormous cavern of a fire place, whence a blazing fire gleamed on rows of suspended stockings, the spinning wheel, the churn, the bed, and walls covered with an array of piled up cheeses, plates, milkpails, and clothes; all clean and all in order; while the older children were dodging about the furniture of the crowded room and the younger ones venting precocious snoring from a box under the bed."

In 1902 Clara May Hurd, elderly and unknown to fame, was writing to her daughter in Massachusetts from her village home in Washington, New Hampshire, and contemplating the bric-a-brac and the busy Victorian decor in the house whose hearth she had first known as a child in the 1830s.

Sitting here and resting this p.m. I went back to my mother's life in this same house—and—it seems at this day and generation to be a life devoid of comforts and plenty. . . . The house was very cold—and how bare and wanting in all the cosiness that more modern furniture and the many pretty little accessories of living as books, plants, pictures, that go to make a home, were not in evidence then and there. And yet these were not missed because they had never been possessed. So their want was not known or felt. She had the home of her day and generation. I have the home of my time.

Rural Places

Normally it is the resident, not the passerby, who claims the authoritative word on the natural environment—the seasons of the year, for example. Summertime activity is put into perspective by Kate Sanborn, a New Hampshire woman writing in the 1890s: "Haying is a terrible ordeal. There's real poetry about emerald-tinted dewy grass, and the waves of growing grain, and the tall and blithely nodding oats, and the stalwart bronzed haymakers, and the merry sun-kissed maidens in broad brimmed hats. But the real man in actual prosaic haying is like a woman on washing day—so outrageously and unreasonably cross and irascible that the very dogs dart out-doors with tails between their legs."

Ellen Rollins, a gifted and forgotten writer of the 1880s, mused on one of her neighbors who was "tied to the soil" and "whose speech was jagged as its rocks." He himself "was almost as stolid as the oxen he drove." She wrote that "he chewed tobacco in meeting-time, and spit into a box filled with sawdust in a corner of his pew." "Uncouth yet honest," his speech like that of his neighbors was "homely, but not coarse," and full of "figures drawn from the soil and devotion to it."

No better orators or writers have ever spoken or written, in this country, than certain ones whose wits were sharpened in the stimulating atmosphere of this quaint, figurative New England tongue. It was truly born of earth and toil, hence its healthy ruggedness. Hence, also, that underlying imagery, borrowed from sun and winds, field and forest, from all forms and aspects of Nature. There was a marrow to it often, inside an outer crust of homeliness, a sweet-meat of sentiment. When the farmer told you that his wife was a "good critter to work," he

This Christmas gathering took place in the Manchester home of Franco-American photographer Ulric Bourgeois in 1907. From the Manchester Visual History collection, Dimond Library, UNH, and Manchester Historic Association (MVHC)

Boston artist Frank H. Shapleigh spent most summers of his professional career living in and painting the White Mountains. At the time he painted this kitchen scene in 1883, he was artist-in-residence at the Crawford House, one of the most famous of the area's "grand hotels." Although best known for his landscapes "full of facts and sentiment" (as a contemporary put it), Shapleigh also moved indoors to paint traditional scenes centered around an open fireplace. Privately owned

When the circus came to Plymouth, circa 1900, tents and flags and colored "murals" lured many residents away from their daily tasks. Even the most Yankee of hill farmers took a day off, recording in their diaries: "To the circus." NHHS

Until well into the 20th century the blacksmith was essential to the community. Not only did the smith shoe oxen and horses, serve as veterinarian, make hinges and hardware, and repair tools, but the smithy served as a village gathering place as well. Arthur Page was Tamworth's last blacksmith. He is seen here holding court in a photograph dating sometime after 1900. NHHS

compared her to his mild-eyed oxen, which he loved, and which to him were the type of patience and meekness. When he said he was having "a hard pull" in life, his words were shaped by the tugging of these same oxen at his rocky farm.

Whether it was a sense of place within a New Hampshire natural environment giving birth to a "quaint, figurative" and eloquent tongue, or whether it was a combination of other reasons—it is clear that a remarkable lot of New Hampshire women writers of the latter 19th century gave especially apt expression to the integrity and the values of life within small New Hampshire communities: Lucy Crawford, Kate Sanborn, Sara Josepha Hale, Edna D. Proctor, Ellen Rollins, Celia Thaxter. Coincidentally or not, it was no less eloquent—though less literary—female voices that also took up in sequence the major social causes of the day: anti-slavery, temperance, women's suffrage. While men excelled in industry and raw politics, women excelled in literature and social causes. Indeed, it came to be widely assumed that, for those capable of it, a woman's "place" was to be a spokesperson for, if not a guardian of, social values. In 1903 a New Hampshire journalist wrote that "the progress of women has proved . . . that the larger the voice women have in affairs the higher are the moral ideals entertained by the community." Not everyone believed this, but no one undertook to demonstrate that it was untrue.

Working Places
In some urban environments a very different sense of place developed. Raymond Dubois reflected on life in Manchester at the turn of the century, "I was brought up in the area of the mill. All our people were mill people, and we didn't know anything else but mills. . . . We lived near the mills, we carried dinners for our parents, and we just were accustomed to the mills. It seemed like this was where we would fall in when we got old enough. I went in a few months after I became sixteen. . . . I didn't like it, and I don't think too many people in there liked it either."

Many urban children knew all too well the meaning of the working place: child labor was standard, with sometimes predictable results. *Foster's Daily Democrat* for August 1, 1874, reported: "Accidents happened to a couple of boys in the mills yesterday. . . . One of them. . . . aged 12 years got his hand caught in the doubler, a machine used in the card room, which stripped the skin and muscle from the wrists to the finger ends. . . . Soon afterwards another boy put his hand into the same machine and came off worse still. Two of his fingers had to be amputated."

The Manchester Coal and Ice Company, which according to its city directory ads sold "coal, wood and Massabesic Ice," delivered its products throughout Manchester in horse-drawn wagons. The employees of the company, with their ice tongs, are shown here about 1915. The photograph is probably by Arthur Boulanger of Manchester. MVHC

Families worked at the Amoskeag Mills, lived in Amoskeag housing, and wore Amoskeag-made cotton. For a long time and for many families it was a satisfactory life. This couple was photographed in 1920, two years before a long bitter strike against the company began. MVHC

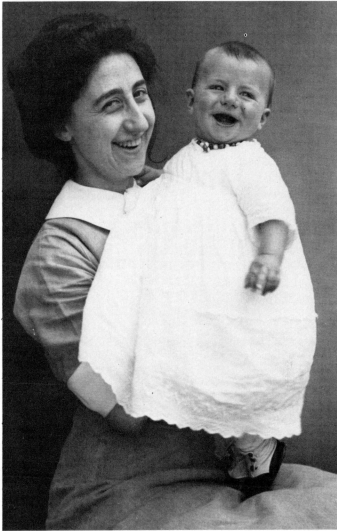

Cora Pellerin of Manchester said: "I came from Canada in 1911. I started working in 1912 when I was eleven . . . my father had a birth certificate made for me in the name of my sister Cora, who died as a baby, because you couldn't go to work unless you were fourteen. . . . I worked in Canada during the strike of 1922, . . . but I never would go back there to live. It was paradise here because you got your money, and you did whatever you wanted to with it."

In some circumstances a sense of place was connected with certain other intangible qualities. The gloom of the Depression hung over the land in 1931 when John Winant gave his inaugural address as governor: "I feel very strongly that certain essential spiritual qualities are needed in order to restore confidence." Winant told his audience that "neither over-optimism nor fear are safe guides . . . in maintaining economic stability. We can do more . . . by undramatic and unselfish effort combined with hard work and quiet faith than through legislative panaceas." This is vintage New Hampshire talking to itself.

That year historian and journalist Bernard De Voto traveled through New England to discover how these tribes had adapted their heritage and the needs of the hour to their own sense of place within the social order. His report appeared in *Harper's*

When photographer Ulric Bourgeois migrated from Quebec to Manchester near the turn of the century, he began the process of documenting the city of Manchester and its working-class people. Nevertheless, many of his best photographs were shots of his own family, which provide the viewer with insight into both family life of the period and the Franco-American experience in New Hampshire. The photographer manages to include himself in both 1910 family photographs on page 70 and in the 1915 photograph, above left, with his wife and daughters. This portrait of mother and daughter, above, is from 1907. MVHC

Manchester's ethnic groups have maintained a degree of cohesiveness over the years. Pictured (above) is a Greek coffeehouse in 1978 (photograph by Gary Samson) and (top) a Greek coffeehouse in 1910 (MVHC).

Magazine in March 1932, "New England, There She Stands." These people, he wrote, have "never thrown themselves upon the charity of the nation. . . . from this frigid north, this six-inch soil sifted among boulders, has come no screaming for relief. The breed has clung to its uplands, and solvency has been its righteousness and independence has been its pride. . . . here are people who have mastered the conditions of their life." At this time New Hampshire had not yet seen the worst of the Depression, and the WPA, the CCC, and the REA all lay in the future, as did the closing of hundreds of New Hampshire mills. But De Voto saw or thought he saw the qualities that would see New Hampshire through.

> *Their ancestral religion told them that the world is a battleground whereon mankind is sentenced to defeat—an idea not inappropriate to the granite against which they must make their way. By the granite they have lived for three centuries, tightening their belts and hanging on, by the sense of what is real. They are the base of the Yankee commonwealth; and America, staring apprehensively through fog that may not lift in this generation, may find their knowledge of hard things more than a little useful.*

Movements Out and In

The temptation to romanticize the achievement of those who stay put and acquire knowledge of hard things is nearly irresistible. The other side of social life, its sense of coming and going, is kaleidoscopic, impressionistic—and subject to its own idealization.

By the middle of the 19th century so many New Hampshire natives had moved to Boston that there were celebrations of remembrance. "Festival of the Sons of New Hampshire" one such affair was called, and of course Daniel Webster was the orator. No one in America could recreate heroic origins like this son of New Hampshire, who had moved to Massachusetts in 1816. People of his native state, he said, were "given to the chase and to the hunt in time of peace; fitted for endurance and danger; and when war came, they were ready to meet it. It was in the midst of these vicissitudes that they were formed to hardihood and enterprise, and trained to military skill and fearlessness. . . . When the march from Boston to Lexington and Concord had spread the flames of liberty, who answered to the call? Did New Hampshire need to be summoned to Bunker Hill? She came at the first blaze of the beacon-fires. None were earlier, none more ready, none more valiant."

In Webster's time many natives of Massachusetts were also traveling north. In 1839 Henry David Thoreau and his brother rowed up the Merrimack River to inspect the New Hampshire interior. Specimens from the Granite State met them coming down: "another scow hove in sight, creeping down the river, and hailing it, we attached ourselves to its side, and floated back in company, chatting with the boatmen. . . . They appeared to be green hands from far among the hills, who had taken this means to get to the seaboard, and see the world; and would possibly visit the Falkland Isles, and the China seas, before they again saw the waters of the Merrimack, or perchance, not return this way forever. . . . What grievance has its root among the New Hampshire hills? we asked; what is wanting to human life here, that these men should make such haste to the antipodes?''

For his part, Thoreau liked the New Hampshire he saw: riverbank farmsteads ''more pleasing to our eyes than palaces or castles'' that were ''surrounded commonly by a small patch of corn and beans, squashes and melons, with sometimes a graceful hopyard on one side, and some running vine over the windows.'' Such dwellings appeared to him ''like bee-hives set to gather honey for a summer. I have not read of any Arcadian life which surpasses the actual luxury and serenity of these New England dwellings.'' Thoreau knows that he sees these New Hampshire homes with the eyes of a poet and an idealist, and he yields to the fancy that ''the employment of their inhabitants by day would be to tend the flowers and herds, and at night, like the shepherds of old, to cluster and give names to the stars from the river banks.''

A few years later, Bostonian Francis Parkman took a coach to Lake Winnipesaukee, and then hiked from Alton Bay around to Center Harbor. In his 1841 journal Parkman wrote that for the first hours of the walk ''we passed no dwellings but a few log-cabins, with a little clearing in the forest around them. But, alas, the little pathway was widened by the junction of others, and farm houses began to appear, first singly, then in clusters, with clearings extending for miles.'' Parkman was amazed to see so much of the lakeside wilderness cleared. He was also annoyed: ''It was almost noon and we toiled up the scorching road, sweating and grumbling at the folly which had deprived us of shelter and comfort by ridiculously burning the forests, in the zeal for making clearings.'' In his eyes ''the burnt lands lay utterly waste and the sole effect of the operation is to ruin the scene and lay the road open to the baking sun.''

Above: Milford's Union Square seems unusually quiet in this late 19th century photograph. Throughout the century Milford was a thriving manufacturing town along the Souhegan River, where mills churned out cotton and woolen cloth, furniture, rugs and rug yarn, ladies' woolen hosiery, plows, and a number of other goods. In addition, Milford's granite quarries provided substantial employment during the second half of the century. NHHS

Top: A few carriages, pedestrians, and cyclists work their way up lower Main Street, Peterborough, in this 1899 photograph. The cleared fields and stone walls on East Hill in the background belie the fact that Peterborough's prosperity in the late 19th century rested upon commerce and a highly diversified manufacturing base. NHHS

Left: Their stylish riggings unbuttoned, this party posed to be photographed on their ascent of Mt. Monadnock. An earlier climber wrote in 1838, "After something of a strain we reached the top of the first peak. As we looked upward we saw another peak at the distance of a mile. So down we go . . . and up we toil to the height of the second peak. To our surprise and disappointment there is a still higher peak beyond . . . So down we go again and up we toil again. Quite exhausted we reach the height of the third peak. We look beyond and upward, and lo! another still higher and more difficult of access . . . We perform another go-down and go-up . . . We look again and the summit is far off still. . . ." NHHS

This group of soldiers from Company F of the Third New Hampshire Regiment had yet to see combat when they posed for New Hampshire photographer Henry Moore near Hilton Head, South Carolina. Before the war was over, however, they would experience their share of combat: the regiment suffered a 54 percent casualty rate. NHHS

Henry Moore's photograph of the regiment's cooks' galley, Company K, suggests that Civil War army cuisine may not have met gourmet standards. Taste aside, however, the cooks of the Third New Hampshire Regiment deserve some credit: the Third was one of the few New Hampshire regiments for which death from disease was less common than death in combat. NHHS

The next year Parkman was tramping around in the old Indian Stream Republic in Pittsburg. Following the common practice of hikers, he and his friend stopped at a house "and asked for lodging and a supper. . . . We went in to supper, which was served in rough style, but had the virtue of cleanliness, as did the whole place—children excepted. There were some eight or ten imps of both sexes." Their host was "a rough-hewn piece of timber enough, but his wife was a perfect barbarian, as far as the entire absence of all manners can make one, but both were equally open and hospitable."

Dr. Albert A. Moulton was brigade surgeon of the Third New Hampshire Regiment when he, his wife, and their young son posed for this Moore photograph in 1862. Moulton, a native of Meredith and a graduate of the Dartmouth Medical School, had been joined by his wife and son in March 1862. NHHS

Tourists and Migrants

Older forms of travel often brought different classes of people abreast of one another—where they could size each other up with a sidelong glance. Nathaniel Hawthorne traveled to the White Mountains, stayed at Crawford's Inn, and formed the plan—never carried out—to spend extensive time there "for the sake of studying the yeomen of New England"; he would mingle with the drovers, lumberjacks, and farmers in their own settings "to see how sturdily they make head against the blast." Later Hawthorne caught a glimpse of New Hampshire people when they were themselves on the move: on the Isles of Shoals in 1852, waiting for Franklin Pierce to arrive so they could discuss the Presidential campaign, Hawthorne watched people arrive by boat from Portsmouth. The first troupe was "apparently from the interior of New Hampshire." Among them "country traders, a country doctor, and such sorts of people, rude, shrewd, and simple, and well-behaved enough; wondering at sharks, and equally at lobsters; sitting down to table with their coats off; helping themselves out of the dish with their own forks; taking pudding on the plates off which they have eaten meat." No doubt he would have preferred these people in their own setting, for people "at just this stage of manners are more disagreeable than at any other stage. They are aware of some decencies, but not so deeply aware as to make them a matter of conscience."

The Civil War brought a new form of travel for New Hampshire's young men. Fourteen regiments went south, probably at least 35,000 men, more than one-tenth of the population. In an 1861 letter published in the Keene *Sentinel* a member of the Second New Hampshire Regiment told of his stop in Reading, Pennsylvania: "I strolled about a while to see the place and people. This is a German city. The name upon every tradesman's sign is a jaw-breaker, and *'lager beer'* is everywhere." He admitted he had tasted that "nauseating beverage in New England, with very wry face, but when I drank in Pennsylvania the real

Dutch brew, I did not wonder that the Dutchmen love it." At this time New Hampshire was hooked on hard cider, and a temperance movement was gathering momentum. Later, better New Hampshire beer probably helped the temperance cause by providing an alternative to "ardent spirits."

"Go West, young man," said New Hampshire native Horace Greeley, editor of the *New York Tribune*. One knows from his autobiography what he was advising these young men to leave: "Picking stones is a never-ending labor on one of those rocky New England farms. Pick as closely as you may, the next ploughing turns up a fresh eruption. . . . youngsters soon learn to regard it with detestation. I filially love the 'Granite State' but could well excuse the absence of sundry subdivisions of her granite." Many who heeded his advice went west in the vigor of youth, dropping the past like a worn shoe, but many others went dolefully. Ziba Crane wrote home to New Hampshire from his stopping point in New York: "Yes, dear brother, I never expect to see you or any of my friends again on earth, nor my native land. I bid farewell. We expect to start next Monday for the west . . . and whether I shall live to accomplish that long journey, it is more than I can say."

Traveling implied meetings and separations and recollections of them: the stuff of nostalgia. A coach which at the time was hot and dusty and jarring is seen in retrospect serenely "wending its course." Already a hundred years ago dozens of town historians were sighing the sigh of the 1878 author who said that the railroad brought a new order of things. "The numerous teams and stages . . . disappeared forever. From that day to the present, no ponderous wagon, with white canvas covering, drawn by eight stalwart horses, has been seen wending its course along [the Fourth New Hampshire Turnpike]." The old stagecoach, he said, with its "passengers, and mountain of baggage, has rolled along the road, leaving a cloud of dust behind: all have gone,—nor will they ever be seen again."

Above: Vigneault and Pigeon's bar and retail liquor store did business in Manchester from approximately 1914 to 1917. The short-lived firm disappeared from its Manchester Street location just before the 18th Amendment and the Volstead Act would have closed its doors. MVHC

Top: One look at Horace Greeley's rustic birthplace in Amherst suggests why he may have advised young men to "go west" in the years before the Civil War. Greeley, founder of the New York Tribune and Presidential candidate, was one of many New Hampshire natives who found fame and fortune somewhere else. His family deserted their New Hampshire hill farm when Greeley was a boy and went west, first to Vermont, and later to Erie County, Pennsylvania. NHHS

Tramping

Always with the coming of hard times came new forms of vagabondage. The "knights of the road," as tramps were called, appeared from nowhere and were going nowhere. "Any person going about from place to place begging and asking or subsisting upon charity" is a tramp, said an 1878 New Hampshire law, and to be "punished by imprisonment at hard labor." This didn't stop the tramps, but it encouraged them to offer to work for a meal. In the New Hampshire countryside itself there was more understanding and sympathy than the state law implied. Many, perhaps most, towns had a tramp house—a roof and usually one meal guaranteed by the town—intermittently active from the Civil War to World War II.

Haydn Pearson's memories of Hancock, which go back to the early 20th century, sum up the experiences of hundreds of communities: "I used to lie awake at night in my small room under the eaves and wonder about them. 'Tramp' was a word we learned to fear." Pearson recalls that "tramps drifted into town from the cities south of us." (If you lived in the country tramps always originated in the city.) "They were ragged, unkempt, and bearded. They plodded up the road on the way to the big orchard farm."

They would come to the ell door and ask Mother if she could spare a bite to eat. If Father was around Mother sent the tramps to him. That was an inflexible rule. The other rule was, when we children were young, that if we saw a tramp coming up the road the girls were to go into the house and Mother was to lock the doors and not answer a knock.

True, the bearded fellow was probably not Parkman or Thoreau or Longfellow doing research and offering to buy a night's lodging. True, tramps were said to be petty thieves, and often unseen tramps were blamed for otherwise unexplained fires; but the basis of these beliefs was usually gossip, not evidence, and fears usually dissolved. Pearson writes:

By the time I was ten I knew the tramps for what they were. With rare exception they were broken, dispirited men. Most of them blamed liquor for their sorry condition. All who came to Hancock were men well along in years. It seemed silly to be afraid of such specimens of humankind.

Some tramps were simply perpetual travelers; some were seasonal and turned up in the same village in the same week, year after year. Sometimes an apple farmer or potato farmer looked over the tramp crop and hired the best of the lot for the picking season. One tramp who stopped at the Pearson farm and stayed the winter as a hired man was college-educated and past middle age, and full of yarns about faraway places. By spring he was uneasy and confided his dark secret to young Haydn: "I don't want you to tell your parents this until after I've left," he said. "I wish I could stay, but I can't. When I have been in a place just so long I get restless and moody. I haven't touched liquor for years, but I've got a disease worse than that. I have to travel."

The biggest hit at Concord's Bicycle Parade of 1896 was the Big Trike from Nashua. Made by the people at Vim Tire, the tricycle weighed 1,900 pounds, and its wheels were 11.5 feet in diameter. It took the muscle of eight men to peddle the contraption to Concord from Nashua—scaring horses the entire way. A punctured tire had to be repaired in Manchester, and, according to newspaper accounts, it took an hour to refill the tire with air. NHHS

For about three decades, from approximately 1880 to 1910, bicycle clubs flourished throughout the state, and cycling was a very stylish sport for both men and women. This carefully posed photograph of the Dartmouth Bicycle Club was made about 1888. DCA

Other itinerants added a regular color to the landscape: the tailor who boarded with a family for a week, made a suit of clothes for each member, and then moved on to the next household; the painter who came to stencil the halls and parlors of the village mansions; the traveling photographer who distributed the family, the horse, and the sulky in front of the homestead and produced in, say, 1890, a wonderfully sharp print, such as is not easily matched even today.

Wheels and Wars

Trains taught Americans that it was possible to move fast and survive, so other forms of high-speed transportation were designed and put on the market. Bicycles were the rage of the

1880s and 1890s, catching the fancy of the public the way snowmobiles did 80 years later. In the 1890s Frank W. Rollins, later governor, dreamed of "skimming like a swallow along perfectly kept bicycle paths." New Hampshire Senator William Chandler developed a reputation in Washington, D.C., for the way he careened through the United States capital on his bicycle, swallowtailed coat streaming in his wake, the terror of horses, dogs, Democrats, and other denizens of the capital city. Back in New Hampshire, Chandler promptly went in for the latest contraption: he bought an automobile. A diary entry for 1902 tells a story many others of the time could tell: "All went well to Warner, when the chain flew off. Got it on again, but within half a mile it flew off and broke. Oscar hauled me home with horse

William Stark of Manchester specialized in domesticating wild animals. At the 1866 state fair held in Nashua, Stark and his elk were the highlight of the day. Henry W. Herrick, a Hopkinton native, sketched and engraved scenes of New Hampshire for New York clients, and this one of Stark and his elk appeared in Harper's Weekly. *Residing in Manchester, Herrick in his later years painted in watercolor and became a distinguished author and landscape artist. NHHS*

Just eight years after the Wright brothers' initial flight Manchester hosted an aviation meet on September 23, 1911. To the surprise of some spectators this flying machine actually got off the ground. NHHS

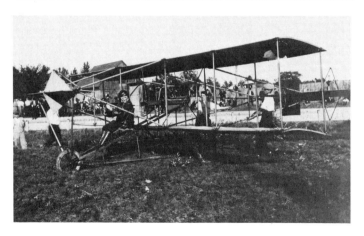

and wagon." As usual, Senator Chandler was too far ahead of his time. He sold the troublesome auto and went back to a bicycle.

For many a remote town the real age of the automobile began when the 1911 Sears Roebuck catalogue arrived: there on page 1266 were four automobiles displayed in all their glory. Sixty-five years later Caroll Farnsworth recalled bringing the first auto permanently to the town of Washington. It was July 6, 1911, when he, his father, and brother went to the freight office in Hillsboro "to assemble our new Sears auto. The wheels were gotten on, and gas in the tank and then we cranked it up. I then took the seat at the steering-bar and headed across the railroad and on to the fair-grounds. Then three laps around the race track for my first driving lesson, then headed for home. Got there safely." In similar ways a new era of mobility came to hundreds of towns.

Just as the Civil War had opened America to New Hampshire eyes, so World War I brought Europe into the consciousness of the Granite State. On May Day, 1915, the Portsmouth *Daily Chronicle* said that "every year large numbers of travellers go abroad and scatter their money lavishly among the people of foreign countries," a practice which is unpatriotic since many of these tourists "have never seen their own country" and also now dangerous: "There is war in the Old World, earnest, bitter and cruel war, and it is the part of wisdom for Americans who are not obliged to go there to keep as far away from it as they can." The war came closer and in May 1916 the Laconia *Democrat* reported proudly on "the biggest civic parade in American history" held in New York City "in favor of preparedness." New Hampshire was represented "by the largest American flag in existence, measuring 100 feet long and 52 feet wide and weighing 500 pounds. It was made, every stitch of it, by the Amoskeag Manufacturing Company." In March 1917, one hundred and eighty towns passed resolutions of support for the national government, and in less than a month the nation was officially at war with Germany. Twenty thousand New Hampshire men served in the armed forces; 697 of them gave their lives.

World War II supplied the pressure by which the New Hampshire outlook merged with the national perspective: it happened to a degree unprecedented then and unequalled since. Most of the familiar, self-consciously New Hampshire terms of reference were suspended: sense of local identity and of place receded, and the dynamics of movement were all related to the war effort. Sixty thousand Granite State uniformed men and women were dispersed to every corner of the earth; 1,600 did not return. Dozens of organizations popped up to guide the war effort, diverting the local will into the mainstream of the national will. Success was imperfect, of course. The *Hillsborough Messenger* reported that Frank Cutting, country store owner, protested: "Mr. Cutting recognized the necessity for regulation and control of business as a war measure, but being an Individualist and never having been used to taking orders and to absentee management, he decided to close the store for the duration."

In the New Hampshire hills a hundred mica mines were opened; on the coast the Portsmouth Naval Shipyard churned out a new submarine every two weeks throughout the war. Like caissons rolling along, the symbols of that time come to mind, each one heavy with memories: victory gardens, the USO, sav-

ings bonds, gold stars, V-mail, draft boards, scrap iron, ration books, the home front, the GI Bill. But they are one and all national emblems and part, not just of the state's, but of the nation's experience.

Some actions stand out as uniquely New Hampshire's. Chief among them was the resolution debated at the March 1945 town meetings, one that suggested a link between the security of New Hampshire hearths and the peace of nations, a referendum no other state put before its people:

To see if the Town will vote to support United States membership in a general system of international cooperation . . . having police power to maintain the peace of the world.

By more than a two-to-one margin New Hampshire people urged the United States to join the proposed United Nations organization.

On October 24, 1950, a block of New Hampshire granite was laid as the cornerstone of the United Nations building in New York City.

Military launchings have been common in the history of the Piscataqua—the first warship built at Portsmouth was commissioned in 1690, the last in the 1960s. To bolster American defense in response to World War I, the Atlantic Corporation was founded in 1918 and contracted with the Emergency Fleet Corporation to produce 10 steel cargo vessels. Completed in record time, the Babboosic *was launched at Portsmouth in 1919, the second ship off the line. From the Historic Photograph Collection of Strawbery Banke, Inc.*

III

E·C·O·N·O·M·Y
A·N·D
I·N·D·U·S·T·R·Y

The legendary Granite State reveals something of itself in outcroppings of gray stone. Veins of granite abound, but at Concord a ledge of superior stone was recognized by 1819 to have quarrying potential. In this circa 1910 view of the New England Granite Company quarry, workers remove granite blocks. Concord granite has been used in the construction of important buildings throughout the country. NHHS

C·H·A·P·T·E·R
E·I·G·H·T

B·E·F·O·R·E
T·H·E
I·N·D·U·S·T·R·I·A·L
R·E·V·O·L·U·T·I·O·N

Before the coming of the railroad the workhorse of Great Bay commerce was the Piscataqua gundalow, in which cordwood, hay, boards and planks, bricks, and other cargo traveled the tidal waters of Great Bay and the Piscataqua River to Portsmouth. By 1900, however, the unique Piscataqua gundalow had seen its day, victim of the railroad and Portsmouth's declining importance as a coastal trade center. The Piscataqua Gundalow Project commemorated the gundalow by constructing one. The Captain Edward H. Adams, *seen here at its launching in Portsmouth Harbor on June 13, 1982, took two-and-a-half years to build, at a cost of over $100,000. Photograph by Gary Samson*

For 100 years after New Hampshire was first settled, the main businesses were fishing, lumbering, and the associated trades, including extensive shipbuilding. For the next 100 years, the 1730s to 1830s, the main occupation was farming and its allied trades, including extensive small-time manufacturing to supply farm needs.

Ships and Farms

Shipbuilding was a significant New Hampshire industry throughout most of the 200 years that led up to the Industrial Revolution. Small vessels for the Boston lumber trade, built on the Piscataqua as early as the 1650s, were soon followed by more and larger ships. There is record of 34 vessels with an average size of 30 tons built on the Piscataqua between 1687 and 1695. Before 1700 larger warships were also built there for the British Navy, one, the HMS *Falkland,* of 776 tons. The lumber and ship-

building businesses, although at first dependent upon the fluid capital produced by the fisheries, soon provided a well-developed economic base for the coastal colony: carpenters and coopers, shipwrights and sailmakers, and a dozen other craftsmen set up business and thrived. The merchants thrived most of all.

Shipbuilding continued to grow after 1700 and so did the size of the ships. In one five-year spurt, 1722-1727, 94 vessels with an average carrying capacity of 60 tons were built at dozens of different Piscataqua shipyards. With the mast trade in full gear, the ships were getting larger and larger: "Masters" had a capacity of 400 to 600 tons. In another five-year spurt, 1740-1745, 142 vessels were built on the New Hampshire coast. On a typical day in the 1750s one could have seen at least one cargo ship enter and another leave the Portsmouth harbor.

Mast shipments to England were halted, of course, by the Revolution, but shipbuilding was only slowed. After the Revolutionary War, shipbuilding in and around Portsmouth continued, with a trend toward still larger ships. By 1790 production was in high gear again, 20 vessels being launched from the Piscataqua that year. Between 1800 and 1860, 575 sailing vessels were constructed at or near Portsmouth. Though this represents fewer vessels per year than during the high point a century earlier (10 per year as compared with 25), because of the ships' increased size it represents more capacity than ever before. The Portsmouth ships of the 1850s averaged over 1,000 tons. But by the time of the Revolutionary War, and certainly by the 1850s, the shipyards were representing a smaller and smaller percentage of an economy that had become increasingly agricultural.

Before the Revolutionary War many of the best forests near the coast had been cut down, the waters around the Isles of Shoals were being fished out, and, indeed, the rivers of the coast were so polluted with sawdust that fish could scarcely spawn there. At the same time, population pressures from Massachusetts and abroad were increasing. By the middle of the 18th century, the interior of New Hampshire, increasingly freed

of Indian troubles, was being rapidly opened up for development by deliberate government policy and by the skillful programs of speculative land merchants. There was land, free or cheap, for anyone who wanted to try his luck subduing it. It took a long time, but before the Revolution the New Hampshire frontier had moved away from the seacoast, and a basically agricultural society had planted roots in the thin and rocky soil of the interior. As measured by the amount of land under cultivation and by the percentage of the state's economy and population tied to the farm, the high point of New Hampshire agriculture came sometime in the 1830s. It had taken 200 years.

From Rural to Industrial Economy

Lumbering, fishing, shipbuilding, and finally and most importantly, farming—these were the premises of the New Hampshire economy from the beginning until well into the 19th century. But by the 1830s the picture was changing. From one point of view—the view that takes the rural yeomanry of Jefferson and Belknap as its ideal—New Hampshire was clearly on the skids before the middle of the 19th century. Town after town in rural New Hampshire reached its peak of population and of rustic, small-town self-sufficiency some time between 1820 and 1850 and then began to shrink as the population escaped to the city or the West.

From another point of view, however, New Hampshire was just getting going. Industrially, the beginnings of modern New Hampshire date from precisely the period when the agricultural economy crested. Looking back from today's standpoint, it is easy to see that after the 1830s all the major social and economic reference points had changed—though not everyone noticed it at the time. Some noticed it then and rejoiced. With their own eyes they had seen the humming factories of Manchester rise suddenly out of pastureland. Daniel Webster, a New Hampshire farm boy who had blazed a path to the centers of power, stood on the brand new railroad tracks in Lebanon in 1847, hailing a new day:

From earliest times the one flaw in the Portsmouth harbor had been Henderson's Point (also known as "Pull-and-Be-Damned Point"), a projection of rock 500 feet into the river's mouth that created vicious crossgrain currents hazardous to navigation. When the Portsmouth Navy Yard was expanded in 1905, the point was removed. First, a dam was built around it, and the layers of rock were hammered and blasted loose and carried away on freight cars. Then it was decided to finish the job with one massive dynamite blast—the largest ever executed. Hundreds of holes were drilled up to 80 feet into the rock and 50 tons of dynamite were deposited. The blast itself was the major tourist attraction of the season. Special trains ran to Portsmouth on July 22, 1905; at 11 minutes past 4 p.m., 18,000 spectators saw Henderson's Point disappear. Courtesy, Dimond Library, UNH

It is an extraordinary era in which we live. It is altogether new. The world has seen nothing like it before. I will not pretend, no one can pretend, to discern the end; but everybody knows that the age is remarkable for scientific research. . . . The ancients saw nothing like it. The moderns have seen nothing like it till the present generation.

Some perhaps heard his words and felt their depth and truth—if only because the great man said them with such force and majesty—yet without really knowing what he was talking about. Had not soothsayers been saying time out of mind that the old way is going or gone, that we live in a new age? Many expected that their sons would farm the same homestead, with the same tools, pretty much as their fathers had—and they were right. Yet vast changes were sweeping through the economy of New England, and social trends were afoot in New Hampshire that would completely alter the state.

Certain symbols of the new age saluted by Webster in the 1840s stand out: water and turnpike had been the basic means of commercial transportation, now it was to be rail; iron had been the basic strong metal, now it was to be steel; the household, shop, and local mill had been the locus of industry, now it was to be factory and corporation; the farmer had always stood out as the representative American, now he was to be flanked by the businessman and the factory worker. New England would still be, numerically at least, a rural region for another century, but it was now to be more and more the city that would focus the ambitions of its youth. As a city, Manchester encapsulates the whole story. It is New Hampshire's representative 19th-century city as Portsmouth is its 18th-century city. Portsmouth, created by politics and a seacoast economy, is an artifact of colonialism; Manchester, created by the railroads and the mills, is an artifact of industrial development.

More generally, the significant economic facts for New Hampshire gather round three major 19th-century themes, in each of which new technology was the decisive element: railroad transportation, textiles, and lumbering. They are stories of risings and fallings. Behind these developments, however, lay the colonial struggles with the challenges of transportation.

Province Roads

In the middle of the 18th century, one could get about fairly well in the seacoast towns, but travel in the rest of the province was difficult and painful. The Portsmouth-to-Boston post road was an exception: it accommodated a weekly round-trip stage and the more frequent mail riders well before the Revolution. Inland, most of the roads were bridle paths or cart trails that wound over ledges, around stumps, and through brooks. The first major road authorized by the New Hampshire Assembly was in 1722—65 miles to Lake Winnipesaukee to build a fort there "for the annoyance of the Indians." The roads themselves annoyed the citizens. Lady Wentworth, writing in 1770 from the governor's Wolfeboro summer home, worried about the trip back to Portsmouth: "I dread the journey, as the roads are so bad."

Until 1770 western New Hampshire was joined to the eastern part by only the most haphazard system of individual town roads—adequate near the villages, then petering out. Selectmen were mandated by the New Hampshire Assembly to keep the town roads in repair, but enforcement was another matter. Towns sometimes complained to the Assembly about their neighbors. The town of Camden (now Washington) wrote in January 1773 to the Assembly about "the greait Deficuly we the inhabitance of Camden, Labour under by Reason of the Roades being So bad in the Township of monadnick No. 7 or Limbrick [Goshen] so Kalled that it is Allmost imposable for a teem to Pess there and Dangorous for a Hors Nothing has Ben Done."

There was good commercial reason for New Hampshire to work for something better. In 1761 the Assembly had noted "...the place called Cohass [Haverhill] ... represented to be in great forwardness, where great quantities of Corn will soon be raised which will be transported down the Connecticut River for sale, unless a good Highway can be made ... into this Province." Accordingly, the Assembly decided to unite the province by constructing a public road northwest to southeast: from Coös to the sea. It was a sound idea, but ideas do not build a highway the way money does.

The Assembly record for January 16, 1770, says: "The Question was put, Whether the Province should be at any Expense for opening and clearing said roads, and it passed in the negative." Let the towns that get the road pay, thought the Assembly. Let the Province pay for what the Province mandates, thought the towns—a refrain that still echoes today. The Assembly prevailed: the road was built, Dover to Cohass (Durham, Barrington, Strafford ... to Haverhill), 100 miles, much of it only bridle path, and the towns were charged through a "Province Road Tax" levied on property holders—10 shillings per 100 acres.

Was this an early version of "home rule" controversies in which home rule lost? Not exactly. Siding with the towns, the governor and his Council (which included Portsmouth merchants with land investments) wanted the Province, not landowners, to pay for the road through towns where they owned much land. Gilmanton, for example, had the longest mileage on the new road, the steepest hills, and a lot of acreage held by the governor and his Portsmouth friends. By laying the tax on the landowners in the towns, the Assembly had also laid the tax on the governor—an opportunity not to be missed.

Nevertheless, Governor Wentworth was a doer, and road building was a thing to be done. The Indian wars were over, the interior was being settled rapidly, lines for supplies and surpluses were needed everywhere. So the "college road" was put through from Dartmouth via Plymouth to Wolfeboro; also the "Governor's road," 60 miles from Wolfeboro to the sea. A new road from Hanover through Concord to Portsmouth was started. A road—or at least a "road"—was put through Crawford Notch. In the early 1770s there was fortnightly mail service across the state from Hanover to Portsmouth. Indeed, the public roads promoted by Governor Wentworth just before the Revolution turned out to be of major importance for keeping the colony united during the Revolutionary War.

Turnpikes and Canals
In the burst of democratic enthusiasm following the War for

In 1813 Lewis Downing, wheelwright, advertised a Concord shop where he would sell "small waggons . . . as cheap as can be bought." From this beginning came the empire of the Concord Coach. In 1826 Downing hired J. Stephens Abbot, and the next year they formed a partnership. By 1830 they had perfected the design of the coach (distinguished by a flat top, rounded bottom and, most importantly, "thoroughbraces" which served as shock absorbers). In 1847 Abbot and Downing split: Abbot continued in the old shops, and Downing set up an operation elsewhere in Concord. Then in 1865 the two firms were rejoined and remained in partnership until the company closed in 1925. Through the years no other coach rivaled the Concord Coach, and the name of Abbot-Downing became known around the world. NHHS

In the summer of 1896 workmen began replacing the old covered bridge at Cornish with a modern steel bridge. At the New Hampshire end of this bridge over the Connecticut River, the steel span was already in place (far right) when this photograph was taken. The roof and siding of the old bridge were removed, exposing the heavy, wooden truss members held together by wooden pins. The unusual frame pictured here served as a crane and derrick in the rebuilding. NHHS

Above: Concord's Abbot-Downing Company was a big business when this picture was taken around 1890. At its height, the company employed about 250 men and turned out about 2,000 coaches and carriages annually, with sales throughout the United States, South America, and Australia. NHHS

Right: This snow roller packed roads in the Hanover area near the turn of the century. DCA

In this lithograph from the mid-19th century, a coach clatters from the "flats" toward the Free Bridge at Concord. Spring flooding made spanning of the Merrimack an expensive proposition: the bridge shown here was the third to be erected at the site. This approach to Concord off Interstate 93 is still called "Bridge Street." NHHS

Independence, it appeared to many that what the government had only halfheartedly achieved in the way of public road building could be swiftly accomplished by free enterprise. It was a venturesome thought, backed by conviction and energy, but not by evidence. Turnpike corporations were formed to build public roads, pay for them from tolls, and return a profit to the investors. By the time the plan had proved to be basically unprofitable, New Hampshire had a fair start on a public road system.

"Proprietors of New Hampshire Turnpike Road" incorporated themselves in 1796 to build a 36-mile road from the Piscataqua bridge, then under construction near Portsmouth, to the Merrimack near Concord, linking nine towns with an almost straight line. Other corporations formed quickly: for the Second New Hampshire Turnpike (Claremont to Amherst) and for the Third (Walpole via Keene to Massachusetts), both in 1799, and for the Fourth (Merrimack River at Boscawen to the Connecticut River at the White River), in 1800. Incorporation automatically conferred right of eminent domain along the proposed

routes. The company was typically empowered to lay out a road four rods wide on a route best combining "shortness of distance with the most practical ground" between the designated end points. Affected towns and the resident farmers almost never objected to their land being bisected by a turnpike—indeed, there was usually competition for the honor. By law, toll rates were to be lowered if profits exceeded 12 percent. No problem.

Entrepreneurs of every sort immediately clambered aboard the turnpike bandwagon: 50 corporations were chartered by 1810. More were chartered during the next half-century, but after 1820 the early roads tended to lapse into public freeways at

about the same rate new ones were opened elsewhere. Parts of the First New Hampshire Turnpike, for example, were being sold to its host towns by 1824, and in 1821 Keene appropriated money to maintain its part of the Third New Hampshire Turnpike. Still, nearly 600 miles of road were constructed in New Hampshire by corporations. One such road, aslant Mt. Washington, still operates as a toll road, as it has for more than 100 years.

Though turnpikes brought poor returns for their investors, they were a boon to the farmers, for they diverted the flow of New Hampshire produce from the Connecticut River toward Boston markets. Farmers went to the seacoast with their own teams in the winter, carrying produce and returning with sleighs full of supplies. As the toll roads became town-owned freeways, public ownership conquering private enterprise, their use and value to enhance free trade increased.

By far the best highway in the state in the early 19th century was the Merrimack River. Before the first turnpike was started, men of Massachusetts were digging the Middlesex Canal from Charlestown, Massachusetts, to the Merrimack near Lowell. This kindled the dream of a direct Concord-to-Boston waterway—though of course only a fanatic would project a canal around the Amoskeag Falls. Judge Samuel Blodget, already past 70 years old, was the required New Hampshire fanatic: in 1793 he bought the land and started digging. Blodget, a noted inventor who had also developed coach lines, traveled through Europe, and raised sunken ships, built along the east bank of the Merrimack a novel system of locks which, when first tried in 1799, were promptly smashed to bits by the river current. Altogether he sank most of a fortune and 14 years of love and labor into the mile-long canal. The state finally authorized a lottery to help pay the bills, and Blodget lived to oversee the completion of the canal and to ride in triumph through the new locks on May Day, 1807. He died in heroic peace just a few months later.

It required, then, but a few short canals in Bow and Hooksett and there it was: a smooth highway from Boston, 85 miles into the heartland of New Hampshire at Concord. By 1815 traffic was heavy and getting heavier every year. The Boston and Concord Boating Company paid for the locks and paid dividends from 1826 to 1842. Long boats, 75 feet by 9 or 10 feet, were poled, two men to a boat, up and down the river, sometimes aided by a square sail, bringing supplies one way and produce the other. Typically, the trip was five days up and four days down. Granite from Concord was one of the main products—down the Merrimack River to all the major seaboard cities, day in, day out. By 1830 the industry of the capital city had given the state a nickname: the Granite State.

Floating the inland freight downstream to the cities on the sea—one is struck by the ageless simplicity and charm of the idea, just as one knows instantly that the Merrimack was finished as a highway as soon as the iron horse sauntered up the banks of the river in the 1840s. Daniel Webster, en route to Lebanon for that speech in 1847, would have glanced out the train window as he careened along at 30 miles per hour, would have watched the freight boats adrift on the Merrimack, and may have suddenly sensed how quaint were all the old ways and how extraordinary the new.

As the old shipping trade declined, most industry moved inland. By the middle of the 19th century, however, the Portsmouth wharves began to see new traffic. The inland transport of coal to the mills of Manchester and other towns began at Portsmouth, where great piles of coal were unloaded from coal packets onto waiting railroad cars, illustrated in this circa 1885 lithograph of the Concord Railroad Wharf. NHHS

At Portsmouth the Piscataqua passes to the sea under a lace of bridges that connect the harbor islands and bind New Hampshire (on the right), to Maine (on the left). Photograph by Bob LaPree. Courtesy, New Hampshire Times

C·H·A·P·T·E·R
N·I·N·E

G·E·T·T·I·N·G A·R·O·U·N·D:
R·O·A·D·S
A·N·D T·R·A·C·K·S

Imagine the lucky citizens of Wakefield, New Hampshire, on January 8, 1833. Not only would they get to see one of their fellow citizens drawn about in a "Rail-road Car," but they would get a firsthand look at a machine which, according to this broadside, was capable of "annihilating distance" and "beautifying our little globe, which to a great extent, has so remained a moral waste." NHHS

Time was when the railroads filled that niche in the public imagination now occupied by super highways, jet airlines, and space travel—fantastic and routine at once.

At first only fantastic. A worn story, nearly forgotten a century ago, has an old-timer visiting the new railway station for his first glimpse of the enormous locomotive. It stands, big as a barn, 50 tons of iron and steel eating piles of hardwood, belching and hissing. Awestruck by the monster, the old-timer confides solemnly to his neighbor, "They'll never get it going." In due course the great iron horse roars out of the station, bells aclang, trailing clouds of smoke and flatcars, takes the bend at easy stride, and, fast as a racehorse, disappears beyond the hill. Old-timer shakes his hoary head and says, "They'll never get it stopped."

If the story died as a joke as railroads became routine, it survives as a metaphor. Who was to suppose in 1800 that the jagged New Hampshire landscape would be trussed up within the century in 1,000 miles of steely bars? How get something so fantastic going? When it was completed at century's end and railroads were *the* mode of transportation, it seemed a permanent achievement: a way of life was then in motion that one could hardly imagine being stopped. Fourteen hundred cars a day passed through Concord. It turned out to be even easier to stop than to start.

In New Hampshire railroad building began in the 1830s. The first railroad charter, granted in 1832, represented a grandiose pipe dream of the Boston and Ontario Railroad to connect Boston—and, incidentally, New Hampshire, Vermont, Massachusetts, and New York—to the Great Lakes. It was never built. In 1835 the first three effective charters were issued, and in 1838 the first trains crossed the southern border and entered Nashua. The charters of 1835 set the pattern for future development: they were independent lines, and in a few decades there were dozens of other railroad companies operating in the state, mostly short lines connected to other lines. Gradually the other lines bought or leased the short lines, as other short lines were built, and were then rapidly absorbed in turn. Just as with the toll roads 50 years earlier, local entrepreneurs wanted to get in on the action, and after a time they wanted to get out. In a few more decades there were essentially only two major companies operating all the lines. And then there was one. In 60 years the Boston & Maine had achieved a monopoly in New Hampshire.

Building Railroads

The first chartered lines of 1835 were these: the Nashua and Lowell Railroad (from Nashua to Lowell, Massachusetts), which opened in 1838; the Boston & Maine Railroad, which opened from Boston to Exeter in 1840, to Dover in 1845, and the next year got to Portland, Maine, by absorbing the Boston and Portland. The Concord Railroad Corporation opened its road on September 6, 1842, with the locomotive *Amoskeag* and three passenger cars roaring into Concord while cannons were fired in the background. It was a death knell for the Boston and Concord Boating Company, which paid no dividends after that year.

Fifteen miles of New Hampshire track in 1840 grew to 900 by 1870, and Concord was the central point in the developing system. From the capital city railroad lines reached toward the interior and through it to Vermont, Canada, and Maine, sometimes meeting other lines coming in. The Northern Railroad Company reached from Concord 69.5 miles to White River Junction; the Boston, Concord and Montreal Railroad went more directly north toward Canada. These lines and several others were chartered in 1844 within weeks after the legislature had temporarily settled the recurring question of what kinds of powers of eminent domain were to be granted to railroad companies. The first charters, which were essentially permissions granted by the legislature to build and operate railroads in the state, had not fully addressed the problem of how to get the farmers to permit the running of a railroad track through one man's back pasture, through his neighbor's potato patch, and past the third farmer's barn door—which was where the needed straight and level lines just happened to go. The people of Dorchester, in the west central part of the state, instructed their Representative in 1842 to "endeavor to prevent, if possible, so great a calamity to our farms as must be the location of any railroad passing through." The 1844 statute created a Board of Railroad Commissioners with power to authorize railroad land-taking and to determine compensation. This Board was a focus of politics for many generations and is the ancestor of today's Public Utilities Commission.

In 1848 the bridge across the Connecticut River at White River Junction was completed, Keene was connected to Boston and Peterborough was connected to Concord. So it went, year after year, farther north, farther inland. The White Mountain Railroad went to Littleton in 1853, and in the same year the Atlantic and St. Lawrence Company completed their line from Portland, Maine, to Island Pond, Vermont, slicing through 52 miles of northern New Hampshire.

In 1844 the Walker Express offered to ship freight from Concord to Boston in one day instead of four for 50 cents per ton, a fraction of river freight cost. The broadside pictured is itself a work of art, the wood engraving in the center an early piece by the renowned engraver Henry Walter Herrick. Shown is the Concord railroad station, built in 1842 and replaced in 1847. The printing, including the virtuoso border, was the work of Morrill & Silsy, whose fancy print shop stood opposite the station. NHHS

Sylvester Marsh made his fortune in the Midwest processing and selling grain, but made headlines when he returned to his native New Hampshire to build a "cog railway" up the side of Mt. Washington. Born and raised in the "primitive environment" of a Campton hill farm, Marsh claimed never to have seen a wheeled vehicle until he was nine years old. Yet by 1869 he had designed and built one of the engineering marvels of his time, a two-and-a-half-mile railroad up the side of New England's highest peak, whose average grade was 1,300 feet per mile. NHHS

A car so crowded with excursionists (above) might test any locomotion, but ascent of Jacob's Ladder (above right) gave proof of Marsh's novel railway. Kilburn Brothers photographs, NHHS

It was not unusual to see a variety of Concord coaches pulling into Marshfield Station in the 1870s, each carrying a load of tourists bound for the train ride to the summit of Mt. Washington. Newspaper publisher and White Mountain aficionado Henry M. Burt described the rustic depot as "an ungainly, unclapboarded, three-story building with a tiny waiting room for passengers and bedrooms for the railway men." It was destroyed by fire in 1895. NHHS

Briefly, the Civil War quieted the railroad boom: it diverted the adventurous spirit of the state, depleted its manpower, and curtailed the textile industry by cutting off raw cotton supplies. But not for long. Before the war was over the railroad business was in full stride again. In 1869, the year the golden spike was driven in Promontory Point, Utah, to complete the transcontinental railroad, the Cog Railway, 2.5 miles to the top of Mt. Washington, was also completed. Together these events (both engineered by New Hampshire men: Sylvester Marsh of Campton designed the Cog Railway, and Samuel Montague of Keene was the chief engineer of the Central Pacific) seemed to certify the faith of the many who supposed that the nation's destiny, and New Hampshire's destiny in particular, was tied to the railroads.

The theory was that all this wondrous technological development would better country life. The fact was that the railroads eventually had the opposite effect. They hastened the breakup of the self-sustaining, community-based husbandry so effectively developed after the Revolutionary War, and the ironic side of progress was soon showing through.

In the 1870s, with 900 miles completed, the railroads kept sprouting and spreading. New Hampshire would be wrapped in rails, come hill or high water. Bridges, trestles, grades unthinkable in neighboring states, were built—if for no better reason than that they could be. Frank Jones, the Portsmouth brewer, adventurer, and politician, brewed up a plan to span Little Bay at Dover Point, and so it was done—with a spectacular 1,646-foot bridge, which opened in 1874. Surely such an achievement would never be superseded. For exactly 60 years it carried the freight and arched the skyline over the water that had borne the freight of an earlier generation. But a relentless logic was now loose in the land: just as the railways had put the inland waterways out of the transportation business, so the highways later would put the railways essentially out of it. In 1934 a parallel highway bridge opened, proclaiming the ascendency of cars and trucks, and the railway bridge across the bay was dismantled and stored away among heroic memories.

Also in the 1870s the railroads opened up the White Mountains: Boston had found a vacationland. Engineers had found a

stunt just as preposterous as putting a railroad up Mt. Washington or putting a freight train on a quarter-mile bridge over the Dover tides. The new idea, too exciting to resist, was to put a railroad right through the heart of the White Mountains, trestle over treetop, up through Crawford Notch. By 1875 it was done, the track rising more than 1,000 feet for the last nine miles on the ascent from Conway to the Crawford House.

Consolidating Tracks

When in the 1850s it had first become possible to travel by rail from Boston to Montreal, six changes of cars were required, for seven companies owned the rails. The "through ticket" had to be invented, but the bookkeeping was so complicated that mergers were not far behind. Sometimes companies merged when their lines joined; sometimes the company of the longer line leased the shorter line. Frequently a branch line was independently chartered and built, failed to turn a profit, and was absorbed by the main artery. Some unprofitable lines—Suncook to Candia, and North Weare to Henniker—were abandoned already before the Civil War. By the early 1880s, with over 1,000 miles of track within the state, charters had been granted to 108 different companies, 35 of which were then in operation, many only as lessors.

Mergers, leases, sales, recharterings, and other complicated adjustments were an inevitable part of this curious kind of "noncompetitive" free enterprise. Competition there was, of course, but two sets of tracks were rarely laid parallel along the same run to compete for the public's business. There *were* competitive routes, Portland to Boston, and Manchester to Boston. But for the most part competition assumed darker forms, involving talents such as these: lobbying the legislature for special favors; anticipating traffic flow and controlling it by pricing; exploiting monopoly situations; extracting subsidies from towns for tracks to their doors; attracting Boston investment capital; cajoling stockholders; and generally exploiting the "double your money" mentality of those with loose cash to invest. All the high spirits

Above left: The Portland & Ogdensburg Railroad through Crawford Notch offered spectacular views of the White Mountains. Frankenstein Trestle, shown here in 1878, was one of the high points of the trip. Guidebook author Moses F. Sweetser described the trestle in 1879: "For 500 feet the line is thus suspended in mid-air, sustained by the spidery network of striding piers, yet as firm and secure as if it rested on a prairie of mid-Iowa." NHHS

Above center: The "gate" of Crawford Notch had to be widened in the 1870s to make room for the Portland & Ogdensburg Railroad. In this photo from a B.W. Kilburn stereograph circa 1880, the famous Crawford House is visible in the background. The P&O served primarily as a tourist railroad, taking sightseers through the Notch to the hotels beyond. NHHS

Above right: Another highlight of the P&O excursion through Crawford Notch was the trip across the Willey Brook Trestle. Mt. Webster looms in the background of this 1880s B.W. Kilburn photograph. NHHS

and middling motives of speculative capitalism and boosterism went into the laying and consolidating of rails.

Within the spreading web of the rail network, the New Hampshire countryside was irrevocably changed. Butter and eggs were suddenly going fresh to market each day; bulky produce like potatoes now had a city market; locomotives were browsing cordwood from the hillsides so greedily that woodcutters could make a good living. For a time it all looked like progress. What was happening was that a secure and self-sustaining husbandry was becoming a market-based agriculture, with all its vulnerabilities. Beneath that impressive fact was the further fact that bringing to the countryside factory-made goods of every sort, from socks to hayrakes to horse collars, at prices below those at the local mills, systematically laid waste a thousand small village manufactories—but slowly, so it was hard to tell just what was

The electric interurban lines and street railways of the turn of the century required users of other forms of travel to be wary of accidents. In the scene pictured, the old gentleman's false beard and hair, and the absence of passengers in the trolley, suggest that this "accident" was staged for a photographer, probably around 1910. MVHC

happening. Even so, most towns directly tapped by railroads flourished for a time, even while their neighbors didn't. A further fact, inscrutable and profound, was that the railroads brought contact with the outside world, and with that grew ideas of an alternative life in the big city with a regular pay check, or life in the Midwest on farmland known to be smooth, deep, rich,

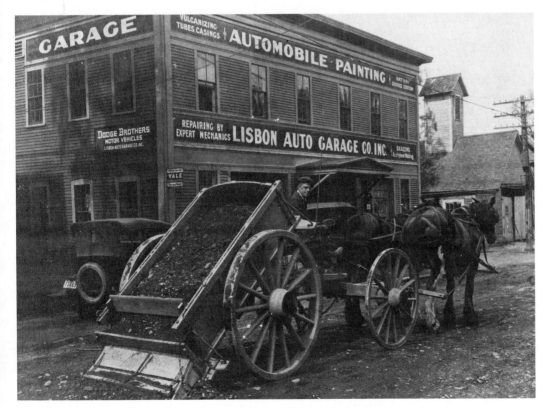

In this circa 1925 photograph the horse-drawn dump truck is still necessary for repairing the streets in Lisbon, although the streets themselves are evidently being readied for automobiles. NHHS

Function and flair are sometimes blended in New Hampshire roadside architecture. This Manchester Esso Station was a well-known landmark when it was photographed in the early 1950s. Photograph by Laurier Durrette. Courtesy, Gerald Durrette

and cheap. Everything tangible and intangible in the life of the New Hampshire countryside was eventually touched by the railroad.

The End of the Line

Were there pots of gold at the ends of the tracks? Only for the few. Building railroads may have been an engineering adventure, but running and consolidating them was an adventure of politics and business tycoons. The major tracks having been laid, the drama shifted from engineering to economics and power politics. By the late 1880s buying, leasing, and merging had, practically speaking, narrowed the field to the two companies which always had the best routes, the Concord Railroad through the state's midsection and the Boston & Maine along its coast.

The Concord Railroad Corporation made money from its beginnings. Its track, running along the level banks of the Merrimack, had been built inexpensively. It had strong feeder lines from northern and western New England, and the granite quarries of Concord themselves originated a considerable freight traffic. Twenty-two hundred flatcars of granite went from Concord to Washington, D.C., to build the Library of Congress. With all the business it could handle, this line had more profits, quite literally, than it knew what to do with. Since developing equitable taxes on profits was beyond the skills or the will of the heavily lobbied legislature, and since lowering the freight rates was beyond the imagination of the owners, there was little to do to relieve the cash problem but to drastically overpay the owners and executives of the railroad.

In one sense the high point of the railroad business in New

Hampshire came only after the Boston & Maine Railroad had achieved a monopoly—in the 1890s and thereafter. Additional track was laid each year, though at a slower pace, until 1920, when there were 1,250 miles in use within the state. But by that time both the drama and the grosser forms of politics had been drained from the network, and the railroad had become a routine form of transportation, suffering increasing competition from the trucking industry. In 1905 a state highway department was created, and the first 125 miles of state roads were adopted. Within a decade 10 cross-state roads had been marked out as state highways, and the annual railroad reports were alluding to competition from motor trucks. By the 1920s New Hampshire was firmly committed to a regular state highway construction program and, inadvertently, the railroads were sent down the long road to ruin.

Gone forever were the days just a generation earlier when the Concord Railroad Corporation had entertained itself by tearing down and building railroad stations in Concord. The fourth and last of these, constructed in 1885 in the grand style of that transient species, was a transportation station befitting a capital city: in 1900, 25 passenger trains left that Concord station daily. The structure served its city well, adding a tincture of nobility to the slightly wild capitalism of that era, and it stood thereafter, when railroad passengers had wandered away, as a fitting monument to an age that was gone, awaiting some other form of service. It was not to be. After the highways and trucks had bankrupted the Boston & Maine Railroad, this fine old building was beaten to dust with a wrecker's ball and buried beneath a shopping mall. An era had ended.

New Hampshire tourism, which relies on the natural beauty of the state, does not always promote beautiful roadways, evidenced by these billboards from the early 1960s. Photograph by John Karol. SPNHF

M·A·K·I·N·G T·H·I·N·G·S: D·E·V·E·L·O·P·I·N·G I·N·D·U·S·T·R·I·E·S

Had you been shopping for a fire engine between 1859 and 1877, you might have taken note of this ad displaying the various products of the Amoskeag Manufacturing Company's subsidiary, the Amoskeag Steam Fire Engine Works. During its 18 years the company turned out 550 fire engines, selling them in the United States, Canada, South America, England, Russia, Japan, China, and even as far away as Australia. NHHS

In the early 19th century textile mills in New Hampshire were mostly woolen mills, though Londonderry had been producing Irish linen since the middle of the 18th century. Benjamin Pritchard erected a small mill on the west bank of the Merrimack River in 1805 near where Samuel Blodget was digging his canal around the Amoskeag Falls. The mill was incorporated as the Amoskeag Cotton and Woollen Manufacturing Company in 1810, the same year Derryfield was renamed Manchester in what seemed an absurd imitation of the great English textile manufacturing city. In the 1820s sizeable textile mills were developed in Dover, Somersworth, Nashua, and Exeter—while Manchester remained a typical small town with a typical mill on a rather atypical site.

The site caught the eye of Boston entrepreneurs who assumed control of the mill in the 1830s, reincorporated as the Amoskeag Manufacturing Company, and started building on both sides of the river. Nothing was typical after that. A huge mill complex and a supporting city (modeled roughly on Lowell, Massachusetts) was laid out on paper, and in less than two decades was transferred to the countryside. Millions of bricks were made in Hooksett—Thoreau, who was there, reports this—and floated down the Merrimack to build Manchester (incorporated as a city in 1846) and its mills. An early branch of the textile company started producing locomotives and steam fire engines. Later, in the 1860s, a new company, Manchester Locomotive Works, took over production of steam engines, and soon the flatcars that took Concord coaches to the West were being pulled by Manchester locomotives. Indeed, between 1850 and 1900 the new city produced steam locomotives and steam fire engines at a rate of nearly one a week—a kind of local sideshow to the main business of Manchester. The main business was cotton cloth.

By 1851 Amoskeag textiles were winning prizes in England's Crystal Palace exhibition; in a few more decades the mills of Manchester, New Hampshire, had surpassed those of its namesake—in size, number of employees, and production. By the turn of the 20th century (when several nearby mills had been consolidated with the Amoskeag) New Hampshire claimed the largest set of textile mills in the world: a stunning mile-long brick row along both sides of the Merrimack River, employing as many as 17,000 workers and turning out cotton fabric at a mile-a-minute clip from 24,000 looms.

The Amoskeag mills lasted just a century—the 1830s to the 1930s. Their creation was a great industrial adventure and their demise was a great economic disaster. During that century the headquarters were in Boston and the board members and shareholders were mostly Bostonians. Though the mills were managed by a hired New Hampshire agent (three generations of the Straw family during one long stretch), the real boss was the Boston-based treasurer of the board, through whose hands passed all the important company decisions.

The Triumph of Amoskeag

In the early mill years, the 1840s, most of the mill operatives were girls from rural New England. Following the Lowell pattern, the Amoskeag company built special housing for the operatives—substantial brick and hardwood structures, some of which are still standing—and sent its agents throughout the state to recruit girls. The mills offered farm and village girls an ambiguously attractive life: secure work in a protective environment, the taste of independence that comes from earning one's own wages, a benign community of one's own kind, life in the city, long hours of regimented work, but also an escape from the boredom of remote hill towns. And the girls came—not only daughters of farmers but daughters of the middle class, too. In the 1840s, 1850s, and 1860s, they came not only to Manchester, but also to Nashua, Dover, Somersworth, and Exeter, where mills offered similar working and living arrangements. Some girls worked to finance a brother's education, or to save for their own; some to support aging parents or to pay off a family mortgage. Many worked in the mills only part of the year, returning to their home villages for the summer work or to teach school. For most, the years in the mill were an interim between school and marriage.

By the 1850s the mills required larger cadres of workers, and waves of foreign immigrants headed for Manchester. First came the Irish families, fleeing the desperation that followed the potato famines in their homeland; Swedes, Germans, and Scots added their skills; then French Canadians were recruited and guided down the new railways from Montreal to set up a new life in Manchester. Later came Greeks and Poles. The Amoskeag mills provided jobs for the whole family, including children. There were 750,000 humming spindles to be tended.

As the recruiting of immigrant families became established policy, various additional paternalist structures were developed: the company providing conveniences and acquiring loyalty in return. By the early 20th century welfare and social programs of all kinds were taken for granted. The mill community had its tex-

The Great Falls Manufacturing Company, founded in 1823, made Somersworth one of New England's leading textile manufacturing centers in the early 19th century. In 1830 Somersworth was New Hampshire's fifth-largest community, surpassing the future manufacturing centers of Nashua and Manchester in population. This engraving of the company's Mill Number One (right) and Mill Number Two (left) was probably made about 1835, prior to the arrival of the Boston & Maine Railroad. Unfortunately, this otherwise excellent look at an early New England textile factory is backwards. NHHS

The Amoskeag Manufacturing Company was almost a society unto itself with its own clubs, social life, athletic teams, newspaper, and educational efforts. Although this 1916 issue of the semi-monthly Bulletin reported that the "English Class is Going Good," it was apparently not going quite so well as it might have. NHHS

tile club, shooting club, baseball team, cooking school, workers' playground, visiting nurse service, company picnics, musical shows, rental privileges in corporation apartments, language classes, concerts, and a company newspaper, the *Amoskeag Bulletin*. Workers and management became bound in a common *esprit*, carefully nurtured by managers, usually accepted with gratitude by the workers. In Manchester itself the different ethnic groups congregated in their own communities: the melting pot was the mills and whatever was allied with them.

For a long time it worked extremely well: raw cotton was cheap, transportation was convenient, production was high, the market for gingham and calico was good. Workers were not notably dissatisfied; if they were, there was not much to do with their dissatisfaction: there was no point in going back to Poland. The Industrial Revolution took a heavier human toll in England's Manchester than in New Hampshire's, but it took a toll here too. The hours were atrocious: 11 hours a day, six days a week, was normal as of the 1860s, and child labor was simply taken for granted. Company profits accruing to the absentee owners were always substantial, sometimes enormous, and during World War I extravagant even by wartime standards.

Opposite page: Photographer Lewis Hine captured images of Americans at work from around 1905 to 1930. The conditions that Hines' work documented made a nation self-conscious and helped lead to some reforms. Hines' photographs of children at work—like these two from the Amoskeag millyards (top) and the workers' district of Manchester (bottom) in 1909—helped to change child labor laws. From the Manchester Collection (MC), UNH

The Amoskeag Millyard complex, looking south from the Notre Dame Bridge in Manchester, is pictured in 1980. Photograph by Gary Samson

The Amoskeag strikers dramatized their cause with a parade across the Merrimack River on April 10, 1922. MVHC

Opposite page: In 1860 Concord streets were already lighted with Concord-made gas. The handsome round brick gasholder on the right was built in 1888 and stored gas until 1957. In the foreground—partially shielded by trees—are some of the outbuildings where gas, tar, and coke were made from coal until 1952. The original gasholder and its indescribable modern successor on the left, built in 1921, operate on the same principle: a heavy steel tank in tracks holds the gas and with its own weight applies the pressure that discharges the gas into the mains and throughout the city. The old gasholder had a complex water seal system and the building was designed to protect the tank and seal from the elements. Though the 1938 hurricane knocked the cupola askew, the building remains the only completely intact gasholder of its kind in the country. Photograph by Gary Samson

The Fall of the Amoskeag

Wartime profits were barely banked when disaster loomed. Relatively high wages, old machinery, excessive production capacity, and Southern competition all pushed the New Hampshire mills from the wartime high to an early version of the Great Depression. Three significant events occurred, and that was the end.

First, in 1922 the Amoskeag company abruptly announced an increase in working hours from 48 to 54 hours per week and a corresponding 20-percent cut in wages. Thousands of workers, by now unionized and united, were immediately alienated from the company which they and their parents had proudly identified with for all their lives. There followed a major strike, lasting nine months and leaving economic and moral wounds that never healed. There were similar strikes for similar reasons in other New Hampshire mill towns.

Second, in 1925 the board of the Amoskeag Manufacturing Company transferred to another corporate entity—the Amoskeag Company, an investment corporation with nearly the same board members—$18 million in assets drawn from company profits. Judgments differ about the meaning of this maneuver. One line of thought offers the blunt verdict that "they took the money and ran," and emphasizes the unwillingness of the parent company to invest in retooling antiquated machinery and in new marketing strategies—the money having been invested instead, through the new corporation, in Southern

textile mills. The other line of thought sees the transactions as an astute business move in the face of the inevitable decline of New England textile milling. At any rate, the parent manufacturing company was economically much weakened, though the severity of the problem was not then evident to the public. What was evident by the late 1920s was that textile mills throughout New England generally were in trouble, and with them most of the New England economy.

The third event (foreseeable from Boston but not foreseen in New Hampshire) was the sudden closing of the Amoskeag mills in 1935, coupled with a promise to reorganize and reopen. Instead of reopening, the Amoskeag Manufacturing Company was ordered to liquidate assets under the bankruptcy law. Nearly 11,000 people in Manchester were jobless, and the economic base of the city was destroyed. (The investment corporation thrived, and still does: in the 1970s it had controlling interest in a large Northern railroad and a large Southern textile mill. Though no longer incorporated in New Hampshire, its assets as of 1980 totalled more than $80 million.)

A group of Manchester citizens formed Amoskeag Industries to salvage the mills. Public Service Company of New Hampshire bought the electrical plant and, thus financially fortified, Amoskeag Industries borrowed money, bought the mill buildings, and began luring new and smaller businesses to occupy the

vast spaces. World War II gave the project a boost and by the late 1940s there were a hundred businesses in the buildings where the Amoskeag mills had been.

All the hardy drama of the Industrial Revolution is to be found in the career of the Amoskeag Manufacturing Company, and all its moral ambiguities too: the story is exhilarating and depressing in turn, and even rather awesome in its full dimensions. Like the Boston & Maine Railroad, Amoskeag was, for the state of New Hampshire, a fatally flawed partner in progress. The company itself roared out of nowhere into the bucolic New Hampshire countryside with eager and vital energy; it burned with a furious and often equivocal glow for a full century; and then it crashed headlong into the Great Depression to sink from sight forever. Echoes linger to this day in poignant reminiscences, recently published, of those who lost jobs at the mills more than 40 years ago.

If our old parents, who worked so much in these mills, if they'd come back today and see how these mills are, it would really break their hearts.

Other textile mills in dozens of other New Hampshire cities and towns followed somewhat similar patterns, though none of them had the size or dramatic contours of the Amoskeag story.

C H A P T E R
E L E V E N

L·U·M·B·E·R,
T·O·U·R·I·S·T·S, A·N·D
T·E·C·H·N·O·L·O·G·Y

Ben Houston's sawmill in Barnstead, photographed in 1905, was typical of the portable steam sawmills found in most New Hampshire towns during the first half of the 20th century. Courtesy, William R. Brickett

Opposite page: Two aspects of New Hampshire's North Country are juxtaposed in this recent photograph: the majestic Presidential Range in the background, and the James River Corporation mills of Berlin in the foreground. The former symbolizes the state's natural beauty, the latter New Hampshire's industrial base. Photo by Bob LaPree. Courtesy, New Hampshire Times

During the half-century of the most rapid development of the New Hampshire manufacturing industry—roughly 1840 to 1890—the state's agriculture was completely transformed. First the frontiers disappeared (so far as tillable land was concerned), and the railroads created upheavals in the rural economy; then the cities growing round the manufacturing centers siphoned the youth from the land; to thousands of others the call of the West and of far horizons proved irresistible. Trains that brought New Englanders to Indiana and Wisconsin returned with reaper-harvested grain that sold in Concord more cheaply than the scythe-harvested grain grown in Merrimack County. Some said that instead of grain they might better import soil from the West. In a hundred rural New Hampshire towns, the population dropped steadily decade after decade.

Portable Sawmills

By the 1870s one could take a train to Michigan and find employment for a dollar a day and decent land for a dollar and a half per acre. Why fight rocks in New Hampshire? Meadows lapsed to pastures, and pastures relapsed to young pine seedlings. During the last half of the 19th century a new crop of timber was growing swiftly to maturity on thousands of acres of abandoned farmland in southern New Hampshire. Inevitably, the farms that remained and remained successful were oriented not so much to rural self-sufficiency as toward markets—milk for Boston, potatoes for the entire East Coast, wool for the mills, and lumber for the cities.

Thus the stage was set: the abandoned farm and the portable sawmill—two memorable New Hampshire symbols moving in tandem across the historical landscape. The settlers of the first generation cleared the land, walled it, and farmed it; their sons and grandsons relinquished it, and *their* sons harvested lumber from it once again.

With their massive steel boilers and powerful circular saws, portable sawmills were exciting contraptions, and they easily eclipsed the small water-powered mills that had straddled the streams for a hundred years. From about 1880 to 1950 the new mills were a kind of moveable fixture in the countryside. A mill operator with his small band of "rounders" (woodsmen who went round from mill to mill) would set up shop on a favorable spot for a year or more, hire additional local hands and teams and then, when supplies were exhausted, would move on to the next town. Since growing timber was taxed at market value until 1949, there was tremendous incentive to sell to the mill operators.

The efficiency of these operations soon raised eyebrows. Joseph B. Walker, president of the State Board of Agriculture and descendent of the Reverend Timothy Walker, wrote that when "a portable sawmill locates in a forest, it is liable to consume all the trees around it for a mile or more, every one of them." Forty bushels of sawdust poured out of a mill for each 1,000 feet of lumber; and mills located, said the 1889 Fish and Game Commission *Report,* "so as to run the refuse into some stream to avoid the bother to take care of it. The greatest injury to our streams by mill refuse is the destruction of the spawning beds and young fry." That had been a New Hampshire rivermouth problem for 200 years: the difference was that it was now happening further up streams, in trout pools and bass ponds.

As portable sawmills multiplied, so did worries concerning them—worries about tax laws that encouraged clear cutting, about the appearance of cutover hillsides, about sawdust, about fires in the slashing. Every Arbor Day elicited public pleas to choppers to spare seed trees. So it went—on into the 20th century.

Stern economic facts had to be weighed against the qualms. The portable sawmill came to the hillsides during a period of prolonged rural decline, and between 1880 and World War II New Hampshire rural communities needed an economic cushion, needed ways to ease the transition to a more varied economy. The cushion came from the woods first of all, for even in the worst of times there were logs to saw, maple trees to tap, and markets for the products: employment for man and team in winter and early spring. Best of all, the crops renewed themselves naturally and time healed the scars on the hills. In dozens of New Hampshire communities the lumber business, although marginal, held disaster at bay. Inadvertently, the forests that crept back to the fields from the inaccessible slopes and valleys to which the first settlers had driven them, had created there a hedge against hard times.

North Country Lumber

Meanwhile, the Industrial Revolution itself—having transformed the countryside and having built cities at Manchester, Nashua, Concord, Somersworth, and Dover—invaded New Hampshire's North Country.

THE BROWN BULLETIN

PUBLISHED MONTHLY BY THE BROWN BULLETIN PUBLISHING ASSOCIATION
BERLIN, N. H., MAY 1, 1922

VOL. III.   No. 11

Left: Throughout the 20th century, the industrial giant of New Hampshire's North Country has been Berlin. The Berlin Mills Company began making paper in 1888, and in the years before World War I operated the world's largest chemical pulp mill. (In 1917 the company changed its title to the Brown Company, casting off the name of the capital city of America's wartime enemy.) NHHS

Opposite page, top: In July 1919 the Brown Company began publishing The Brown Bulletin, *which documented social life, sports, company news, and other items of general interest in the company town. NHHS*

Above: In the 1920s untold numbers of pulpwood logs found their way down the Androscoggin River to Brown Company mills. The logs were cut from company-owned lands totaling about 6,000 square miles — an area somewhat larger than the state of Connecticut. By the Brown Company's standards, the amount of lumber pictured is quite small. NHHS

"The North Country"—it stretches from the southern edge of the White Mountain National Forest northward, to encompass essentially the entire upper half of the state: all of Coös County, and most of Grafton and Carroll as well. Today it is 2.5 million acres of forest land and a few thousand acres of farmland; its population is about 135,000, barely 15 percent of the state's. Only a small percentage of the timber in this land had been harvested before the Civil War—along the Connecticut River on the west and along the Androscoggin River and Lake Umbagog on the east—but once serious lumbering began in the North Country, it accelerated swiftly.

Several things made these northern timber operations possible, probably inevitable. The first was the transfer of large tracts of public timberland into the hands of private corporations: lumbering was now to be not just an individual but a corporate business. Another was the railroad—to the lumberman a double blessing in that it provided access to markets at one end and access to the remote valleys at the other. The Atlantic and St. Lawrence line, for example, reached north from Berlin to the otherwise inaccessible regions of North Stratford in 1853; on the other hand, spur lines from main tracks could poke into a dozen remote valleys where the rivers had been too steep or swift or small to ferry the logs. At last the loggers could take genuine satisfaction from Ethan Allen's maxim that even God cannot

make two ranges of mountains without a valley between. The third fact was the development, after 1880, of papermaking processes from pulpwood, which itself transformed the northern timber industry. Trees once disdained as too small for lumber were now salvaged for paper: entire mountains of spruce that might have been left were swept into the pulpwood mills.

In the beginning of the 20th century, when the world's largest textile mills were operating full tilt in Manchester, the world's largest newsprint paper mills were operating full tilt some hundred miles north in Berlin. The northern "infinite thick woods" of earliest legend were being thinned at last.

Many elements combined to make 1907 a notable year in the annals of the New Hampshire timber industry: the science and the technology of papermaking had been fully developed; railroad spurs had reached into most of the wooded valleys; the legislature had not yet seriously restricted either railroading or timber cutting; the first pine growth on the pasturelands of southern New Hampshire had come to maturity; and the technology and economy of portable steam sawmill operations had been worked out. 1907 was the all-time record year for timber harvesting in New Hampshire.

In the 1980s there are more acres of woodland in New Hampshire than at any time in the last 200 years, and more professional foresters per acre than in any other state. Besides several

hundred thousand cords of pulpwood, 150 to 200 million board feet of lumber are harvested each year—less than the annual new growth and also less than the normal harvest a generation ago. Fifty to seventy-five thousand gallons of maple syrup also come from the woodlands each year—less than a generation ago. But forests remain a major economic resource—in addition to being a great treasure of botanical, biological, aesthetic, and recreational diversity.

Hotels, Farms, Tourists

A very different kind of influence upon the New Hampshire economy came from the tourist industry. Like the lumbering industry, tourism once meant different things to different regions of the state. In the North Country, in and around the White Mountains, the principal symbol and locus of the tourist industry was the "grand hotel"—elegant structures in mountainous settings that catered to the well-born, the well-connected, and the well-heeled.

The first tourist stops in the North Country, well established already by the 1840s, were simple inns, and the most famous of them were run by the Crawfords in the notch that bears their name. These taverns were superseded in the 1850s by much larger establishments. In the last half of the 19th century dozens of major hotels were built in the North Country, confirming the

Above: The city of Berlin, home of the Brown Company, was photographed early in the 1920s. NHHS

Opposite page: Whitefield was the lumber capital of New Hampshire at the end of the 19th century. When this picture of the city was taken in the early 20th century, small concerns like the Whitefield Manufacturing Company, shown here, still operated as sawmills, and in this case, also as a manufacturer of bobbins for the state's textile mills. A lone employee was photographed surrounded by logs in 1925. Courtesy, Forest Service, White Mountain National Forest, U.S. Department of Agriculture

White Mountains as the major recreation area of the Northeast, a role they have increasingly occupied ever since.

Whereas the earliest taverns had been accessible only to coach or foot travelers, the grand hotels were built for the railroad era. Each of the major establishments, such as Crawford House, Fabyan House, Profile House, The Maplewood, The Waumbek, The Glen House, had its own train station or livery service, and its own versions of comfort and elegance: gas lighting, fancy dining, lawn tennis, coaching parades, mountain guides. Each of the above houses—the largest among many others—had a guest capacity of 400 or more, each was built entirely of wood, and each was eventually destroyed by fire. The last to be built of the truly grand hotels, one of the largest and one of the few still operating today, is the Mount Washington in Bretton Woods. It opened in 1902, in an era when New York corporate executives commonly sent their families to the White Mountains for the summer months and trained in to visit them on weekends. Presidents and foreign dignitaries came too—a way of seeing America. Mrs. Pullman came each summer in her own private railroad car.

By the beginning of the 20th century the recreation industry was well underway in the southern part of the state as well, actively promoted by state officials. In a few areas of the south— the seacoast, the Jaffrey-Peterborough-Dublin areas, the Cornish-Plainfield regions—summer visitors had been present in substantial numbers as soon as the railroads came. But around

the turn of the century the "summer industry," as it was called, took on major economic significance and, outside cities, it formed a place beside lumbering and dairying as one of the three or four staples of the rural economy. While White Mountain tourism was primarily sponsored by Eastern seaboard money and catered to people of means, tourism in the south, with some few notable exceptions, was more a middle-class phenomenon. Hotels began to show up on the edges of village greens in dozens of small hill towns.

The summer industry was welcome in rural New Hampshire, where the last decades of the 19th century had been depressing. The journals of that day regularly carried articles whose titles are indicative: "A Good Farm for Nothing" (1899); "The Decadence of New England" (1890); "The Deserted Homes of New England" (1893); "The Doom of the Small Town" (1895); "The Rural School Problem" (1896); and dozens more. In 1889 the New Hampshire Department of Agriculture produced a booklet titled *Price List of Abandoned Farms in New Hampshire.* This represented a break with past policy—which had indulged the pretense that nothing was wrong with New Hampshire farming that a little Yankee resolution could not cure. The aim was now to advertise the fact, throughout the country and abroad, that cheap farms were available in New Hampshire. In 1891 a new booklet bore the upbeat title: *Secure a Home in New Hampshire—Where Comfort Health and Prosperity Abound;* it listed and described farms for sale town by town. In that same year a New

Above: Plymouth's second and most famous Pemigewasset House was built in 1863 by the Boston, Concord, & Montreal Railroad. Pictured in a John H. Bufford lithograph shortly after it opened for business, the Pemigewasset House became a favorite resting place for tourists on their way to the White Mountains. It was here that Nathaniel Hawthorne died in 1864 while traveling to the mountains with his old college friend Franklin Pierce. The hotel burned in 1908. NHHS

Opposite page: The Notch House, located just to the north of the gate of Crawford Notch, was built by the Crawford family in 1828 and run by Thomas Crawford until it burned in 1854. This particular print appeared in the book American Scenery *(1840) and is based on a drawing by William H. Bartlett. NHHS*

Left: The 1893 Baedeker guide informed potential tourists to the White Mountains that hotels varied "from the large and fashionable summer caravan-serais down to small, unassuming, and inexpensive inns and boarding houses." The writer especially praised "the waiting of the students (male and female) at some of the larger hotels." The starched staff of Fabyans line up to receive guests circa 1895. NHHS

Late each summer throughout the 1880s and 1890s, hotels in the White Mountains sent their decorated entries to the Bethlehem Coach Parade. Gaudily dressed Concord Coaches, pulled by gaudily clad teams of matching horses, made their way up and down Bethlehem's main street to the sound of bands, coach horns, and the applause of passengers and spectators. NHHS

These four unidentified gentlemen, photographed around 1910, were guests at the Crawford House. Bridle paths for sure-footed burros were common throughout the White Mountains. NHHS

Above: Salt haze and languid air are fused in a summer day at Wallis Sands, circa 1890. New Hampshire's coast on the Atlantic is just short of 18 miles. But the attraction of the beach has been no less because of its brevity. By the third quarter of the 19th century cottages and grand hotels on the beach were catering to a major tourist trade; and with the advent of the automobile, daytrippers began to come as well. Courtesy, John P. Adams

Left: There are various kinds of "camps" in New Hampshire's past. Along with military camps, church camps, children's summer camps, and sportsmen's camps of various descriptions, there were the lakeside summer camps to which urban Americans migrated annually. Harry Jones' cottage on Sewall's Point, Wolfeboro, was typical of many lakeside camps in 1908. From the Wolfeboro Collection. UNH

Hampshire woman, Kate Sanborn, wrote a how-to book, *Adopting an Abandoned Farm*. The book sold well, but not quite so well as did her next book, *Abandoning an Adopted Farm*.

The emblem of the new summer business became Old Home Week—instituted by Governor Frank Rollins in 1899. He caught the nostalgia then adrift in the New Hampshire air and focused it upon a simple and seductive idea: spruce up the town and invite the wandering sons and daughters back to the villages for a week of remembrance and celebration of rural values; they may reclaim an interest in their roots, may even buy up the family homestead before it falls down, perhaps endow a school or library or put up a cottage on the pond. After all, it was an era when nearly everyone—the president of Harvard and the captains of industry included—was making the most of the fact that he too had been schooled in a village and reared on a farm, sprung from the communities of virtue.

It worked extremely well. Hotels, inns, and guest houses

The automobile brought a new class of tourist to New Hampshire's White Mountains in the years after the First World War. This group from Connecticut is in Franconia Notch viewing the Old Man of the Mountains. NHHS

cropped up; farmhouses were remodeled into guest houses. Many towns of 500 people listed a half-dozen guest houses in the *Guide* Rollins published in 1902, and many other farm families made it a practice to take in city guests, a week or two at a time, during the summer. The New Hampshire Department of Agriculture started to sponsor "workshops" on how to attract and serve the summer guests. In 1925 the state legislature first appropriated money ($25,000) for publicizing the attractions of the state for tourists. A few years later the state began publishing booklets, such as the 1930 *New Hampshire by Motor*. Such publications were more successful than those of an earlier generation, which had tried to rescue the abandoned farms by attracting immigrants to the hill country.

For nearly a hundred years now, tourism has been a central element in the state's economy, though with the coming of the automobile the forms changed significantly. The grand hotels of the north were dying out slowly from early in the 20th century, as soon as automobiles in numbers reached the mountains. A few carry on the grand tradition: the Mount Washington in Bretton Woods, the Balsams in Dixville Notch, The Mountain View House in Whitefield, and far away in Newcastle, Wentworth-by-the-Sea; and there are a few others on a lesser scale. Elsewhere the guest house tradition lasted until the 1930s, and after World War II the overnight motel became ubiquitous.

State officials say that today more than six million tourists visit New Hampshire each year and that they spend $750 million,

Above: Recreational skiers are shown on Mt. Moosilauke in the 1930s. Mt. Moosilauke has a special place in the history of skiing in America. On March 12, 1933, the Mt. Moosilauke Carriage Road was used for the first U.S. National Downhill Championship. Of the 80 contestants, only 69 finished the 2.8-mile course. DCA

Left: The first Dartmouth Winter Carnival in 1911 not only began a proud tradition in Hanover, but helped to popularize the little-known sport of skiing in the United States. Pictured are students who won prizes in the various competitions of that first year. In the center of the front row and wearing the Dartmouth sweater is Fred Harris, a founder of both the Winter Carnival and the Dartmouth Outing Club. From Fred Harris, Dartmouth Out O'Doors, *1913*

accounting for 10 to 15 percent of the gross state product. Whatever the actual numbers, tourism is central to the state's economy. Two particular circumstances make it doubly important. A seven-percent tax on rooms and meals has been carefully arranged by the legislature for visitors, and the state liquor monopoly has placed stores near all the state's entrances and exits. If there have been times when New Hampshire wealth was drained into Massachusetts, there are also times when New

By the middle of the 19th century and for long thereafter granite quarrying at Concord was a major industry, employing at times more men (and more oxen) than any other Concord industry aside from the railroad. NHHS

It is midnight and the idyllic New Hampshire landscape and coastline are out of sight. This is Seabrook, where round-the-clock crews are building a nuclear power plant—the largest, most costly, and most controversial project ever undertaken in the Granite State. Photograph by Bob LaPree. Courtesy, New Hampshire Times

Hampshire ingenuity has siphoned Massachusetts cash into Granite State coffers.

Tourism is seasonal, but it occupies most of the seasons. Summer or winter the White Mountains are the main attraction, and 35 percent of the tourists are reported to be skiers and other snow seekers. In autumn, as the foliage colors edge southward from Canada, streams of sightseers edge northward from Boston. In early October they meet on schedule in the byways and notches of the White Mountains in some of the most scenically positioned traffic jams known to modern civilization.

The Recent Economy

Different manufacturing industries have jostled each other for supremacy in the New Hampshire economy of the 20th century. In 1920 the manufacturing field was led by textiles—40,000 were employed in it; the leather industries, shoemaking in particular, occupied second position. Many New Hampshire cities, such as Manchester and Nashua, Rochester and Dover, developed major shoe factories in the late 19th century. Leather overtook textiles in the late 1930s. In 1955 the order was leather goods, textiles, and paper products, with electronics moving up fast after the stimulus of World War II. The Brown Company, a timber firm, was the largest single employer in the state in 1955; today the largest is Sanders Associates Inc., an electronics firm.

In the 1980s New Hampshire relies upon a mixed industrial economy weighted toward small manufacturing. The business climate is widely regarded as favorable, with its low taxes, nearby markets, and reliable work force, and in some areas the booster mentality prevails again. The state's population expanded rapidly in the decade of the 1970s, from 737,000 to 918,000, and the work force expanded even faster—both well ahead of national averages. Growth areas in the state's business economy of the 1980s are in metal products and electronics; areas of decline, both relatively and absolutely, are in the indigenous industries, those that rely essentially on native raw materials. The woolen industry, lumber and wood products, food production, textiles generally, paper and allied products, leather goods—these employed fewer New Hampshire people in 1980 than they did in 1970. Minor indigenous industries such as stone and clay products and fishing have increased marginally during the same time. The quarrying of granite in the Granite State, though much reduced from former times, is on the upswing again in the 1980s. The main granite markets are in monuments, building blocks, and curbstones—in that order. Sixty-five years ago two-thirds of those employed in manufacturing were connected with textiles or leather goods, but in the 1980s word processing supersedes wool processing, silicone chips supersede wood chips.

The diversified economy evolves within a reasonably predictable framework, though it seems pointed toward a dependence upon high technology and defense-related industries in the way it once was upon the textile and leather business. If the armaments industry were sharply curtailed, a large sector of the New Hampshire economy would suffer. The world's war machine is a major partner in "progress." Interesting juxtapositions abound: the Seabrook nuclear power plant, by far the largest building project in the state's history, proceeds apace in round-the-clock shifts, employing 10,000 construction workers. Meanwhile, in an interesting echo of times past, Portsmouth has been officially designated (January 20, 1983) a Foreign Trade Zone, thus to encourage the use of domestic facilities, materials, and labor in the processing or shipping of products in and out of the country. By this administrative device Portsmouth harbor comes full circle, 360 degrees, to the point where it was, in effect, declared a foreign trade zone by John Mason in 1623, 360 years ago.

IV

M·I·N·D
A·N·D S·P·I·R·I·T

Mythic New England is packed with very definite images of place and order, of tradition and geography; and New Hampshire, with its close linkages of land and art, contributes more than its share to that composite. Embodied in these images of New Hampshire are various impulses created by the encounter of the Puritan heritage and the new land. Striking contrasts abound: not only of wilderness and garden and industry, but also of a yeomanry beleaguered by a stern and rocky nature and blistered by cold and toil who, whatever they themselves felt, were represented to themselves in theology and art and sometimes in education as laboring in a Promised Land—living lives somehow continuous with Biblical drama. This part looks at some of the data that support these images, that connect the facts of history with the artifacts of mind and spirit.

The smell of pine still strong on the stumps, the Reverend Eleazar Wheelock establishes Dartmouth College in the wilderness. This 1839 engraving shows the original log building that preceded the grander Dartmouth Hall of 1791. DCA

C H A P T E R
T W E L V E

E·D·U·C·A·T·I·O·N A·N·D
T·H·E S·C·H·O·O·L·S

Since New Hampshire was part of Massachusetts from 1641 to 1680, its educational and religious climate was set by the laws of Puritan Massachusetts. Puritans knew their enemies: education would help to keep barbarism and irreligion at bay. The first education law affecting New Hampshire was a very general pronouncement of 1642 that obliged town selectmen to have "a vigilant eye over their neighbors" to see that "none of them shall suffer so much barbarism" as not to teach "their children ... to read perfectly the English tongue."

Solid Puritan advice—but lacking in details. Those came five years later in a 1647 law that included both a religious and a secular imperative for schools. First, since it was a "chiefe project of ye ould deluder, Sathan, to keepe men from the knowledge of ye Scripture" and, secondly, in order that "learning may not be buried in ye grave of or fathers," the law provided that every town of 50 householders appoint someone to "teach all such children who shall resort to him to write and reade." Further, a town of 100 householders was to "set up a grammar school" to instruct youth "so far as they may be fitted for ye university."

The basic intent of this law was reenacted by New Hampshire after its separation from the Bay Colony. This New Hampshire law of 1693, which lasted through the next century, obliged towns to provide by taxation for a schoolhouse, and a schoolmaster's salary. Schools and schoolmasters were mandated, but attendance was not. The law was neutral as to the sex of the children, but a school was nearly always run by a master, perhaps a young man still in college, and his scholars were usually boys. The early law also included stiff fines on a town for noncompliance and, after 1721, even upon the selectmen themselves for their town's failure to provide a school. Nothing suggests that miracles were expected from the schools; there was merely a commitment that they were absolutely necessary. The statutes set forth an ideal more than they described a practice. Governor John Wentworth II, a Harvard-educated man, may have been unduly harsh when he told the Assembly in 1771:

The promoting of learning very obviously calls for Legislative Care. The Insufficiency of our present Laws for this purpose must be too evident, seeing nine tenths of your towns are wholly without Schools, or have such vagrant Masters as are much worse than none; being for the most part unknown in their principles & deplorably illiterate.

Constitutional Beginnings

As boys they attended the New Hampshire public schools; as men they drafted the state Constitution of 1784. New Hampshire's founding fathers had faith in education, and they wrote that faith into the document.

Knowledge and learning ... being essential to the preservation of a free government ... it shall be the duty of the legislators and magistrates ... to cherish the interest of literature and the sciences ... to encourage private and public institutions, rewards, and immunities for the promotion of agriculture, arts, sciences, commerce, trades, manufactures, and natural history of the country.

The U.S. Constitution contains no such sentiment, and only a few of the early state constitutions speak of education. These particular New Hampshire words echo a similar passage written into the Massachusetts Constitution a few years earlier by John Adams.

Hundreds of laws since then have shaped these ideas into policy. Concern for teacher quality emerged early, and a 1789 law obliged towns to have prospective teachers examined by an "able and reputable" person (normally a minister) to insure that they were qualified. In the midst of the rapid development of the New Hampshire countryside, an 1805 law authorized the individual towns to set up multiple school districts within their borders. Before this some towns had made similar decisions on their own: in 1801 the town of Hampton voted: "That the North

District shall have Jonathan Sanborn's Barn for a school house." In 1827 the legislature took school matters out of the hands of town selectmen, where they had been since 1647, and put them into the hands of a separate school committee. In 1846 the state created the office of Commissioner of Common Schools—a general supervisor with a special mandate to focus upon teacher education—and secured a Dartmouth professor to fill it. The result was a series of teachers' "institutes"—two-day to four-week sessions in various parts of the state for the recruitment and training of teachers. In 1847 the Commissioner reported:

Every Institute that has been held has sent a wave of elevating influence to every retreating cove and every shadowy eddy where mind lay sleeping and stagnant.

In 1854 there were 2,294 such coves and eddies—separate school districts in New Hampshire, every one of them an independent fiefdom.

It was the schools that opened the door to female suffrage. An 1877 law held that "female citizens of adult age may hold and discharge the duties of prudential or superintending committee." The next year women were even allowed to vote in district school meetings. In 1883 at the height of the temperance movement a new law said that "physiology and hygiene, including special reference to the effects of alcoholic stimulants and narcotics upon the human system, shall be prescribed in all schools sufficiently advanced." The last two words were a loophole that left the matter up to the teacher.

In 1885 a new law changed the scene drastically. By that time the school year in many a one-room district school had dwindled to 10 weeks of haphazard classes kept by an ill-prepared teacher for a half-dozen children in a collapsing building. The new law obliged the independent school districts within a town to consolidate into one town district. Separate district schools were permitted but only under a single town board—a major shift away from what was then called "local control." The state superintendent wrote that "as long as the idea prevails that every man must have a school-house within a few rods of his door, regardless of *what* that school may be, so long there will remain a great obstacle to the complete education of all the children of the state."

A by-product of the 1885 law was that New Hampshire women for the first time had a vote in a townwide meeting. Long since, of course, women teachers had come to far outnumber men, one reason being that it was cheaper to hire women: their salaries were invariably one-third to one-half lower than those of men. Thus during the 19th century the schoolmaster of folklore gave way to the schoolmistress of memory.

Teachers and Academies

For a long time public high schools—after Portsmouth's early beginning in 1830—were a rarity in New Hampshire. Private aspiration and enterprise, not state policy, led the way in secondary education. The 19th century witnessed the bright, brief flowering of classical academies all over the New England countryside. The first example had been set shortly after the Revolutionary War by Phillips Exeter (1783), and it was

SCHOOL EXHIBITION.
Last Thursday Mr. Eastman closed his School in this town, and entertained the inhabitants with an exhibition, by his scholars, consisting of Orations, Dialogues, Poetry, &c. &c. The judicious manner in which the scenes were arranged—the display of his whole School, upwards of 70 in number, on the stage,—and the ingenious performances of the scholars—did honour to the Tutor and his Pupils, and gave great pleasure to the parents & spectators. A numerous audience manifested their approbation by repeated clapping of hands, and other tokens of applause.

Like most schoolmasters of his day, Edmund Eastman, Concord's schoolmaster in 1793, was little appreciated and poorly paid; his annual salary in 1793 was £18. Nevertheless, Mr. Eastman and his students had their day in the sun with a "School Exhibition" that was reported in the Concord Herald *of April 3, 1793. NHHS*

Phillips Exeter Academy is pictured here as it appeared in 1831. The academy opened in 1783, having been founded by John Phillips, an Exeter merchant and "worthy gentleman" who had done well in banking and finance. The main part of the building shown was constructed in 1794-1795, with wings added between 1821 and 1829. After the building burned in 1870, other Exeter Academy buildings in the neo-Georgian style were designed by New Hampshire native Ralph Adams Cram. NHHS

The arrival in New York of the "Vacation Special from St. Paul's School" brought crowds of anxious mamas, papas, and coachmen to Grand Central Station. The scenario was depicted with some humor in a December 1889 issue of Harper's. *NHHS*

followed soon thereafter by academies at New Ipswich, Chesterfield, Charlestown, Atkinson, and Amherst. By 1850 there were 46 incorporated academies in the state and at least as many unincorporated private secondary schools. Many offered both a classical course based on languages and literature and a teacher preparation program. By 1860 many of the elementary schools of the state were "kept" by young women, and occasionally by men, who had spent a part of one or two of their teenage years in such an academy. Some of these academies began under direct religious auspices. For example, New Hampton Academy (1826) and New London Academy (1853) were Baptist; Tilton School (1845) was Methodist; and St. Paul's School (1850) and Holderness School (1878) were Episcopal.

New Hampshire academies waned as fast as they had waxed, and their decline was a setback for female education. In 1877 an essayist for *The Granite Monthly* wrote: "The Academies have dwindled away like the mountain streams when the forests are cut down. A few have survived and have been specialized into expensive college preparatory schools. Boys alone are the students. . . . the tendency of the population toward the cities and the preference for machinery over individual labor . . . have killed the academy." Some survived and are thriving still a century later.

From a private academy a candidate often went to employment in a district school in a neighboring town, so much of what transpired in education was outside the sphere of state government. The New Hampshire legislature liked this arrangement, and it long resisted any further involvement in teacher preparation. From 1850 onward a State Teachers' Association and others tried to get a normal school, or teachers' college, bill through the legislature and even pledged money on a matching basis to pay for it. These efforts finally bore fruit after the academy movement crested. The first state normal school was established at Plymouth in 1870, and the legislature fastidiously stipulated that it was to be run without expense to the state. New Hampshire educators of the time found it hard to square the passive and reluctant legislative stance with the categorical statements of legislative duty toward education written into the state constitution by an earlier generation.

Official Views

The 20th-century habit, in New Hampshire and elsewhere, of looking to the public schools as either the cause or the remedy of all our social ills is rooted in the remarkable 19th-century faith in schooling as preventive medicine. The *Annual Report* for 1857 declared that had the teachers for the past 200 years "been in heart and head what they ought to have been, today we should have no need of an organized police in any city, a prison, an asylum, or a house of reformation in any State, or a standing army to guard domestic tranquility. Can anyone deny this?" (The founders of New Hampshire's school system 200 years earlier would have denied it.) The next year's *Report* bespeaks a better insight and a calmer eloquence: "A mind undeveloped by culture is a captive, and walks round its narrow cell of thought from childhood to the grave in unconscious servitude. But knowledge breaks the shackles from the soul and permits it to

rise to a higher and better life." During the 19th century the annual state *Report* was often a well-written and well-documented analysis of New Hampshire's educational needs. However, by the turn of the century, the practical problems faced by a state undergoing urban immigrant population growth and rural decline were dominant: transportation, teacher quality, public apathy, dilapidated buildings, finances. The "abandoned farm" and the "rural school problem," two verses of the same song, echo down the decades well into the 20th century. The 1906 *Report* recapitulated the problem of teacher quality:

> *In earlier days the schools were kept . . . by college students, usually men of force and character and often of qualities destined to make them famous. They were succeeded first by women scarcely inferior to themselves in ability and forcefulness, but afterward by an increasing generation of girls without education, training, or maturity, and more often than not without ability.*

Perhaps the most persistently disconcerting problem addressed by these officials year after year was the inequality of education among the different towns and the lack of adequate state financial support. "New Hampshire is dependent upon direct local taxation for support of schools to an extent scarcely equalled in any other state," stated the *Report* in 1906. This sentiment has been voiced countless times thereafter, even to the present day.

The Twentieth Century

By 1901 there were laws on the books concerning compulsory school attendance up to age 14, forbidding the employment during school hours of anyone under 16 who could not read and write, and obliging towns to pay minimal high-school tuition costs for anyone attending high school out of town. Beyond that New Hampshire lacked a coherent education policy in the early decades of the 20th century. Standards were often haphazard, teacher quality varied greatly, and the school term differed among towns from a few to 30 weeks per year. No law prescribed a minimum school year. The best small schools, those in academy towns, were sometimes very good. But they were very few.

Something deeply ironic was at work in the educational system: it was precisely the schools that were draining the talent from the countryside. The better the school, the better the chance that it would awaken interest in life beyond the hillside communities and lure the more promising young people from the farm to the city. It was, of course, an ancient dilemma, poignantly reenacted from one end of New Hampshire to another for more than a generation before and after 1900. Even in the cities, school problems were complex: Manchester, for example, had to cope with large immigrant groups. And everywhere the lack of minimum standards enfeebled the schools. Good advice could not supply what laws had left undone.

The early Puritans, convinced that Satan himself had a vested interest in human ignorance, assumed that growth in Christian virtue required secular learning—an assumption later transmuted into the grand and bland educational optimism of the 19th century. Though these complex impulses had largely spent themselves in New Hampshire by the beginning of the 20th century, there remained the perennial, thoroughly American, idea that illiteracy is not only a regrettable waste but is politically dangerous as well.

Toward the end of World War I, all this high-toned ideology, coupled with the lowly practical facts about the state's schools, gave birth to a new doctrine in New Hampshire. Public opinion had been startled by the reports that hundreds of New Hampshire wartime draftees "were unable to read the orders they were expected to obey." On March 28, 1919, the General Court passed a comprehensive law that emphatically acknowledged the state's responsibility for promoting educational standards. Education officials had long pleaded for this, and Article 83 of the state constitution had long suggested it, but not until 1919 did the law embody it—this during an otherwise politically dry and infertile time. The new law created a five-person State Board of Education to oversee the state's public education, with a Commissioner of Education responsible to the Board. It mandated 36 weeks of school per year, reorganized the supervisory unions, tightened requirements for teacher certification, gave the state responsibility for approval of private elementary schools, and made the physical welfare of students a concern of the public schools. Historian J.D. Squires calls it: " an epochal law, reflecting the trends of the time, yet actually going further in some ways than had been anticipated. At one jump, New Hampshire went from a condition of relative backwardness in public educa-

tion to a status of being somewhat of a pioneer."

Thus New Hampshire education entered the 20th century. Though much amended, the 1919 law has for more than 60 years supplied the essential framework within which New Hampshire conducts its public education. In the 1980s there are 53 superintendents and about 160,000 pupils in the public schools. The school programs are unimaginably more complex than anything foreseen in 1919, the costs still continually outrun resources, and the lack of substantial statewide tax support for schools is still a sore spot diagnosed in almost the same terms, only more pessimistic, as were familiar generations ago. The isolated rural school is but a marginal issue now; the problem of teacher quality, no longer the disaster it once was, is dealt with by an educational bureaucracy that manages a thousand other matters and, just as the law intended, is responsible through a commissioner to a five-person State Board of Education.

A century before, the Toleration Act of 1819 had been both a revolutionary and a successful redrawing of the lines between church and state; similarly the State Board Act of 1919 was a

Above: New Hampshire's village schools often put several grade levels into one classroom. In 1948 Lavina Dole's Campton classroom contained grades 5 through 8—and one dog. Courtesy, New Hampshire Department of Fish and Game

Opposite page: Concord's Cogswell Elementary School was photographed in 1906. Just a few years earlier the schoolboy hero of The Real Diary of a Real Boy, *by Henry Shute, had confided to his diary: "tonite i had to studdy Colburn arithmatic. It is the wirst book i ever studded . . . . i had rather be a merderer if nobuddy gnew it than be a feler whitch rote a arithmatic." NHHS*

This posthumous portrait of the Reverend Eleazar Wheelock, founder of Dartmouth College, was commissioned by the trustees of the college in 1793. It is the work of Joseph Steward, who had graduated from Dartmouth in 1780. DCA

Intercollegiate athletic rivalries were well established by the end of the 19th century. Here Dartmouth entertains the Amherst College baseball team in 1890. There are still those in New Hampshire who shake their heads and say that the decline of farming in New England coincided with the rise of baseball as a national pastime. At the turn of the century nearly every town in New Hampshire had its own uniformed baseball team. DCA

revolutionary and successful redrawing of the lines between school and state. If at the outset, early in the 17th century, church and school had been viewed by the law in almost the same way, 300 years of New Hampshire experience had steadily awarded the churches more independence and accorded the schools more supervision.

Dartmouth College

In the 1740s the Reverend Eleazar Wheelock, a Yale-educated Congregational minister serving in Lebanon, Connecticut, began tutoring nearby Indian children in the Christian religion with remarkable success. As more Indians came to him in the next decade, Wheelock began to contemplate an enlarged school, perhaps far off at the edge of the wilderness, where English and Indian boys could be educated together in a Christian community. Ironic backdrop for this noble dream was the French and Indian War, then raging in New Hampshire and elsewhere. In the 1760s Wheelock sent one of his early Indian converts, Samson Occum, to England to raise money for the project. Occum and renowned New Hampshire Indian fighter Robert Rogers arrived in England at about the same time, and each was a spectacular public-relations success. Rogers spun embellished tales of exploits fighting Indians; Occum elaborated the Reverend Wheelock's dream to educate Indians and embodied in his own person the fruits of such a plan. Lord Dartmouth, Secretary of State for the Colonies, contributed money for the school, energetically organized dozens of others to do the same, and persuaded George III himself to put up £200. The college was Britain's last best gift to New Hampshire before independence.

Word of the planned school had filtered to New Hampshire. In 1762 the Congregational Convention of Ministers in New Hampshire endorsed Wheelock's plan, and shortly thereafter the citizens of Hanover, a young Connecticut River town, offered him a large tract of land. On December 13, 1769, Governor John Wentworth signed a college charter "for the education and instruction of Youth of the Indian tribes . . . and also of English youth and any others." Wentworth College was the preferred name, but the governor shrewdly deferred to his English friend and fund raiser, Lord Dartmouth. Wheelock journeyed to the frontier with several transfer students from Yale and began the college in 1770 in a log building, a voice in the wilderness. The next year, 1771, the first class of four was graduated, with Governor Wentworth in attendance. Subsequently the training of Indian scholars and missionaries was only sometimes successful, but the training of "English youth and any others" has been very successful for two centuries.

Early on, Dartmouth entered vigorously and contentiously into the political life of New Hampshire, and its graduates and faculty did much during the 19th century to energize the political and cultural tone of the state. Characteristically, New Hampshire's first statewide public-school administrator came from the Dartmouth faculty, and when New Hampshire came to revise its educational system in the early 20th century, the principal intellectual force behind the 1919 statute turned out to be President E.M. Hopkins of Dartmouth. During the recent half-century Dartmouth has been rather less oriented toward the affairs of New Hampshire than it was formerly—in deference, perhaps, to the emergence of the University of New Hampshire during that same period. Today, at age 214, Dartmouth College is a small "university" of some 4,000 undergraduates with about 800 graduate students in three professional schools and several arts and sciences doctoral programs.

An invaluable link that has emerged in recent decades between Dartmouth and the people of New Hampshire is the Dartmouth-Hitchcock Medical Center, the distinguished descendant of the Dartmouth Medical School, which was itself founded in 1797. Today the Medical Center trains physicians at its Medical School and serves patients at the Hitchcock Clinic, the Mary Hitchcock Memorial Hospital, the Veterans Administration Hospital, and its outreach clinics in area communities.

The University of New Hampshire

Like many other state universities, the University of New Hampshire owes its origins to the 1862 Morrill Act of the U.S. Congress, which earmarked money derived from the sale of Western public lands for what became known as "land grant colleges." Each state was offered 30,000 acres per Congressman for maintaining "a college where the leading object shall be, . . . such branches of learning as are related to agriculture and the mechanic arts, . . . to promote the liberal and practical education of the industrial classes." Each state had five years to take it or leave it. The New Hampshire legislature hesitated. Was this a gift or an imposition? Where put such a college? Taking courage, the legislature incorporated the New Hampshire College of Agriculture and Mechanic Arts in 1866, and decided that it would be in Hanover, leaning on Dartmouth, now a vigorous enterprise.

The new trustees hired Ezekiel Dimond of Massachusetts as head of the new college; they gave him $3,000 for equipment and sent him to Hanover to set up the new institution with its practical course of study, alongside Dartmouth's classical curriculum. By nearly a century Professor Dimond was following the footsteps of Eleazar Wheelock to Hanover, to carry out an educational mandate that was, like Wheelock's, both a deep personal commitment and a broader mandate of his culture. Neither mandate bore bounteous fruit in quite the way intended—one did not rescue New Hampshire Indians, and the other did not rescue New Hampshire farming. They succeeded in other terms.

Professor Dimond distributed 2,000 circulars throughout the state, hired an associate, planned his courses, borrowed his classrooms, set up his gear, and waited curiously to see what would happen when he rang the bell in the fall. On September 4, 1868, ten young men came to register, and what was eventually to become the University of New Hampshire was on its way. In a few years the college had a building of its own, a faculty of two, the land grant endowment of $80,000—and still only a very few students. Professor Dimond, a versatile man and a strong leader, correctly insisted that the Morrill Act specifically encouraged "other sciences and classical subjects" as well, and from the first he regarded the institution as a state college. Dartmouth viewed its adoptee otherwise, mixing bemusement and disdain. During

Twenty-nine years after Dartmouth's first Winter Carnival, collegians in 1940 put the finishing touches on their impressive Winter Carnival ice sculpture, The Starshooter. *DCA*

Harvard president Charles Eliot once called the organized summer camp "the most important step in education that America has given the world." Throughout the late 19th and early 20th centuries, city youths flocked to New Hampshire's lakes each summer, where summer camps offered them a unique educational and recreational experience. Hebron's Camp Pasquaney, founded in 1895, featured a wide range of programs in its early years, from baseball (opposite page, top) to "backpacking"—finding this Civil War veteran and his wife was a bonus (above). Courtesy, Camp Pasquaney

its 25 years spent in Dartmouth's shadow, the college never had more than 14 graduates in a year.

Once more fortune smiled. In a will drafted long before the Morrill Act, Benjamin Thompson, a prosperous farmer in Durham, New Hampshire, bequeathed his land to the state for an "agricultural school, to be located on my . . . farm . . . in said Durham, wherein shall be thoroughly taught . . . the theory and practice of that most useful and honorable calling." When the will was probated in 1890, there was again considerable hesitancy about accepting a gift with its implied faith that agriculture had a bright future in New Hampshire. Journalists opposed starting up another such school. According to one voice: " . . .all the agricultural colleges between here and the setting sun will not convert the rocky hills of New Hampshire into gardens of Eden."

At this point common sense intervened, disguised as genius: the Thompson tract in Durham and that struggling college in Hanover, each a mixed and fragile blessing in itself, could be combined into one solution. A legislative act in 1891 lifted New Hampshire's state college from the shades at Dartmouth and sent it down to Thompson's farm in Durham. There, a fine red-brick Gothic academic building was erected in the pasture, and duly dedicated as Thompson Hall in 1893. Nearly a century later it still presides grandly over the academic landscape, and the university property, once within a farm, now has a farm within it.

In May 1917, with the nation going to war, the faculty of UNH decided to launch a patriotic potato patch under the supervision of Frederick W. "Pa" Taylor, seated at left in the wagon. While the launching may have been fun, the work was to follow. The faculty harvested 260 bushels of potatoes in 1917 and 324 bushels the following year. UC, UNH

Early growth at Durham, though moderate, was much more rapid than it had ever been in Hanover, and by the turn of the century there were nearly 200 students at the college.

Slowly, inexorably, like many another land grant college in many another state, New Hampshire College developed an inner logic which, propelled by outer circumstances, headed it in the direction of a university. Founded in Hanover and refounded in Durham in terms of explicit service to the state, the college had new demands laid on it—in teaching, research, and dissemination—by the New Hampshire citizenry. By the 1920s it had become clear that while Dartmouth might continue to dwell in the luster of its ivy, New Hampshire College would stick closer to its grass roots; it had become clear, too, that a liberal-arts impulse, frail at first, was coming alive in the center of the college, earnestly poking a taproot toward the veins of traditional academic culture. Eventually, like the other New England land grant colleges that were planted in the shadows of powerful private colleges, this one became a modern university. The transition came in stages.

In 1923 the General Court redefined the college as the University of New Hampshire, composed of three colleges: Agriculture, Technology, and Liberal Arts; a graduate school was formally added in 1928. In 1939 the standard two-year agricultural program became the Thompson School of Applied Science. A new burst of expansion and reorganization came in the 1960s. The Whittemore School of Business and Economics was founded in 1962; in 1969 the Agricultural College became the College of Life Sciences and Agriculture, and a new School of Health Studies was added; in 1975 the College of Technology became the College of Engineering and Physical Sciences; and at the end of the decade the School for Lifelong Learning was created.

One of the most significant changes during this time was the 1963 creation of the University System of New Hampshire, which officially brought the Plymouth and Keene state colleges, née normal schools, into one system with the University of New Hampshire under a single board of trustees. By the early 1980s enrollment at Durham was over 10,000; at Keene, well over 3,500; and at Plymouth, just under 3,500. Approximately two-thirds of these students are from New Hampshire.

Above: This is how the University of New Hampshire looked as it began its second century in 1968. Thompson Hall is near the center of the picture, Dimond Library to its left. UC, UNH

Left: The circa 1893 view of New Hampshire College of Agriculture and Mechanic Arts was photographed shortly after Thompson Hall (upper left) was completed. At the time Thompson Hall housed all of the college's non-agricultural academic disciplines. Today it is the central administrative building at the University of New Hampshire. UC, UNH

Wallace Nutting may have loved the New England countryside, but he had little love for the region's road signs, complaining in his 1923 book, New Hampshire Beautiful, *that it "would require a year's course at a university to become thoroughly posted on the signs in New England. . . ." Fortunately this very readable 1921 Durham road sign was near a center of higher learning. UC, UNH*

CHAPTER
THIRTEEN

R·E·L·I·G·I·O·N
A·N·D
T·H·E C·H·U·R·C·H·E·S

In colonial New Hampshire there was no such thing as separation of church and state: worship service was town meeting at prayer.

Unlike the Puritans and the Pilgrims farther south, the early settlers in the Piscataqua region were not seekers of religious freedom. Most of them were Anglicans like their sponsor, John Mason, who had taken care to send over a pulpit Bible, copies of the *Book of Common Prayer,* and communion silver. An Anglican parish was established at Strawbery Banke (Portsmouth) in 1638, but Anglicanism virtually died out there during the next decades as New Hampshire towns united with Puritan Massachusetts Bay Colony. The remaining Anglicans were taxed in support of the Congregational Church, which was to become virtually the established church of New Hampshire.

Nearly a century later, in 1732, the Anglican communion was reconstituted in New Hampshire (an attempt in the 1680s had failed) with the beginning of Queen's Chapel (now St. John's) in Portsmouth. Since the Anglicans were a minority in Portsmouth, their church taxes went routinely (until they got exemptions in 1740) to the Congregationalists, and they paid their own minister's salary. Prior to the Revolutionary War many important Portsmouth merchants and politicians were Anglicans, including the last two Wentworth governors. As was to be expected, a number of prominent Loyalists, or Tories, during the Revolutionary period came from among the Anglicans. Samuel Livermore of Holderness, an ardent Anglican and an ardent Patriot, was a notable exception. Later, in 1791, Livermore became president of the New Hampshire Constitutional Convention.

Quakers also appeared early in New Hampshire, fleeing persecution in Massachusetts Bay. After one bizarre incident in 1662 in which, in accordance with the law and under the orders of Magistrate Richard Waldron, three Quaker women were publicly whipped in Dover, simply for being there, one hears no more of persecution of Quakers in New Hampshire. A Quaker Society was formally established in Dover before 1700, and tolerance, offically expressed in a Royal decree as "liberty of conscience," was then the norm. Laws requiring oaths made exception for Quakers, who conscientiously objected to oath-taking, which they viewed as an act of worship not to be forced upon anyone. Despite the early persecution, Quakers prospered in Dover during the 18th century.

But the vast majority of New Hampshire churches were Congregational. By the time of the Revolutionary War, there were nearly 120 organized churches in New Hampshire. Eighty-four were Congregational; two were Anglican; 15 were Presbyterian; 11 were Baptist; and 5 were Quaker. Other denominations appeared soon after the Revolutionary War: Freewill Baptists, 1780; Universalists, 1781; Shakers, 1790s; Methodists, 1790s; Christian Church, 1803. Until well into the 19th century there were no Catholics or Jews in New Hampshire to disturb the comfortable Protestant bias of the laws and the state constitution. Each new denomination, however, was one more tug away from the center of the Congregational "establishment."

Church and State

From the start religion and education in New Hampshire were undergirded by a common assumption: school and church are social necessities to be supported by public taxation. There were also further assumptions: schools should be required; churches should be encouraged. Accordingly, the New Hampshire laws that required a schoolmaster for a town did not mandate hiring a minister (as they did in Massachusetts), but they did require that the meetinghouse be public property and that the minister, if any, be paid through town taxes in exactly the same way as a schoolmaster. Moreover, most township grants and most town charters given by the governor included—as a condition of

Top left: The Shaker Village at Enfield, one of two in the state, lasted from 1793 to 1923. The brothers and sisters pictured here are standing on the steps of the office of the South Family around 1870. The family's ruling Eldress and Elder stand in front. From the Leavitt Collection, NHHS

Top right: The interior of the minister's dwelling at Enfield's Church Family was plain, but by no means uncomfortable. Elder Abraham Perkins, photographed circa 1870, had ministerial duties in several Shaker communities, which might explain the map of New England on his study wall. From the Leavitt Collection, NHHS

Above: Canterbury Shaker Village, founded in 1792, may have had as many as 300 residents at its largest. Pictured in this H.A. Kimball photograph are the buildings of the Church Family circa 1870. The meetinghouse is the gambrel-roofed building on the right. NHHS

Above: A classic New Hampshire meetinghouse, one of hundreds, this building was erected in the late 18th century, photographed by Gustine Hurd in the late 19th century, and is still in daily use in the late 20th century. Courtesy, Ronald and Grace Jager

Opposite page: Both inside and out, the Sandown Meetinghouse remains a superb example of 18th-century architecture and craftsmanship. It was built between the summer of 1773 and October 1774; construction was briefly interrupted at one point when the workmen ran out of rum and walked off the job. Between 1778 and 1929 Sandown held its town meetings here, although regular church services stopped in 1834. NHHS

ownership, not as a matter of law—requirements that a minister be secured within a certain period of time. It was simply taken for granted that the minister was a civil officer of the town.

Thus, until well into the 19th century a New Hampshire town decided by majority vote which religious denomination it would support; the minister was called, his salary set, and the church expenses decided at town meeting. Unless they secured exemptions—rare during New Hampshire's first hundred years (granted only to Quakers), difficult to obtain during the next 50 years, and widespread during the following 50 years—all taxpayers supported the church, whether they went to it or not, whether they liked it or not. The 1693 New Hampshire law that set the general pattern for well over a century was careful about loopholes, intending that no one

> *under pretence of being of a different perswassion be Excused from paying toward the support of the settled Minister . . . but only such as are Conscientiously So; and Constantly attend the publick worship of God on the Lords day according to their owne P'rswassion; And they only Shall be Excused from paying toward the Support of the Ministrey of the Towne.*

New Hampshire had followed the example of Massachusetts, and Massachusetts had followed England. The American innovation lay in allowing each town to decide *which* church to support. The New Hampshire innovations in 1693 lay in allowing individual exemptions and in not mandating a town minister. At the time these provisions were the most liberal of their kind in New England. Indeed, to a thoughtful person of open mind the New Hampshire colonial church/state system seemed like a good idea. Yet the system crumbled slowly over the course of two centuries; the fact that it became unworkable and therefore unwise probably did as much to break it down as did the conviction that it was unjust. In a more general sense, however, the system fell victim to its own virtues—one of which was liberty of conscience.

"Liberty of Conscience"

Shipped over from England, "liberty of conscience" embodied a noble sentiment of uncertain meaning. It was affirmed for New Hampshire citizens, "Papists" excepted, in the Royal charter of the province in 1679; it was repeated in laws and was regularly reaffirmed in the commissions of the Royal governors. It meant at least this: no one, not even a Quaker, is to be persecuted for religious beliefs. (The implications for Catholics were not worked out, for there were then no Catholics in New Hampshire.) "Liberty of conscience" in this sense was valued and practiced, thus inoculating New Hampshire against the witchcraft hysteria that swept through the less tolerant Bay Colony. No one then would have suggested that paying taxes to support a religion not one's own was a violation of conscience any more than one would have suggested that paying taxes to educate children not one's own was a violation of conscience.

Liberty of conscience helped to undermine the established system. For example, tax exemptions encouraged non-Congregationalists. Encouraged, they multiplied; discouraged,

they complained to the Selectmen, to the Assembly, and to the courts. The more denominations that were recognized, the more complicated became the system, and the more burdened became town and state governments with religious and church affairs. In Newton, in 1769, Baptists and Quakers ganged up, took control of the town meeting, and voted themselves the tax exemptions they had been denied. In a more characteristic case, in 1801 the New Hampshire Supreme Court had to decide whether the Universalists qualified as a "sect" within the meaning of the law that authorized the exemptions. They didn't. So Universalists continued to pay taxes to the support of Congregational or Presbyterian ministers. Sometimes the unchurched simply joined together, as they did in Durham in 1805, and voted to inform Mr. Coe, the town's Congregational minister, "that his preaching is no longer beneficial to the Inhabitants of Durham." A way to ax the tax.

The opportunities for quibbling about tax exemptions were endless, forever new and forever the same: Was last Sunday's gathering at the Jones farm a "publick worship" or just a murmuring of malcontents? And does the MacGregor family go "constantly" to the Presbyterian Church, 30 miles away in Londonderry? Deny them exemptions and they may enlist others and incorporate a Presbyterian parish right here in

Chester and then petition the Assembly and the Selectmen for their share of the town taxes. In Bedford and Londonderry it was easy: the Presbyterians were in a majority and "established" their church and let the Congregationalists off free; in Goffstown and Pembroke it was hard: Presbyterians were only a large minority and so the legislature eventually created special parishes for them. The system was a frequent headache for the towns, for the legislature, and for the courts, where grievances piled up, and for the churches, when squabbles about where to locate a church or whether to call a pastor or change his salary, and disputes about doctrine or morals easily became townwide issues. After 1800 many towns voted somewhat evasively, as did Durham in 1814, "that each Religious Denomination in this Town raise their ministerial money in their own way and manner." This peace-keeping maneuver was probably illegal and probably wise.

Slowly, inexorably, the venerable "liberty of conscience" idea began—especially in the latter days of colonial New Hampshire—to assume a profounder meaning: not only "no persecution" but also "right to worship as one chooses."

The Constitution and the Law
The New Hampshire Constitution of 1784 was not designed to change any of the basic assumptions and practices of "estab-

lished" town churches. Yet it did—almost imperceptibly at first, but permanently.

Liberty of conscience, the "constitutional" principle of colonial days (affirmed in the Bill of Rights of the Constitution), had begun the subtle subversion of the established system. However, a new principle present in the 1784 Constitution worked quietly and efficiently to subvert the system further. The new principle was that all churches should be treated equally by the law. "No subordination of any one sect or denomination to another shall ever be established by law," says the Constitution. It was difficult to reconcile this ideal with many of the town practices or with the fact that the same Constitution, until changed in 1877, restricted state offices to Protestants.

The surprising thing is that the *theory* of state/church relations, despite strife in practice, was not really controversial at the time. The topic was scarcely debated in the several conventions that led to the final text of the 1784 New Hampshire Constitution, which declared that "the best and greatest security to government" lay in "morality and piety," to be achieved by "the institution of the public worship of the Deity." Since a *state* church was unthinkable, there seemed to be no genuine alternative to the publicly supported town church.

The 1784 New Hampshire Constitution also empowered the *legislature* "to authorize from time to time the several towns . . . to make adequate provision . . . for . . . Protestant teachers of piety, religion, and morality." Thus the legislature could change the practice without changing the Constitution, and they did so by the Toleration Act of 1819. The new act resulted from a growing consensus that the town-church idea was outdated, and it resulted too from years of journalistic and political agitation against tax support of churches by Democratic-Republicans William Plumer and Isaac Hill. A town's right, granted by the legislature, to hire and dismiss its own ministers, initially the greatest privilege, had become the greatest burden.

The 1819 Act repealed the towns' authorization to support ministers and churches; it left existing contracts between towns and ministers in place; and it provided that "no person shall be compelled to . . . support or be classed with . . . any congregation, church or religious society without his express consent." In addition, anyone resigning from a religious society and so notifying the town clerk "shall thereupon be no longer liable for any further expense" of that society.

The 1819 Toleration Act was *the* watershed law in the history of New Hampshire church/state relations. Many problems remained—disposal of church property, use of meetinghouses, and the like—but the major intent of the act was soon absorbed into the everyday assumptions of the people: towns were now out of the church business. Suddenly it was quite obvious that the way for the government to treat the churches equally and subordinate none of them was not by financing them equally but by financing them not at all. So complete was the change of mind during the period from 1791, when church/state matters were first seriously debated at the Constitutional Convention, to the time of the new law in 1819 that it seemed superfluous to change the Constitution. Nearly 150 years later, in 1968, a badly muddled constitutional amendment finally withdrew from the legis-lature the power to authorize towns to support ministers.

The Great Awakening

The arrangements of religion are one thing; the religious life another. For a time New Hampshire people organized religious practice with a few laws, a few central ideas. Then the arrangements wore out, their breakdown contaminated religious life itself, and the local dramas that ensued are left as the principal stuff of record. Easily lost to memory and to history, or drowned in the melancholy din of neighborhood clashes, is the texture of religious life itself: the flow of feeling and passion and the faith, piety, and pride that the churches labored to refine into the living worship and service of God. Something of the force of this spirituality may be suggested by two other dimensions of New Hampshire church history: the Great Awakening, a representative and revealing 18th-century episode; and the rise and fall of theological seminaries, obscure but revealing episodes of the 19th century.

In the early 1740s intense religious revivals swept through the American colonies, especially throughout New England. Religious life had become cold, formalistic, complacent—according to the critics of the day. Moreover, in the frontier communities of New Hampshire many people were out of touch with an established church: it might be hard to get to, without a settled pastor, not worth the trouble, or not yet established in a town. The Puritan zeal for righteousness that had burned so fiercely in the 17th century was often submerged in the strenuous secular business of wresting a living from the wilderness. In many places active church members were a minority of the townspeople. Though religion died almost nowhere, it often moved to the margins and slept.

A critical instrument of awakening was the "itinerant," a traveling evangelist, usually gifted in direct and dramatic Biblical oratory aimed at the emotions. An itinerant's success in a community was marked by numerous conversions, by a great intensification of religious interest, Bible study, prayer, and, frequently, by extended, emotional, sometimes disorderly religious meetings lasting late into the night, sometimes night after night. Most itinerants active in the New Hampshire of the 1740s—perhaps a dozen at different times—pale beside the eloquent George Whitefield, an English evangelist who preached up and down the American coast with enormous effect, and the incomparable Jonathan Edwards, a central American figure of the Awakening, whose powerful preaching in his own church in Northampton, Massachusetts, was indirectly felt in all the towns of New Hampshire.

Supporters of the Awakening, called "New Lights" (they would be called the "born again" today), focused on the slumbering and unfeeling orthodoxy of the churches and on the forthright faith and vigor of the awakened. Critics, or "Old Lights," focused upon the excesses of religious commotion, often deliberately cultivated, in the souls of the New Lights and deplored the "enthusiasm" (18th-century word for fanaticism) that boiled and bubbled in the wake of the fiery preaching of the itinerants.

The Great Awakening of 1740 began in New Hampshire a

dozen years early. It started with an earthquake at 10 p.m., Sunday evening, October 29, 1727. The next Sunday and periodically for years thereafter hardly a preacher failed to remind his congregation regularly that this dramatic sign from the Lord should prompt repentance and rededication. And it did. Contemporaries and statistics tell the same story: every congregation for which records are available shows an upsurge of membership in 1727 and 1728. Fifteen years later William Shurtleff of Portsmouth expressed the common opinion, declaring that the "Earthquake in the Year 1727, that put the whole Country in such a Surprise, was a Means of Awakening a great many here: and . . . the Impressions have remain'd."

Two of New Hampshire's most prominent clergymen remained Old Lights. It was no surprise that Governor Benning Wentworth's pastor, Anglican Arthur Browne of Queen's Chapel, Portsmouth, was not amused by the goings on. He wrote to a friend in London that

Impressions, Impulses, Experiences are altogether in vogue & become the Test of Regenerate men; whilst the true Scripture works are quite out of request . . . . He is the best and most edifying Preacher who is most presumptuous and unintelligible.

The Reverend Timothy Walker, a Congregationalist of Concord who preached and published two anti-Awakening sermons in 1743, was concerned after seeing "one Vain Boaster after another start up," that the "Form of Godliness would be destroyed, under Pretence of farther advancing the Power of it." Nevertheless, most New Hampshire ministers supported the revivals and attempted to redirect the excesses. A number of hell-fire itinerants, like Daniel Rogers of Exeter, eventually settled into regular pastorates and became solid churchmen. Some of the New Lights became Old Lights as they aged.

The Awakened infused the churches with valuable spiritual energies; new openings for other denominations, Baptists especially, were created, as perhaps was a keener sensitivity to certain democratic attitudes. Intense piety before a Biblical God, almighty and forgiving, who is "no respecter of persons," is an effective social leveler. Though the fine links from religious revival through social attitude to democratic revolution are tenuous, complicated, and hard to track, they are essential threads in the tapestry of the New England experience.

In the Wilderness

Some itinerant preachers of the Great Awakening were notable, occasionally notorious, for being essentially self-educated—supplying with zeal what they lacked in knowledge. Leaders of New England churches, themselves usually alumni of Harvard, Yale, or, occasionally, Oxford or Cambridge, were perennially concerned about the supply of educated pastors in remoter regions such as New Hampshire. They were haunted and inspired by the idealism voiced as far back as 1636 in the founding rationale of Harvard College: "dreading to leave an illiterate Ministry to the Churches, when our present Ministers shall lie in the Dust." The 1812 ecclesiastical convention acknowledged that more trained pastors were needed lest "new settlements, where they

This posthumous portrait of Mary Baker Eddy was painted by J.N. Marble in 1916. A native of Bow, Mrs. Eddy formed the Christian Scientist's Association in 1876; the church of Christ Scientist was chartered in 1879. In 1889 Mrs. Eddy returned to New Hampshire from Massachusetts, living in Concord until 1908. NHHS

The Baptist churches in New Hampshire originate from the Great Awakening and the successive visits to the state by the evangelist George Whitefield. The first of these churches was organized in Newton in the 1750s, and by 1800 there were 16 others. During the Revolutionary War a Free Will Baptist Church—inspired indirectly by Whitefield's 1770 visit to New Hampshire—was founded in New Durham. Pictured is the community's church building, erected in 1818-1819. NHHS

have not faithful ministers, will be left a prey to sectarian preachers, who disseminate errors . . . who create divisions, which weaken society."

By the 1830s, with the state's population rising rapidly, there were 50 New Hampshire Congregational churches without full-time pastors. In those days of unsettled church/state relations, it was difficult to know how to go about supplying church needs. Should the state government do something for ministerial education? Who should develop a seminary and by what authority? Should it be denominational? How should it be financed?

The New Hampshire response, reiterated in different ways and places, came directly from Biblical impulse, not from organizational theory. The brick and mortar that emerged was firmly laid upon a unique pillar of New England theology, namely the Biblical concept of the "wilderness," or "desert": a place of testing as well as the providential setting for the eventual strengthening of the true church. Millenialist theology—the belief that Christ would soon return and usher in the end of the age—was frequently a part of the concept. New England, including New Hampshire, though an alien and unpromising wilderness, was to be God's instrument for working out his kingdom in America, a promised land destined to be a blessing to all nations. The planting of a seminary in the desert, a seed plot of teachers and preachers awaiting "showers of divine blessings" of which the revivals were an emblem, was not only a practical necessity but a reenactment of Biblical history, trial, and blessing. It was to be God's way of building up "the waste places of Zion," that is, the unpastored towns of New Hampshire.

The rich ambiguity and inspirational power of these Biblical metaphors lie behind a good deal of the spiritual history of 19th-century New Hampshire, spilling over into education and eventually into art as well. The motto of Dartmouth College, plucked from the Bible by founder Wheelock, was fitting: *Vox clamantis in Deserto.* But the hope that Dartmouth would strongly supplement the small trickle of trained clergymen from Harvard, Yale, and Andover, had faded unfulfilled. Something more was needed.

A cold summary of the main institutions that emerged from all the warm theology looks like this. *Baptists:* Calvinist Baptists set up an Academical and Theological Institute at New Hampton in 1825, with a three-year academy and theological course. When that school moved to Vermont in 1853, the building was taken over by the Free Will Baptists as New Hampton Biblical and Literary Institute; in 1870 it joined Bates College in Maine, where it was renamed and where it eventually died. *Methodists:* A Vermont-based seminary moved to Concord, New Hampshire, in 1847 and became the Methodist General Biblical Institute. For 21 years it was housed in the old North Congregational Church, and 211 young men graduated from its three-year seminary course. In 1868 the Institute moved to Boston to become the Boston University School of Theology. *Congregationalists:* Kimball Union Academy was established in Meriden in 1813 to prepare young men to enter college with advanced standing so as to enter the ministry more quickly. In 1835 the Academy of Plymouth (founded in 1804) added a theological department, renamed itself Plymouth Literary and Theological Seminary, but, partly because of competition from a more carefully planned seminary effort at Gilmanton, it soon petered out.

The Gilmanton Seminary was academically the most formidable of the New Hampshire seminaries. Founded in 1835 and attached first to the academy that had existed there from 1794, the Seminary soon erected a fine three-story brick building, assembled a good library, admitted students from any orthodox denomination, and graduated its largest class of 10 in 1841. "The wilderness has become as the garden of God," exulted the Reverend David Lancaster, longtime Gilmanton pastor, leading promoter of the Seminary, and short-term Hebrew teacher there. The faculty was distinguished and the course of study solid, largely post-collegiate, with Dartmouth and Harvard graduates among the students. On the faculty prolific scholars such as Herman Rood, Isaac Bird, and William Cogswell stood out. Cogswell left his Dartmouth history professorship to head the Seminary in 1844, and while there he founded a quarterly, which eventually became the *New England Historical and Genealogical Register*. He later edited several volumes of the New Hampshire Historical Society's *Collections*. A half-dozen different journals were started at Gilmanton during its Seminary days. In 1846 activities were suddenly suspended for lack of funds. The Congregational churches, clutching their independence, had never formally and financially backed the project. David Lancaster left Gilmanton for Concord to become chaplain of the legislature and of the insane asylum. The Biblical metaphors had finally failed.

Yet, for a time these various theological institutions had supplied New Hampshire with educated clergymen, and to many they visibly embodied the striking vision of *Isaiah:* "the wilderness and the solitary place shall be glad—and the desert shall rejoice and blossom like a rose." Like many of the classical academies in whose image they were created, the seminaries faded or failed financially or moved away as transportation and communication problems eased. Moreover, the distinctive theological outlook that prompted the seminaries became permanently blurred in New Hampshire as an utterly different kind of moral wilderness, that of an industrial economy, came to prominence on the landscape.

With the influx of immigrants in the beginning of the 20th century, several Eastern Orthodox congregations were formed in New Hampshire. Today the state has a dozen Greek Orthodox and three Russian Orthodox congregations. Pictured is the Holy Resurrection Orthodox Church in Claremont. NHHS

The Seventh-Day Adventist faith, which now sponsors a worldwide missionary service, was born in the New Hampshire hill town of Washington in the 1840s, when several Adventist members of the Christian denomination in that town elected to worship on Saturday. The original Seventh-Day Adventist Church was subsequently organized there in 1862. Today there are 14 churches of this denomination in New Hampshire. Courtesy, Ronald and Grace Jager

C H A P T E R
F O U R T E E N

A·E·S·T·H·E·T·I·C A·N·D
L·I·T·E·R·A·R·Y
H·A·U·N·T·S

New Hampshire has nourished the aesthetic life in dozens of ways, not just in paint and print and photograph and sculpture and architecture but also in crafts and arts innumerable—from Dunlap chests to Prescott violas to Stoddard glass to Graves clarinets.

In the 20th century three very different vehicles have stimulated artistic creativity. The most recent is the publicly funded New Hampshire Commission on the Arts, which supports individual and group projects in music, dance, theater, and related arts. Another is the League of New Hampshire Craftsmen, which, since its founding in 1932, has variously supported its members' work through exhibitions, access to markets, support of the educational aspects of crafts, and by sustaining high standards of craftsmanship. A very different vehicle, whose influence on artistic effort has spread far beyond Granite State borders, is the MacDowell Colony in Peterborough. Created in 1907 by the musicians Marian and Edward MacDowell, its cluster of woodsy workshops and cottages provides short-term retreats for artists, composers, writers, and others. From this colony have come more than two dozen Pulitzer Prize-winning works. Some colony residents have settled in Peterborough and nearby Dublin—the latter town being associated especially with Abbot Thayer and other distinguished painters. Together these two towns may have sheltered more notable musicians, writers, and artists than any similar small communities in America.

In three centuries New Hampshire has produced aesthetic riches too many and too varied to survey. One way to sense the aesthetic impulse within the state is to observe the creativity inspired at just three quite dissimilar locations: the White Mountains, the Isles of Shoals, and the rolling hills of Cornish and Plainfield along the Connecticut River. Each was at one time (and, in a sense, the White Mountains continues to be) a special kind of aesthetic haunt—like the MacDowell Colony, but more spontaneous, and each formed a unique response to the allure of the hills or the sea or the land.

Somewhat apart from these colonies of artists, a counterpoint to them, is the solitary figure of New Hampshire's greatest poet, Robert Frost. Others were caught up in the spell of the landscape, but his was "a road less traveled by," an attachment directly to the land itself, to its people, and to the particular places where their dreams had been.

White Mountain Images

Jeremy Belknap was the first writer in America to give expression to the romantic view of mountains, which had originated in Europe in the late 18th century. He had not yet read Wordsworth on the Alps when he wrote of the White Mountains: "A poetic fancy may find full gratification amidst these wild and rugged scenes. . . . Almost every thing in nature, which can be supposed capable of inspiring ideas of the sublime and beautiful, is here realized. Aged mountains, stupendous elevations, rolling clouds, impending rocks, verdant woods, crystal streams, the gentle rill, and the roaring torrent, all conspire to amaze, to soothe and to enrapture."

That was the view of the White Mountains that lured the first artists there in the early decades of the 19th century, and among them Thomas Cole is preeminent. Both a painter and a writer, Cole saw in mountains the place where "the savage is tempered by the magnificent." Many of his paintings after his first trip to the White Mountains in 1827 explore this view of nature raw, extravagant, fearful, where intimations of morality and religion lurk. Mountains, he wrote, are "a fitting place to speak of God." Towering cliffs, gnarled trees, and stormy skies dominate his best White Mountain canvasses, while analogies dominate his essays: "the broad sheets of untrodden snow that capped the mountains above us were like emblems of nature's purity."

Many other writers and painters picked up these dramatic perspectives on the wilderness. Travel books, such as those of Theodore and Timothy Dwight, highlighted the romance of the White Mountains, as did even such London books as Nathaniel Willis' *American Scenery* published in 1840. Among painters the work of Alvan Fisher, Jasper Cropsey, and Orford's Henry Cheever Pratt supply outstanding expressions of the same themes. Thomas Cole and these others were attracted to the most intimidating aspects of the mountains: to the Crawford and Franconia notches, to cataracts and avalanches, to the peaks and shadows of the Presidentials—to what was called the "sublime" in nature.

Artists who came later in the century often sought out another view, the softer aspect of the slopes, the velvet hills, and cultivated valleys and pastured uplands—the pastoral side of romanticism. Here the mountain peaks provided a distant and stately setting for meadows, cultivated and tame, beside quiet rivers— nature more beneficent than overpowering. If this art suggests an idealization of rural America, it is no wonder: after the Civil War rural New Hampshire was heading for the city faster than at any time in history. It thus also hints of wilderness not merely as a savage thing to be dominated, but as a resource to be

In the mid-19th century, Concord was a center of musical instrument making. Much of the activity was spurred by Abraham Prescott, who had been born in Deerfield but moved to Concord in 1831 to expand his manufacture of bass viols, double bass viols, cellos, and violins. Praised as "the Stradivarius of their type," Prescott viols (such as the bass viol shown here) were sold worldwide and, along with Abbot-Downing's overland coach, made Concord famous around the globe. NHHS

Opposite page: By the 1840s Abraham Prescott was manufacturing melodeons and reed organs as well as his famous stringed instruments, as seen here in this Concord City Directory advertisement from 1856. The business stayed in the family until 1917. NHHS

Exhibition of
PAINTINGS.
FOR THREE WEEKS ONLY.
(Open on Monday next.)

THE Public are respectfully informed that a number of Paintings will be exhibited at No. 4 State street,—among which are 6 Views of *Niagara Falls*, a View of the *Notch of the White Mountains*, a View of *Lake Winnipissiogee*, a Likeness of Sir William Pepperel,—together with a great variety of other Paintings.

Admittance to the whole, 12 1 2 cents, Children half price; season Tickets 25 cts. Tickets for sale at Mr. B. Hutchings' store.

N. B. The entrance to Mr. Blunt's Painting Room, will be (for the present) through Mr. Hutchings' Store.

Portsmouth, Oct. 18, 1828.

John S. Blunt was a Portsmouth artist and sign painter in the 1820s. Breaking out of the restrictions of sign work, Blunt advertised this exhibit of paintings in 1828. NHHS

Below and below right: Various exhibitors demonstrate their crafts at a League of New Hampshire Craftmen's fair around 1940. Courtesy, League of New Hampshire Craftsmen

cherished—an intimation just breaking into the industrial consciousness of the Granite State in the last quarter of the 19th century.

At about the time of the Civil War, Benjamin Champney settled in North Conway and there gathered around him a group of artists often called the White Mountain School. Among them are the familiar names of Ashur B. Durand, Aaron D. Shattuck, John F. Kensett, Thomas Hill, Albert Bierstadt, Winslow Homer, and many others. The last half of the 19th century also saw the publication of many distinguished illustrated books for the White Mountains fancier—paintings, drawings, engravings, and finally photographs, often accompanied by rather florid texts. "The Switzerland of America" was the phrase that was supposed to make hearts flutter. Moses Sweetser's *Views of the White Mountains* (1879) is a classic example of these books. In prose, nothing excels the loftiness of rhetoric and feeling that was poured into Thomas Starr King's *The White Hills* (1859), wherein piety toward God and nature are remarkably combined but not confused. His special talent, or compulsion, was to describe in exact detail the scene from the best viewing spots and then to quote a bit of verse to heighten the experience.

These artists and others gave form to different and competing conceptions of New Hampshire wilds. One extols wilderness *as wilderness*—provided that it is distilled in painting or prose or even framed by the window of an excursion train crossing the Frankenstein trestle or climbing Jacob's Ladder. The other is a more contemplative view, wilderness itself is domesticated, some order has been imposed, and the central landscape is at peace with itself.

Such contrasting images are also summaries of historical realities. For it is plainly true that the White Mountains as first found were ragged and raw, that Mt. Washington undeniably has a certain stolid and durable majesty, and that the region as a whole has a climate Arctic enough to keep the treeline at 4,000 feet (compared with 10,000 feet in the Rockies), just as it is also true that by mid-century this region was partially subdued—roads and railroads had brought in people, farms had crept to the base of the slopes, and villages had sprouted in the valleys.

In the wake of the stock market crash of October 1929, Manchester put the finishing touches on the State Theatre, billed as the largest theater north of Boston (with 2,187 seats) and extolled for its "futuristic design." Workmen (left) put the finishing touches on the theater's figurehead. On Wednesday evening, November 27, 1929, the theater opened to an overflow audience (above), including Governor Charles Tobey. For those lucky enough to get in, an orchestra seat cost 40 cents and a balcony seat cost 30 cents. MVHC

The Sea and the Shoals

Here is a very different sort of landscape—hardly a *land*scape at all. These isles are piles of irregular green-crowned and treeless granite off the coast of Rye: eight small islands, nine miles out, together only a few hundred acres. "A stern and lovely scene," wrote Nathaniel Hawthorne. Bleak in appearance, rich in historical association, their record goes back to 1614 when Captain John Smith noticed "the remarkablest isles . . . a heap together . . . a many of barren rocks." Their destiny has turned with tides and time: in the 17th century a major fishing station with hundreds of residents; in the 18th century intermittent fishing and a washed-out maritime community; in the 19th century a tourist retreat and a haven for artists and writers; and in the 20th century a center for marine biology and religious conferences.

During the middle of the last century two large hotels on the Isles were often filled the summer long. Visitors sought island seclusion, sought stern and lovely scenery, and they also sought each other. For a chosen few the center of attraction was Celia Laighton Thaxter, who had grown up on the Isles, married there, and became a much-published poet. For 30 years, from the Civil War onward, she spent most summers on Appledore Island, gardening, writing, painting, and playing host to a coterie of "beauties and geniuses" (as a contemporary called them) from all over New England, who were captivated by her talents, her friends, her gardens, her island setting, and her hospitality. A salon of latter-day transcendentalists thrived at her cottage, including artists who came to paint her flowers, the seascapes, the rocks, and to illustrate her books, musicians who came to play, and writers who came to talk. Many returned year after year. Among the writers were John Greenleaf Whittier, Oliver Wendell Holmes, Ralph Waldo Emerson, James Russell Lowell, James Whitcomb Riley, Harriet Beecher Stowe, Sarah Orne Jewett, and Thomas Bailey Aldrich.

One visitor, John Albee, later reminisced: "She could make the musician play his best, the poets and scholars say their best—even Mr. Whittier could be vivacious and communicative. . . . To see Celia Thaxter so surrounded by her flowers, lovers, pictures, books, and souvenirs, to listen to the speech and music of her gifted friends, was the most picturesque and exciting spectacle afforded in this part of the country." "Picturesque"—it had become a favorite term of approval by the latter part of the 19th century.

Celia Thaxter's own verses were well known at the time and much admired. If today they appear to be somewhat dewy with sunsets and dawnings, the sweet voice of 19th-century femininity, her other work is of more universal appeal. John Greenleaf Whittier coaxed, cajoled, and flattered her into writing a small volume on the Isles themselves. Her book, *Among the Isles of Shoals,* first published in 1873 and much reprinted, is a graceful prose poem that catches and blends the austerity and romance of the Isles. No one has captured more feelingly than she the sublime aftermath of a dark storm over the Isles: "this solemn gray lid was lifted at its western edge, and an insufferable splendor streamed across the world from the sinking sun. The whole heaven was in a blaze of scarlet, across which sprang a rainbow unbroken to the topmost clouds, 'with its seven perfect colors chorded in a triumph,' against the flaming background; the sea answered the sky's rich blue, and the gray rocks lay drowned in melancholy purple. I hid my face from the glory,—it was too much to bear."

Above: The Isles of Shoals had been a center of fishing and commercial activity throughout the 17th and early 18th centuries, but by the time this picture was taken, circa 1875, the tiny church at Gosport was serving the needs of very few. Built in 1800, the church stood up to many Atlantic storms, although its wooden tower pictured was blown down in 1890, to be replaced by another of stone. NHHS

Opposite page: "Swept by every wind that blows, and beaten by the bitter brine for unknown ages, well may the Isles of Shoals be barren, bleak, and bare." Nineteenth-century poetess Celia Thaxter knew the islands about which she wrote and understood why the stranger might be "struck only by the sadness of the place,—the vast loneliness; for there are not even trees to whisper with familiar voices,—nothing but sky and sea and rocks." From the Historic Photograph Collection of Strawbery Banke, Inc.

By the third quarter of the 19th century, Celia Laighton Thaxter was a poet of renown well beyond Portsmouth, the town of her birth, and Appledore, the locale of her summer salons. It is indicative of both her literary standing and the attitude toward women's writing at the time that her publisher, Houghton Mifflin, rejected a submission from Emily Dickinson because they already had "a female poet." NHHS

The Flowering of Cornish

As the Thaxter circle at the Shoals faded and the White Mountain School of artists dispersed, another New Hampshire flowering, not connected with the others, opened at another place.

A New York lawyer bought up several thousand acres of cheap, abandoned farmland near the Connecticut River in Cornish in 1884. One tract featured a bleak old brick structure, and this property he sold to a fellow New Yorker, the sculptor Augustus Saint-Gaudens. Other New Yorkers came to visit and some stayed to paint the scenery, whereupon the countryside itself began to work its spell upon a whole train of voluntary exiles from New York. Something oddly wonderful was going on: farmers' sons were seeking the city for a new lease on life; city artists were seeking out the abandoned farms for a new inspiration.

Some of the earliest to come to Cornish were assistants of Saint-Gaudens, sculptors on their way to important careers of their own. Among the early painters were George de Forest Brush and Thomas Dewing, and after them were others, including Charles Platt and Stephen Parrish, both distinguished etchers with other talents, too. The latter's son, Maxfield Parrish, came to Cornish in 1898 and found there a perfect setting for his extraordinary talent as illustrator and artist. From his studio (just over the Cornish line in Plainfield) flowed a stream of illustrations for everything from chocolate boxes to children's books, to magazines and calendars, all in a wonderfully personal style, colorful, droll, and dramatic. There came too a stream of paintings, stunning portrayals unlike anything seen hitherto, at once accurate and romantic: beige hillsides and exquisite blue skies and haunting purple dusks. Fortunately it was work more than good enough to survive the indignity of having been immediately and highly appreciated: not for Parrish the doleful legends of the struggling artist starving in a garret; most of his life he was rich and famous. Parrish's landscape work—his favorite subject—is largely untouched by the traditions of White Mountain painting and constitutes today the major 20th-century New Hampshire answer to that great tradition of the 19th century.

Writers migrated to the Cornish hills as well—the poets William Vaughn Moody and Percy MacKaye, and the novelist Winston Churchill, who later went on to a bright brief political career in New Hampshire, were joined—sometimes for just a summer or two—by a dozen other critics, authors, playwrights, and editors. Arthur Whitney, the composer and musician, came and went as did others. Charles Platt, who was first an etcher and a painter and then a landscape artist and architect, designed houses for his Cornish friends, many with hillside terraces or Italian gardens. By the turn of the century there was a "little New York" on the banks of the Connecticut, and Augustus Saint-Gaudens was its most distinguished citizen. Indeed, right from the time he came he was perhaps the best-known sculptor in the nation—with such memorable achievements as *The Puritan, The Standing Lincoln, Sherman,* and others which, like Parrish's landscapes, are now a permanent part of the American artistic canon.

The other eminent national sculptor of the time was Daniel Chester French of Exeter, and he, too, spent several summers of the 1890s in Cornish. Dublin, New Hampshire, was the base of

an older and, by some accounts, a somewhat stuffier artistic colony. George de Forest Brush did leave Cornish for Dublin when he joined the painter Abbot Thayer. Barry Faulkner of Keene bridged the two colonies, being a student of both Saint-Gaudens and Thayer. A Dublin friend wrote to Mrs. Churchill, wife of the novelist, asking what clothes to bring on her proposed visit to Cornish, and Mrs. Churchill replied in a private letter: "In Cornish we wear our oldest clothes, and when we go to Windsor, the little Vermont village across the river, we wear nothing at all." In 1879 the Windsor paper had written: "We continue to absorb all the noted artists and sculptors in America."

The Cornish colony lasted little more than a quarter-century. Homer Saint-Gaudens, a writer and son of the sculptor, observed that the colony as a separate entity had already peaked by 1907, the year Saint-Gaudens died; a new generation of artists went elsewhere, sought other inspirations. But for a time something had "called strongly to these artists," he wrote; perhaps it

Beginning in 1900, Augustus Saint-Gaudens made Cornish his home and around him developed a colony of artists, writers, and summer guests— attracted as much by the ambience he evoked at "Aspet" as by the "further vales and big irregular hills" along the Connecticut. This portrait by Kenyon Cox, a summer colonist, shows the sculptor at work in 1908. Courtesy, The Metropolitan Museum of Art, gift of friends of the sculptor, 1908

was the "peace and dreamlike ripeness of the hills . . . their dark clumps of trees . . . their river winding south" before Mt. Ascutney. The grip of the place was strong: Maxfield Parrish declined an invitation in 1913 to head Yale's art department and continued to live and work productively at his Cornish home and studio for many decades after the colony had dispersed. In a sense he outlived his early fame and carried on, still painting, into his "rediscovery" in the 1960s. He died at his home, The Oaks, in 1966 at age 95.

The Italian gardens have been abandoned. Some of the houses have burned. The pastured fields have turned to trees. The old beloved scenes are mostly gone. Some of the houses and a few of the studios remain, hidden now behind the new-grown forests. A Maxfield Parrish museum and studio still stands near where his home, which burned, has been rebuilt. And the old brick tavern that Saint-Gaudens turned into a magnificent house, "Aspet," stands regally amid mowed fields surrounded by his yard and studios, open to visitors. Well preserved and well cared for, it is now a National Historic Site.

Frost Country
While the Cornish colony flourished in western New Hampshire there lived on the opposite edge of the state an awkward and shy young farmer, who had a great gift within him but no very cer-

tain sense of direction. He was Robert Frost of Derry. He had probably never heard of the Cornish colony, wouldn't have been in the slightest interested anyway, and would have found such company and setting no inspiration at all. Unlike the young Frost, the artists of Cornish knew who they were and what they were about. They were nourished by the scenes of Cornish—which might have been anywhere but happened to be in western New Hampshire. Frost was not moved by scenes, but by things he saw.

Robert Frost was born in California from an old New Hampshire family and came to New England at the age of nine. He had little talent for conventional study; he tried two colleges, Dartmouth and Harvard, and left them both. He took up farming at a time when New Hampshire farming was going downhill. On the Derry farm, which he had inherited from his grandfather, he was, by 1906, working harder at his poetry than at his farming; neither was producing a decent living, so he sought employment at Pinkerton Academy. Part of his application was "The Tuft of Flowers," read aloud by a friend, and someone glimpsed there a spirit that could be turned to advantage in a classroom. Weak as a student, Frost proved strong as a teacher, and best of all as a teacher of teachers. His stint at Pinkerton and later at the State Normal School at Plymouth, where he went in 1911, were only stopping places, stages on the way to his liberation as a country poet.

Having sold the farm in 1912, Frost gathered his courage, his unpublished pieces, and his family, and went to London to make a stab at a literary career. To a New Hampshire friend he wrote: "My dream would be to get the thing started in London and then do the rest of it from a farm in New England where I could live

Left: Birches line an unpaved road in New Hampshire's "Frost country." SPNHF

Opposite page, left: In 1827 Sarah Josepha Hale of Newport published the novel Northwood, which became a bestseller. Subsequently she became editor of the Ladies' Magazine, a new Boston periodical, and later of the original Godey's Lady's Book where she worked for close to 40 years. She was involved with a number of social causes, including raising money to complete the Bunker Hill Monument, persuading President Lincoln to declare a national Thanksgiving Day, and promoting higher education for women. NHHS

Opposite page, right: Boxed in by the attitudes and cultural constraints of the 1950s, Grace Metalious (who was born in Manchester and lived subsequently in Belmont and Gilmanton) wrote of futility, alienation and hypocrisy in her 1956 novel Peyton Place. The book sold more copies than had any previous American novel; even among those who did not read it, "Peyton Place" came to stand for all the dark undercurrents of small-town life. Photograph by Larry Smith

cheap and get Yankier and Yankier." He did just that. His first two books of poetry were published in England, and he returned to New Hampshire in 1915 to find his reputation established. He settled in Franconia, lived cheap, and got Yankier. In a 1916 interview he said: "You can't be universal without being provincial, can you? It's like trying to embrace the wind."

Perhaps no province of the country has ever been more carefully or more profoundly rendered into poetry than New Hampshire has been in the poetry of Robert Frost. He captured the cadence and diction of his neighbors and the actual ingredients of their lives—moving rocks and cutting trees and mowing hay and feeding chickens—using the furniture of land to let us in on the meaning of life. He wrote of loneliness and tragedy and of the simple silent satisfaction of doing a small job well, and he wrote the tang of the New England weather and the seasons into his poetry. He constantly caught country people being human—sad, elated, perplexed—and he caught them speaking poetry unawares, and slyly told on them. "Poetry is simply made of metaphor," he declared, "saying one thing and meaning another, saying one thing in terms of another." He almost made his New England, his New Hampshire, America's metaphor. In the course of a very long career that lasted into the 1960s, there fell to Frost a vast responsibility he had never sought and which no one conferred: he formed and handed over to the American public an image of New England that is now inescapable. "The land is always in my bones," he said. Fortunately, even natives acknowledge that he was on pitch: a singular but accurate voice, halting at first in those Derry years, but soon flowing clear and strong as if arising directly from the New Hampshire soil, limpid and natural as a sidehill spring, speaking the land's own language.

Wilderness and Village

Landscape is what catches the eye of the New Hampshire artist: landscape, robust, sublime, and irresistible, like an avalanche in a howling wilderness, or landscape pastoral and reposed like a village in a rolling countryside.

"Wilderness theology," that blend of faith and hope, was sowing seminaries and academies into small towns just when the actual wilderness of New Hampshire, driven to a corner in the northern part of the state, was being redeemed in another way—by being reaffirmed in art. Nathaniel Hawthorne and others came to Crawford Notch, picked up bits of mountain history and legend and turned them into story. Throughout New Hampshire, wilderness as a fact of life became also an artifact of imagination, a mixture of record and myth. For a generation artists produced canvases and reproduced engravings of the scene of the Willey slide, the avalanche of 1826 that destroyed a family and left their home intact. From 1830 onward, painters, poets, and writers came north to revel in mountain gloom and mountain glory.

As for the wilderness, so too for the countryside: record merged with myth. The self-sufficient farm of the early 19th century was extracted from the forest and hillside, framed with stone walls, presented to the village by a winding road, made a pillar of a rural economy, and promptly entered into history and fable at

Lotte Jacobi's father, grandfather, and great-grandfather had distinguished careers as photographers in Germany. She began her own photographic career in 1927, spending most of her time in Berlin, New York City, and (since 1955) Deering. Internationally known for her portraits of Albert Einstein, Robert Frost, and a host of others, she allowed Gary Samson to turn the camera on her in 1981. Photograph by Gary Samson

one stroke. The family farm became a tenet of American theology; town government, the political emblem of the village community, became the touchstone of New Hampshire politics, giving to everything a sense of place. Jeremy Belknap, New Hampshire historian, praised the simplicities of a "happy society" of rural villagers. And so on and on. All this sentiment poured out upon the soil seeped into New England's self-image, there to work its wonders and then to spill out eloquently in many places, including such oddly contrasting crossroad towns as Northwood, Coniston, Grovers Corners, and Peyton Place.

That at least was the general shape of things as delivered to the mid-20th century.

It is not quite the same today in the last quarter of the century. For one thing, the wilderness of New Hampshire as summed up in the White Mountains seldom evokes that old rapture and awe—the majestic, the terrible, and the sublime are ideas we now associate with the mountains more through art and literature and history than through direct experience. In our day the main experience linked with the mountains is recreation—a social commodity in which New Hampshire specializes and a valid mode in its own right. But recreation does not reenact the original confrontation with "nature red in tooth and claw," nor is it the old 19th-century encounter with gloom and glory. We have changed at least as much as the mountains. For a thousand related reasons the New Hampshire small town too, beloved and beleaguered as it is, is also now an ambiguous locus of value. Half of those shapely colonial homes in the village are owned by the folks from Connecticut.

But the aesthetic eye in New Hampshire—especially of the writer and the painter—is artfully selective, and when it wanders over the images that simplify and distill the state's historical drama it settles again and again on the associations of wilderness and village. They embrace New Hampshire's earliest and longest experiences. As images these survive partly through the effective way in which they mix and contrast with other facts and other images: for here, there, and everywhere the machine crept into the village garden and the red-brick factory rose up on the river-bank beneath the elms and willows; tourists trouped in and reminded natives of what is all about them; technologies and their economies swept into the southern regions of the state and prevailed, and by prevailing reminded everyone of what had once been.

And Robert Frost—who had lived in villages and near mountain wilds—came and blithely took for granted this whole century-long dance of general truisms about the landscape, and started gazing hard at the land itself to see what particularly was true of it: bent birches and ax handles and broken paths to cellar holes and hayfields and mud season, and also poetry lived and spoken inadvertently by people as real as the neighbors.

Nevertheless, village and wilderness, and the intricate web of experiences that radiates over the centuries from them, have supplied New Hampshire artists and writers—custodians of our imagination and thus of our history—with their most durable raw material. Even were wilderness and village themselves to pass away entirely, as they emphatically have not, their place in New Hampshire landscape and memory is intact.

C·O·L·O·R P·L·A·T·E·S

Opposite page: An 18th-century New Hampshire town is depicted in the overmantel of the Gardiner Gilman house in Exeter. Painted circa 1775 by an anonymous artist, the work was long thought to be a view of Exeter and the Squamscott River. It is currently held that the painting is a compilation of various elements of a New Hampshire town rather than a representation of Exeter itself. Courtesy, Amon Carter Museum, Fort Worth

Opposite page, bottom: A native of Holland, Bartholomew Van Dame overcame the language barrier, poverty, poor health, and a permanently crippled right arm to become one of New Hampshire's most active teachers, preachers, and moral reformers. Itinerant painter Joseph H. Davis prepared this 1836 ink and watercolor likeness of Van Dame at Bow Lake, Strafford. Courtesy, Currier Gallery of Art

When Concord schoolteacher Benjamin Thompson was chased from New Hampshire for his "Tory" sympathies in 1774, he apologized to his family, saying, "I thought it absolutely necessary to abscond for a while and seek a friendly Asylum in some distant part." His quest for a "friendly Asylum" led him throughout Europe, where he gained a reputation as one of the great scientific minds of the 18th century. In Bavaria he was knighted "Count Rumford" in 1791, in honor of the New Hampshire town that forced him to leave 17 years before. This William Lane chalk drawing of Rumford was considered by Rumford's daughter Sarah to be "the best likeness to my fancy, that was ever taken of him." NHHS

Above right: Ezra Woolson of Fitzwilliam painted this portrait of Jesse Kittredge Smith, "a skilful surgeon and physician" in Mont Vernon. The pink, blue, and green potions identify Smith's profession, and the scene out the window is probably of his dwelling. Woolson's career as a painter was brief. Born in 1824, he died suddenly in 1845 at age 21. Courtesy, Old Sturbridge Village

Right: Franklin Pierce was only 27 years old when he became speaker of the New Hampshire House of Representatives. By the time he became the 14th President of the United States, he had served in the United States House of Representatives and Senate, and the U.S. Army—as a brigadier general in the Mexican War. As President, he tried valiantly to hold North and South together, yet his belief in the limited constitutional role of the federal government doomed his efforts. At least he was a good-looking President. This circa 1852 portrait is attributed to the artist George P.A. Healy. NHHS

Left: This circa 1825 watercolor shows a parlor in the home of Moses Morse, a cabinetmaker in Loudon. The floor is painted in a checkered pattern, and the walls are decorated with stenciling, popular because it approximated the color and motifs of more expensive wallpaper and provided charms of its own. The desk to the right is typical of late Federal inlaid furniture, which was fashionable in New Hampshire until the 1830s. Privately owned

Above: Although discovered in New Hampshire and titled Piano Recital at Count Rumford's, Concord, N.H., *this stylish circa 1800 watercolor may well depict an English setting. Nevertheless it presents a charming picture of the fashions of the day. Courtesy, National Gallery of Art, Washington; gift of Edgar William and Bernice Chrysler Garbisch*

Above: It is appropriate that English native and Concord resident John Burgum painted this circa 1868 picture, Shipment of Thirty Coaches to Wells Fargo. *He also painted the coaches—all 30 of them. Burgum, and later his son Edwin, made their living (or at least much of it) painting the world-famous Concord Coach. Burgum based this painting on a photograph of the train leaving Concord and heading down the Merrimack River Valley. NHHS*

Top: Artist Enoch Wood Perry, Jr., painted The Pemigewasset Coach *probably around 1899. Unlike Crawford Notch, Franconia Notch was never violated by the railroad. Hence, tourists wishing to get to the Profile House or the hotels in Bethlehem often took the coach north from Plymouth or North Woodstock, much to the delight of children living along the route. Courtesy, Shelburne Museum, Shelburne, Vermont*

Above: The Concord Coach, a product of Concord's Abbot-Downing Company, gave 19th-century travelers around the world the best ride one could expect on 19th-century roads. This circa 1852 coach was used for many years in Massachusetts, until it appeared in the New York World's Fair of 1941-1942. After second-generation coach painter Edwin G. Burgum (son of John Burgum) redecorated the vehicle in 1942, it was "retired" to the Boston & Maine Railroad Station in Concord before coming to the New Hampshire Historical Society. Photograph by Bill Finney

Cutting wood—saw wood and cord wood—provided income in the wintertime for many New Hampshire farmers, occupying their days from mid-November even until early April if spring thaws held off. Edward Hill's Lumbering Camp in Winter *is dated 1882; Hill and his better-known brother Thomas were among the most prolific of the White Mountain artists. NHHS*

This circa 1860 lithograph shows activity at Amoskeag Falls with the new city of Manchester on the horizon. NHHS

Top left: At a time when skill in needlework was an important social grace, the making of a sampler was as much a part of a young women's education as learning to read and write. This florid show of silk embroidery on linen was worked by Hannah Foster of Canterbury when she was 12 years old. NHHS

Top right: Crazy quilts made of scraps of fabric were much admired in the late 19th century for their novel embroidery and design. A detail of one such quilt by Margaret Slack Gilman of Canterbury is seen here. This quilt won second prize at the state fair in 1903. NHHS

Above: Stickney's was Concord's favored tavern, but around 1840 the swinging Stickney signboard came down, for taverns had belonged to another era. NHHS

Above right: First held in 1886, the Tilton Fair was an annual summer event for the rest of the 19th century. NHHS

Opposite page, bottom left: Fire was a constant threat in congested towns whose frame buildings kindled quickly. As early as the 17th century progressive communities adopted laws requiring homes to keep fire buckets ready so that water brigades could be formed quickly when fire broke out. A brightly painted leather example is shown, from the Portsmouth household of William A. Vaughan. NHHS

Opposite page, bottom right: This jolly model represents a 1922 fire truck marketed by Abbot-Downing. Although their last horsedrawn vehicle was delivered in 1919, by the turn of the century Abbot-Downing was already in trouble as other forms of transport had made the coach and buggy obsolete. In 1915 the firm added motorized trucks and fire equipment to its line. The reorganized Abbot-Downing Truck and Body Company continued in business a decade more, but, unable to compete with franchised manufacturers and dealers, the corporation was dissolved in 1925. NHHS

Above: Maxfield Parrish came to the Cornish colony in the 1890s, and in 1898 he built his home and studio nearby in Plainfield where he painted for almost 70 years. Afterglow, *painted in 1947, effectively explains the attraction New Hampshire had for Parrish. Privately owned. Photograph courtesy, Vose Galleries*

Left: Politely dismissing the difference in their ages, these dolls—once owned by New Hampshire children—take morning tea at an elegant tea table dating from the 18th century. NHHS

Opposite page, top: Amusement parks were often built outside city limits to increase the use of car lines. Burgett Park in Somersworth, an attractive example located between Dover and Great Falls, was developed in 1890 by H.W. Burgett. NHHS

Opposite page, bottom: Although the Amoskeag Manufacturing Company went on to become the world's largest manufacturer of textiles, this circa 1856 John H. Bufford lithograph extols one of Amoskeag's other interests, the manufacture of locomotives. Prior to the Civil War Amoskeag machine shops turned out over 200 locomotives. NHHS

In 1826 Thomas Cole was the first major American artist to visit the White Mountains. The scenery, he wrote, furnished "a rich profusion of the sublime and beautiful." Through the remainder of the 19th century artists in great numbers followed. Pictured, clockwise from above, are The Notch of the White Mountains, *painted in 1839 by Thomas Cole (courtesy, National Gallery of Art)*, *Albert Bierstadt's circa 1862* Moat Mountain, Intervale, New Hampshire *and Jasper Cropsey's 1857* Indian Summer Morning in the White Mountains *(both courtesy, Currier Gallery of Art)*, and Autumnal Snow on Mt. Washington, *painted in 1856 by Aaron D. Shattuck (courtesy, Vassar College Art Gallery)*.

Left: The founding of the League of New Hampshire Craftsmen in 1932 prompted a renaissance of traditional crafts and their increased popularity. This poster, celebrating the League's 50th anniversary, was designed by Lance Hidy. Courtesy, League of New Hampshire Craftsmen

Opposite page, top: This view of the Portsmouth waterfront at Mechanic Street sums up much of the lore and legend of the city. At the center is the Wentworth-Gardner house, built in 1760 for Mark Hunking, brother of Royal Governor Benning Wentworth. Though the river in the foreground still harbors commercial traffic, the reflection suggests a certain stillness in the water. Photograph by Peter Randall

Opposite page, right: Since it was built in 1902, the Mt. Washington Hotel in Bretton Woods has carried on the tradition of the "grand hotel" in the White Mountains. In July 1944 the 44-nation Bretton Woods Conference that framed monetary policy after World War II was held there. Photograph by Peter Randall

The waters of the Atlantic still provide a living for lobstermen and commercial fisheries, and a fishing shack at Rye speaks of a way of life as old as the first New Hampshire settlements. Photograph by Bill Finney

V

P·A·R·T·N·E·R·S
IN P·R·O·G·R·E·S·S

CLOUGH WIRE CORKSCREW CO.,
ALTON, N. H.
Write for Samples and Prices of Wire Corkscrews of all sizes.

E. B. CRAPO'S
TRIMMING STORE,
70 NO. MAIN ST.,
CONCORD, N. H.

NEVER MIND JOHNNIE I'LL SEW IT UP WITH
CLARK'S O.N.T. SPOOL COTTON, IT WILL
BE AS GOOD AS NEW AND MA WONT KNOW!

With the Best Wishes

Of Lothrops, Farnham & Co.
THE OUTFITTERS,

FOR BARGAINS IN
MILLINERY AND FANCY GOODS
VISIT J. B. ESTEY & CO'S
BEE-HIVE,

Above: A craze for colored tradecards dominated American advertising during the second half of the 19th century. The lithographed cards were cheap and effective, sporting pictures that ranged from sentimental, to comical, to plainly descriptive. NHHS

Preceding page: In Richard Whitney's award-winning Edges of April Sky, *painted between 1976 and 1978, New Hampshire's landscape is seen as a blend of urban and rural. Thriving town and city centers, which mix the old and the new, are surrounded by forested hillsides. The artist is a 1968 graduate of the University of New Hampshire and a resident of Keene. Courtesy, Richard Whitney*

In 1827, only a few years after the first great textile mills began to operate on the power of New Hampshire's rivers, a group of farmers in the state petitioned the United States Congress for protection against less-expensive imported cloth.

"Of our climate and the fertility of our soil, we have little to boast," they wrote. "But, unkindly as our soil is, we are blessed with streams, which afford a water power inferior to that of no State in the Union. . . . Our hills, too, may be covered with flocks to their summits."

That was no exaggeration in the days when forests were plentiful and the farms seemed promising. New Hampshire's small factories making cotton and woolen cloth, shoes and boots, lumber, and paper went hand in hand with forestry and husbandry. Flax was grown to make linen, paper, and oil; sheep were pastured for their wool. Timber was cut for masts and lumber (and later for pulp), and it was burned on the farmer's cleared land for potash to make soap, glass, and fertilizer.

Yet in the years after the Civil War, the failed and abandoned farm became a sad fact of life in a state that had betrayed its true industrialism early in the 19th century. "The state lives by manufacturing, and by manufacturing only can there be any advance," one Charles C. Coffin wrote in *The Future of New Hampshire* in 1881. "There must be something besides rocks and trees to make a state."

Industries have grown up in New Hampshire and have been part of a consistent record of industrial innovation: The medical X-ray, the paper towel, and the video game were all, for example, invented here. But alongside them are industries that have managed to thrive on what some think of as the state's eternal liabilities. The rocks made its remarkable granite industry; the trees are the stuff of numerous New Hampshire wood products and of its recreational charm. The soil that disappointed farmers created the largest silver polish manufacturer in the country; precipitous slopes in two of the state's smallest towns are home to its largest ski area and one of New England's two four-star resorts.

Even in the late 1930s, when the widespread failure of textile mills might have seemed like the state's last gasp, New Hampshire was far more industrialized than the average of all 47 other states. And within two decades, new businesses came to fill the empty mills and shoe shops and employ people whose work ethic seems uniformly to have impressed out-of-staters. New Hampshire historian Jeremy Belknap described their traits as early as 1797—"firmness of nerve, patience in fatigue, intrepidity in danger, and alertness in action."

And for many companies, it is not so much the able population, the historically favorable attitude toward business, or the tax structure as much as it is simply New Hampshire that draws them and keeps them here. Some of the principals of these companies summered here as children, honeymooned here, went to college here, supervised campers here, hiked and skied here. They have come to live in what Robert Frost called "a most restful state," a place that remains quite rural despite the impressive statistics about New Hampshire's industry.

The New Hampshire Historical Society

In 1912 the New Hampshire Historical Society moved from the Merrimack County Bank building to its own facility in Concord's civic district. Here, building committee chairman Benjamin A. Kimball reads an address at the 1909 laying of the cornerstone.

When the nation was not yet 50 years old and, as one historian later said, "history was mute," 17 New Hampshiremen met at Emery's Tavern in Exeter to talk about how to celebrate the bicentennial of the state's first settlement.

It was March 1823, and even if the meeting produced no result on that question, its record would have been accomplished enough: it created the fifth statewide historical society in the United States, chartered by the New Hampshire legislature for the "laudable purpose of collecting and preserving such books and papers as may illustrate the early history of the state."

To the New Hampshire Historical Society's first president, William Plumer, former U.S. senator and four-time governor, preservation was best achieved by the publication of historical material. Plumer's determination was followed by the appearance of several volumes of *Collections and Proceedings* during the 19th and 20th centuries. His vision has been pursued most seriously since 1944, when the publication of the first issue of the Society's quarterly magazine, *Historical New Hampshire,* marked the beginning of a regular publications program. Twenty years later the *NHHS Newsletter* made its first appearance, and over the past decade exhibition catalogs, guide-

books, bibliographies, and edited collections of the papers of important New Hampshirites have expanded the publications program.

Collecting books and papers, initially in recording secretary John Farmer's Concord apothecary shop and librarian Jacob Bailey Moore's bookstore, developed the Society's library even before it settled in its first permanent home in 1841. Collecting also has come to embrace artifacts—fine and decorative arts, manufactured goods, farm and household equipment, and other items relating to New Hampshire people and events—that comprise a museum collection of more than 15,000 objects.

Despite its state charter and the "public encouragement" the legislature gave the Society by giving it temporary use of a "small and low" room in the State House, the New Hampshire Historical Society has no official connection with the state of New Hampshire. As a privately supported, nonprofit organization, it has always depended upon its members and friends, who have helped create a modest endowment over the past 160 years, and upon dues, gifts, and grants to sustain its collections and activities. The Society's supporters often have pooled their resources to buy significant objects and keep them in the state, as they con-

tinue to do today.

Aside from preserving and collecting objects, books, and papers, interpreting the state's past through these holdings has become the third principal activity of NHHS. Since 1964 the Society has had an active school program, bringing the state's fourth-graders to Concord every spring and taking programs into the classrooms in the fall. Programs for adults include courses on New Hampshire history and crafts, preservation workshops, bus and walking tours, and traveling workshops and exhibits reach out all over the state.

From one part-time librarian, the Society's staff has grown to 15 full-time professionals working the library, the manuscripts department, the museum, publications and programs, and administration. And while membership originally was limited to 50 persons, it has been open to everyone interested in New Hampshire history and in the Society's efforts on its behalf since 1850.

At the New Hampshire Historical Society's annual Christmas party, Old Sturbridge Village's Robert Olson recreates the early 19th-century magic of Richard Potter, for whom the New Hampshire village of Potter Place is said to be named.

Nashua Corporation

In 1848 a Nashua bookstore owner named Charles T. Gill came up with an idea for coating and printing on paper so that the East could profit from the Gold Rush boom in the West.

The firm that eventually became the Nashua Corporation never made good on its brainchild—playing cards for gold miners—because the cardboard manufacturer who had agreed to provide stock for the new enterprise withdrew his offer on moral grounds when he learned what the final product was to be. Nonetheless, the business was known as "The Card Shop" for years and counted among its customers companies that did manufacture the sinful items.

Be that as it may, the basic notion of converting a substrate such as paper to other uses by coating or otherwise treating it has stayed with Nashua Corporation since its birth. And its complicated evolution has been accompanied by almost bewildering product diversification based on that original manufacturing principle.

The firm—first known as Gill, Murray and Gage—began making cardboard and

At Nashua Corporation's Merrimack facility, an aluminum disc enters an ultrasonic cleaning station before its magnetic coating is applied.

When the Nashua Corporation was Nashua Card and Glazed Paper Company, "some of the help" posed on the curb outside the Franklin Street plant for this photograph.

glazed papers in 1848. In 1904 the venture was purchased by Carter, Rice and Company of Boston, a paper merchandising enterprise run by James R. Carter, whose sons and grandsons would figure centrally in the development of Nashua Corporation in the 20th century.

The making of printed waxed packaging was Nashua's largest single product line until 1960, chiefly due to the inventive reasoning of one employee who saw that the way to compete with cellophane, first commercially produced in the United States in 1924, was to make waxed paper more opaque, thus making it more effective than transparent packaging for display advertising. That approach to the market carried Nashua through the Depression, the full flowering of the "self-service" age when consumers turned their purchasing faith from shopkeepers' recommendations to brand names on packaging.

However, as the waxed paper business declined, the substrate coating principle led Nashua Corporation into the growing computer, office products, and photofinishing markets. While paper conversion was the great bulk of the company's volume in 1960, it comprises only 29 percent of its volume today.

With three New Hampshire plants and 14 branch plants around the world, Nashua Corporation now manufactures carbonless paper, pressure-sensitive tapes, office copy systems and supplies, and memory discs, cartridges, and disc packs for the computer market. It employs 5,400 people worldwide (one-third of them in New Hampshire) and recorded sales of $598 million in 1982.

Paper coating has been transfigured into "discrete particles technology," stored in substrate coating particles— "reactions" that are activated by heat, light, pressure, electric current, and other forces. Nashua Corporation's old standby, waxed paper, has not been manufactured for nearly a decade.

After the death of James R. Carter in 1923, his son Winthrop became president. Another son, Eliot, became vice-president in 1944, and it was his donation of more than half the necessary funds that created the present Nashua Public Library. Nashua Corporation is also responsible for a $400,000 donation to the University of New Hampshire to sponsor a professorship at the Whittemore School of Business and Economics.

Sanders Associates, Inc.

It is a story one often hears about how today's electronics and computer companies came to be: Already employed engineers have an idea, work on it on their own time in someone's basement, and develop it into a multimillion-dollar enterprise.

The story of the founding of Sanders Associates, Inc., in Nashua could be the one on which this stereotypical origin is based. In September 1951, 11 members of the Industrial Research and Development Group at Raytheon, all of them key engineers in the company's missile and radar work, established a venture to develop, manufacture, and sell advanced technology electronic systems and products. They began in a basement of a foundry in Waltham, Massachusetts.

The small enterprise moved to an abandoned textile mill in Nashua, New Hampshire, in 1952. Thirty years later it

A year after its move to Nashua, the accounting department of the young company, on the fifth floor of an old textile mill, included four people who are still with Sanders Associates today: Mary Sarameta, in the foreground; Eddie Arnold, standing at the rear talking to Sue Kobzik; and Roland Breault, at far right in the back row.

was the state's largest private employer and one of the top 50 electronics companies in the United States.

Sanders grew quickly, largely on the strength of defense electronics contracts. Just as it was casting about for a large space in which to relocate, a task force of Nashua citizens approached the company with an offer to set up shop in the city's Jackson Mills, left vacant between 1948 and 1951 by Textron, which moved its blanket and sheeting operation south.

Sanders brought 80 commuting Massachusetts residents to Nashua in 1952. By August of the next year nearly 200 of the area's industrial work force, 25 percent of whom had been left without work by the Textron move, had been employed by Sanders Associates. Growth continued to be very rapid.

Throughout its history, Sanders has been a leading designer and manufacturer of electronic defense systems including electronic countermeasure systems for aircraft, ocean surveillance, air defense and signal processing systems, training and simulation, and microwave devices.

In the 1960s Sanders developed innovative computer graphic display systems for NASA and its space program. This technology later was applied

Antenna testing on the roof of Sanders' Canal Street building.

to other advanced computer graphic applications such as air traffic control, and the firm became one of the largest manufacturers of graphic displays.

At the beginning of the current decade, under president Jack L. Bowers, Sanders made a major expansion into the computer graphics market which was at that time beginning a period of long-term, substantial growth, and a technology with which Sanders was not only familiar, but which it had helped develop with many key advancements.

In 1980, to be able to offer the most complete line of computer graphic systems and products, Sanders acquired two leading computer graphic companies. One, CalComp in Anaheim, California, manufactures a broad line of plotters that are widely used in computer-aided design and which produce detailed contour maps, bar graphs, perspective drawings, and finished schematic drawings from data and rough sketches. The second company, Talos Systems of Scottsdale, Arizona, manufactures digitizers which extract information from graphic representations

Manufacturers Graphic Display Systems in the north wing of Sanders' South Nashua facility.

and store it in memory for subsequent design work.

Sanders now is about equally devoted to government systems and products and graphic systems and products, and its sales growth has exceeded 20 percent per year for several years. The firm employs 7,400 people, 5,400 of whom work in the firm's New Hampshire facilities.

In 1968 Sanders constructed the seven-story building in South Nashua which serves as its corporate headquarters, while expanding its original facility on Canal Street in downtown Nashua. It also has extensive engineering and manufacturing facilities in Manchester and Merrimack, New Hampshire, in addition to the recently acquired subsidiaries in California and Arizona.

In the course of its extensive research and development work, this diverse company has made many significant technological contributions to both defense electronics and computer graphics. In display technology, for example, Sanders recently produced the first four-color air traffic control display in the United States, this one used by the U.S. Navy. In addition, Sanders has recognized the potential of its research in allied fields; for example, the firm holds the basic patents on video game technology, the basis of most of the video games on the market today.

These are only two of many examples which show that "Creating New Directions in Electronics" is as valid for the future of Sanders Associates, Inc., as it has been for the past 30 successful years.
Copy supplied by Sanders Associates, Inc.

The firm's corporate headquarters in South Nashua was built in 1969. Military component systems still are manufactured in the original Canal Street facility in downtown Nashua.

Monadnock Paper Mills, Inc.

When the Scotch-Irish left Ulster to settle in Londonderry, New Hampshire, in 1719, they brought with them a thriving native industry—raising flax and weaving it into linen.

A century later a man named Moody Butler took flax left over from making cloth and thread, boiled and beat the fibers in a vat, and made paper from them. Butler's handmade paper was the first ever made from flax in this country. And it was the beginning of one of the oldest continuously operating paper mills in the United States—Monadnock Paper Mills, Inc., of Bennington.

The "Great Falls" of the Contoocook River had been put to use since 1782 to support a variety of local industries— lumber and grist milling, blacksmithing, tanning, carding and clothmaking, and fowling-piece manufacture. The paper-making enterprise Butler started there was one of the three earliest paper mills in a state known for its paper mills, and Monadnock is the only one of those three still in operation.

By the time Monadnock Paper Mills (not so known until 1880) had turned

from handmade paper to machine-made paper, flax had also ceased to be used in favor of linen rags, and, later, wood pulp. After passing through a number of hands in its early history, the mill was bought in 1870 by William T. Barker, who widened its markets vastly. He also took as an apprentice one Arthur J. Pierce in 1900, the man who would succeed him as owner of Monadnock Paper Mills upon his death in 1903.

Under "Colonel" Pierce, as he was known locally, the old wooden mill building was replaced in 1905 with a brick structure still in use today. Pierce died in 1948, at which time Gilbert Verney, a native Englishman with a history of success in textile manufacturing, bought the mill from the Pierce estate.

An aerial view of Monadnock Paper Mills, Inc., situated on the banks of the Contoocook River. The main section of the mill was built in 1905.

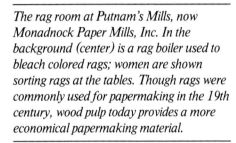

The rag room at Putnam's Mills, now Monadnock Paper Mills, Inc. In the background (center) is a rag boiler used to bleach colored rags; women are shown sorting rags at the tables. Though rags were commonly used for papermaking in the 19th century, wood pulp today provides a more economical papermaking material.

Gilbert Verney's son, Richard, is now president of Monadnock, which remains privately owned.

Gilbert Verney and his son saw that a small mill in a major industry could survive only by continual diversification of its markets and specialization of its products. Monadnock Paper departed commodity markets in the late 1950s in favor of specialty printing and converting grades of paper. Now known as one of the finest small specialty paper mills in the country, it devotes half its effort to the manufacture of premium text and cover papers and half to papers for technical/specialty uses.

Its technical papers include abrasive-backing papers, medical-packaging papers, chart papers, latex-treated stocks, and filter media. Its graphic arts papers are designed for fine limited-edition books, annual reports, and other markets that use high-quality, uncoated paper. Catering to both specialty printing and converting markets, Monadnock's equipment is utilized to accommodate custom orders; its papers were used for the Reagan inaugural invitation in 1981.

Concord National Bank

In 1863 the need to pay 500,000 Union soldiers and to settle the mounting debt of the Civil War created the nation's first national banks.

First National Bank of Concord was the 318th national bank to be chartered by the federal government. In fact, its charter was signed on the first day that the National Currency Act of 1863 went into effect.

It is not entirely fortuitous that Concord's First National Bank got in on the ground floor of its industry. After all, Salmon P. Chase, a native of New Hampshire, was Abraham Lincoln's Secretary of the Treasury. Another New Hampshirite, William P. Fessenden, chaired the Senate Finance Committee at that time and assumed Chase's Treasury position in 1864. And Hugh McCulloch—who as Comptroller of the Currency put his signature to the new bank charters—was a college friend of Franklin Pierce, New Hampshire's only U.S. President who was, in 1864, practicing law in Concord.

First National Bank's first president was Asa Fowler, Pierce's former Concord law partner. By 1865 Fowler also was a director of the newly chartered National State Capital Bank, which, in its original form as State Capital Bank, was Concord's fifth at its founding in 1853.

Both banks have had their share of illustrious presidents. George A. Pillsbury, First National's second president for 12 years, later "went west" to Minnesota and helped found the Pillsbury Company, originally a flour manufacturer. And financing the manufacture of Concord Coaches, the vehicles that effectively opened the West, was in large part undertaken by National State Capital Bank. Lewis J. Downing, Jr., one of the bank's presidents for a time, also was president of Abbot-Downing Company,

builder of the Concord Coach and once Concord's largest employer.

Edgar Hirst, New Hampshire's first State Forester in 1909 and the third president of the Society for the Protection of New Hampshire Forests, became First National's president in 1939. At that time the bank began its long tradition of financing the then-infant forestry industry, now one of the state's largest. Another National State Capital president, Josiah Fernald, was personal financial advisor to Mary Baker Eddy, the founder of Christian Science. At her death, Fernald was named one of three trustees under her will, the largest probate trust in Merrimack County's history.

After the merger of the two banks into

Concord National Bank in 1956, the institution became one of the first to open a branch bank in the state in 1960. Since joining First NH, a multi-bank holding company, in 1974, Concord National has maintained its position in the areas of commercial, industrial, and personal finance, financial performance, and community involvement. Current president Caleb W. Whiton continues Concord National's tradition of community-based economic growth as a primary objective of the bank.

This photograph shows the teller's cage and bookkeeping department of the First National Bank of Concord in 1894.

Erected on the site of the former National State Capital Bank at Main and Warren streets in Concord's business district, Concord National Bank's present building was constructed in 1958.

Manufacturers and Merchants Mutual Insurance Company

In 1885 a spate of fires thought to have been set deliberately destroyed a great many buildings across the state of New Hampshire. That year's legislature responded swiftly to the needs of property owners by passing what is known as the "valued policy" law; insurance companies had to pay damages equal to the sum insured, whether a property had been intentionally overinsured or not.

The passage of the law caused all 58 insurance companies doing business in New Hampshire at the time to pull out, leaving the field wide open for enterprising New Hampshire businessmen.

Lyman Jackman, a veteran Civil War captain and native of Woodstock, New Hampshire, suddenly found himself with an insurance agency but no firms to provide policies for his clients. He promptly invested his life savings in four New

One Sunday morning in November 1935 smoke was seen billowing from the steeple of "Old North," Concord's oldest church. Manufacturers and Merchants Mutual carried the insurance on the church and paid 100 cents on the dollar toward a new building, despite its business slump in the Depression.

Hampshire-based insurance companies. Manufacturers and Merchants Mutual was one of them.

The organization received its charter from the New Hampshire legislature at the end of 1885 and began doing business immediately with Jackman as secretary and Edward Giles Leach, Franklin lawyer and Meredith native, as president.

Manufacturers and Merchants Mutual's 1886 surplus of $2,800 was eaten away only a year later by a huge fire in Lebanon, New Hampshire, which almost forced the company out of business. Eighty buildings burned in a conflagration that leveled the center section of the town and caused nearly $350,000 in losses.

The Concord-based insurance company had to pay out nearly $6,000 to cover losses from the Lebanon fire; Capital Fire Insurance, another of Jackman's companies in Concord, insured buildings whose total losses were even greater. As secretary, Jackman convinced the directors of the two firms to allow him to borrow money to cover these losses. By the end of 1887 Jackman not only had repaid this bank loan but showed a company profit.

Lyman Jackman—with whom local

lore also credits the accidental discovery of Lost River, an underground cavern that has become a major tourist attraction in New Hampshire—remained secretary and vice-president of Manufacturers and Merchants Mutual until 1914. Leach remained its president until 1928. Upon Leach's death, Charles Lyman Jackman, Lyman Jackman's son, became president of the company and remained so until 1957, when his son-in-law, Carl G. Gesen, assumed the position. Manufacturers and Merchants Mutual's current president is Gesen's son, Charles, who has occupied the position since 1975.

Manufacturers and Merchants Mutual does business in all New England states and in South Carolina and still views itself as a property insurer. After its difficult infancy, the firm managed to accrue a surplus of $21,000 by 1895. That surplus stood at more than $7 million by the end of 1982.

After nearly 70 years in the Acquilla Block on Concord's Main Street, Manufacturers and Merchants Mutual Insurance Company had its own building constructed in 1970 on Pleasant Street.

New Hampshire Distributors, Inc. ————————

Now chairman of the board and chief executive officer, James H. Hayes stands in front of the awards New Hampshire Distributors, Inc., has earned over the years.

Just before World War II, when Jim Hayes stopped traveling across the country organizing and training state police forces, he wanted to come back to New Hampshire, where he had spent his college years.

Hayes wanted to be a soft-drink bottler, but wartime sugar quotas got in his way. A friend from his native Massa-chusetts suggested that he go into the business of distributing his brand of ale, Holihan's, since the brewery had moved out of New Hampshire to escape grain shortages during the war years.

The first week on the job, Hayes sold only 27 cases of Holihan's ale. Yet in little more than three decades, Hayes built his New Hampshire Distributors, Inc., into the second largest beer distributor in the state. For three years running, New Hampshire Distributors, Inc., has won Dimensions of Excellence Awards from Anheuser Busch, Inc., whose products it now markets, for being that firm's best wholesaler in the nation for the volume of beer it distributes.

New Hampshire Distributors, Inc., began in 1946 in the basement of the Leddy Block in Epping, New Hampshire. The next year the company moved to Concord and leased space for 10 years, and in 1957 it built a new warehouse on the shores of the city's Horseshoe Pond.

New Hampshire Distributors, Inc., now covers 38 percent of the state and sells more beer in a week than it sold all year in 1947. Its Concord warehouse has grown from 10,000 to 51,000 square feet over that time, and the firm moved into an 86,000-square-foot controlled-environment warehouse and office building in February 1983.

New Hampshire Distributors, Inc., has sold a variety of beers in the past 30 years, some of which disappeared from the marketplace long ago. The company took on Anheuser Busch products in 1949 and has stayed with them ever since. The proliferation of Anheuser Busch brands and the ability of the brewery to capture a greater share of the overall market has helped fuel New Hampshire Distributors' healthy growth. In 1982 the organization sold in excess of 2.4 million cases.

As president of the firm for 27 years and now as its chairman of the board and chief executive officer, Hayes has managed to sustain his original interest in history. His company's logo includes the Concord Coach, the New Hampshire-made vehicle credited with opening the West. Hayes also bought nearly 800 copies of a recent history of the New Hampshire legislature (in which he once served) to distribute to every school, library, and historical society in the state.

Hayes also served under four New Hampshire governors on the executive council. His 18-year term was the longest ever served on that advisory body. And the state's new Department of Safety building was named for him in 1976.

In February 1983 New Hampshire Distributors, Inc., moved into this new facility at 65 Regional Drive, Concord.

Simplex Wire and Cable Company

From its riverfront location along the banks of the Piscataqua just outside of Portsmouth, Simplex Wire and Cable Company builds and ships products that have applications worldwide. The sole manufacturer in the Western Hemisphere capable of producing transoceanic undersea cables, Simplex has nearly half a million square feet of manufacturing and storage area on approximately 100 acres of land.

Hardly a newcomer to the seacoast, Simplex traces its origins to a one-man wire-working firm established over a century ago in Boston, Massachusetts. There, in the late 1800s, the firm built its first insulated wire for electric power transmission. Crude in construction by today's standards, it soon became widely used by public utility companies newly established to control and distribute this technological marvel.

As early as the 1890s Simplex placed an emphasis on submarine cable technology. By the turn of the century the firm had manufactured an unparalleled five-mile-long underwater telephone cable that was installed across the Straits of Mackinac in Lake Michigan.

World War II brought increased

At the forefront of marine technology, Simplex's unique capabilities serve both the commercial and U.S. Navy defense sectors. The plant is situated on nearly 100 acres of land purchased from the late Louis de Rochemont, the cinema magnate of the silent film era.

demand for greater capacity and sophistication in undersea cables. During this critical period Simplex supplied much of the deep-sea cable required by the U.S. defense establishment. Among these was a cable built for the Air Force missile range between Florida and the Bahamas that was considered to be a prototype for the first commercial ocean telephone cable.

Simplex began construction of its present Newington facility in 1952, the first American plant specifically designed to produce long lengths of undersea cable. In 1955, when Her Majesty's telegraph ship *Monarch* laid the first transatlantic telephone cable linking North America and Europe (TAT 1), Simplex cable made up the American portion of the system. More recently, Simplex has built

ocean cable systems which have expanded telecommunications between Taiwan and Guam and linked Greece to Egypt.

In 1974 Simplex became a wholly owned subsidiary of Tyco Laboratories, headquartered in nearby Exeter. Tyco's ownership has fostered a progressive, growth-oriented philosophy.

Over 40,000 miles of ocean cable have been manufactured at this unique New England facility. Its deepwater pier enables the largest cable-laying ships in the world to dock and load cable directly from the massive storage facilities at the Simplex plant.

Continuing its century-old commitment to the advancement of undersea technology, Simplex has expanded its research and development into several new areas: fiber optics, high-voltage underwater power, and flexible pipe. Working under contract to the Bell System, Simplex is developing and manufacturing fiber optic undersea communications cables. With installation of the first fiber optic transatlantic cable system slated for 1988, Simplex research efforts will help to usher in a new era of telecommunications technology. In the area of underwater power, Simplex is designing, manufacturing, and testing prototype high-voltage power cables for use at ocean depths more than three times any existing installation. Most recently, Simplex development efforts have been focused on an entirely new product line—flexible pipe. Utilizing well-established techniques gained through years of cable manufacture, Simplex has developed a high-pressure, reliable pipe that is ideally suited to offshore applications by the oil industry. This product capability is unique in North America.

Throughout its history in the seacoast, Simplex has provided significant growth opportunities both for the state and the company's local employees. From its first insulated electric wire to today's most sophisticated fiber optics, Simplex's influence has been felt far beyond the borders of New Hampshire.

—Leslie Grommet

Chubb LifeAmerica

Starting a life insurance company in New Hampshire, albeit the state's first, does not in retrospect look to have been a propitious move to make in 1913.

Only three years after United Life and Accident Insurance began to sell its policies in Concord in 1914, the United States began sending men to fight in World War I. And even before the war ended late in 1918, the nation was scourged with an influenza epidemic that left in its wake nearly one-half million fatalities. New Hampshire, which lost almost 700 in World War I, lost another 2,500 people in the epidemic.

Even though it did not pay its stockholders a dividend in 1918, United Life and Accident Insurance Company (now Chubb LifeAmerica) managed to weather those early storms—and later ones, such as the Great Depression—even while acquiring one North Carolina insurance company and offering an unusual triple indemnity life insurance policy to its customers.

Starting off with an office manager and two secretaries in a small office over Woolworth's on Concord's Main Street, United Life and Accident Insurance had $36 million of life insurance in force in 1936 and built itself a new headquarters—the site of what is now Franklin Pierce College's Law Center—by 1941.

United Life embarked on its first "long-term plan" in 1955 under the presidency of Douglas B. Whiting, who had joined the firm as assistant to the

Built in 1850 and considered one of the finest homes in Concord, the J. Stephens Abbot home at 24 South Main Street was bought late in 1913 to house United Life. Abbot was a principal in the Abbot-Downing Company, the carriage maker that produced the Concord Coach. United Life occupied Abbot's former home until 1941.

actuary in 1930. Designed to double the amount of life insurance in force over five years' time, the plan's goal was achieved in less than four years. By the end of its third long-term plan in 1967,

1975 the firm had more than two billion dollars of life insurance in force. In 1976 a new headquarters facility was built on 143 acres of land formerly owned by the city.

The operations of United Life and the Colonial Life Insurance Company of America of Parsippany, New Jersey, also a Chubb subsidiary, were consolidated in 1980 with their executive office in Concord and they began marketing their products under the common service name of Chubb LifeAmerica in order to more closely identify themselves with their parent company.

The consolidated entity operates in all 50 states, the District of Columbia, and Puerto Rico. In addition to traditional life insurance, Chubb LifeAmerica markets individual disability income and annuity plans, group life and medical plans, mortgage life and disability coverage

Rapid expansion prompted Chubb Life's move from 2 White Street to 1 Granite Place, a road created on former City of Concord property for the new headquarters. Built in 1976 at an estimated cost of $4 million, the facility houses more than 400 employees.

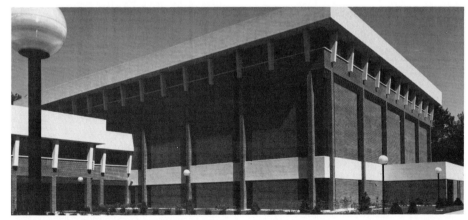

United Life had one billion dollars of life insurance in force.

In 1971 United Life was purchased by The Chubb Corporation of New York City, and between 1973 and 1975, 100 new jobs were added to the Concord home office work force. By the end of

through lending institutions, corporate pension plans and retirement plans for self-employed individuals and partnerships, and business and estate life insurance protection. Through its subsidiaries it makes available mutual funds and tax-sheltered investments.

Kingsbury Machine Tool Corporation

The history of Kingsbury Machine Tool Corporation is the story of a series of innovations that, quite accidently, led the company down new avenues of commerce, avenues its founders could not possibly have foreseen in 1888.

Kingsbury is the direct outgrowth of the Triumph Wringer Company, which started making washtub wringers in Keene in 1888. As a sales gimmick, one enterprising member of the company made a cast-iron wringer in miniature to heighten interest in the labor-saving device. But sales of the toy wringer soon outstripped sales of its parent, and the Wilkins Toy Company was born of that success in 1890.

Then, in 1894, a Keene Bicycle shop proprietor named Harry Thayer Kingsbury bought Wilkins Toy Company and turned it into one of the most reputable and popular toy manufacturers in the country.

Kingsbury's toys always stayed in step—perhaps it is better to say in gear—with whatever mundane or glamorous vehicles Americans happened to be riding in, whether on roads, in the air, or on the water. Introduced to the toy-buying market in 1895, Kingsbury toys included a horse-drawn road sprinkler, a steamboat, streetcars, hansom cabs, and a rowing shell with oarsmen.

Kingsbury made the first toy automobile in 1900 and was, by 1901, the largest manufacturer of toy cars in America. As the nation's cars increased in complexity, so did Kingsbury toys. Some models had motors, rubber tires, electric lights, and music-box radios. And they were the only toy cars in the country so exact in their replication of real ones that they were allowed to sport a miniature "Body by Fisher" emblem.

Kingsbury also made a submarine during World War I, a parcel post cart and driver in 1915, a tractor in 1918, and exact miniatures of record-breaking racing cars in the 1930s. In the same decade the firm, which had changed its name from Wilkins Toy Company to Kingsbury Manufacturing in 1918, made a different toy Chrysler "Airflow" every year to emulate changes in its larger counterparts. Kingsbury manufactured sturdy fire trucks, trailer trucks, airplanes, and Desoto sedans. And, to promote thrift during the Depression, it produced a bank clock that registered coins, locked after the first deposit, and unlocked between $9.95 and $10.

But Harry Kingsbury's son Edward, who joined the organization after graduating from the Massachusetts Institute of Technology in 1915, was more interested in how the toys were made than in the toys themselves. One particular problem interested him—how to drill a hole through a cast-iron toy wheel to fit an axle while taking into account differing hardnesses in the metal. Up to that point all the wheels had been drilled by hand.

Edward developed a friction-drive machine with two drill heads and a weight feed, so that drill pressure could vary with hardness. The machine, developed in 1917, was so successful that it was marketed to other manufacturers. With the sale of the first one in 1920, the Kingsbury Machine Company was created.

Edward and Gunnar Swahnberg, a Detroit engineer who joined the firm in 1921, developed other ingenious machines. In 1923 they developed a rotary index machine, which could take a piece of metal and perform a variety of milling, tapping, boring, or drilling operations on it. The operator could put the rude part on and take the finished part off from the same position. The Nash and Dodge Brothers, automobile

Although the firm produced toy printing presses, appliances, and banks, vehicles of all kinds were the forte of the Wilkins (later Kingsbury) Toy Company.

Kingsbury's main plant is one of three in Keene, together comprising 500,000 square feet.

manufacturers, purchased a rotary index machine in 1925 and began Kingsbury's long association with the auto industry—still its major market.

In 1942 the sheet steel Kingsbury used to manufacture its toys was diverted to wartime production. Kingsbury retooled to produce machines for fuses, aircraft engine parts, rifle bolts, and gun parts. And in 1947, envisioning a future in which molded plastic would take over the toy market, the toy part of the company sold its patents and equipment and turned its attention strictly to machine tools. Edward Kingsbury's division, swamped with orders from a burgeoning auto industry, immediately took over the vacant plant space.

Kingsbury now custom designs and builds precision machines for the mass production of parts. At rates anywhere from 300 to 800 parts per hour, the indexing machines make parts for, among other items, washing machines, refrigerators, typewriters, lawn mowers,

meters, and cars. Other divisions of the firm produce machines to automatically assemble parts and rebuild and retool used Kingsbury machines. The company now employs 700 people, has plants occupying 500,000 square feet in the city of Keene, and remains locally owned. Presidents of the company since 1920 have been Edward J. Kingsbury, Gunnar Swahnberg, Henry J. Frechette, Walter M. Burkart, Charles J. Hanrahan, and James L. Koontz.

Kingsbury has done its share for the Keene area, as well. The Cheshire Hospital sits on land donated by Edward Kingsbury and his wife, and the firm supplied the money and machinery to equip the vocational area of nearby Monadnock Regional High School. A large collection of its remarkable toys, now valuable collector's items, are on display at The Colony House Museum.

Gunnar Swahnberg, originally chief engineer and later president of Kingsbury Machine Tool Corporation from 1955 to 1962, stands between one of the firm's popular rotary index machines (at left) and Edward J. Kingsbury's original friction-drive drilling machine. Kingsbury stands on the right.

Nashua Federal Savings and Loan Association _____

"There is no rent day," the motto went, "for the man who owns his own home."

In 1888, when the streetcar and railroad helped bring about a swell of suburban development across the nation, the slogan of the newly incorporated Nashua Building and Loan Association carried the promise of home ownership to Nashuans who yearned to put the worry, insecurity, and rootlessness of renting behind them.

Thirty-nine of Nashua's citizens created the Building and Loan Association to gather together peoples' savings for the eventual purchase of homes and other real estate. Begun in room seven of the city's Goodrich Block, the bank had $1,000 in assets by May 28 of its first year. Ten years later, in 1898, assets had reached $231,000.

Nashua Building and Loan was the second largest cooperative bank in New Hampshire by 1928. During the tenure of its first president, John A. Fisher, the bank moved to the Odd Fellows Block, one of the largest buildings in downtown Nashua at the time, in 1894.

The bank changed its name to the Nashua Building and Loan Association and Cooperative Bank in 1949 and short-

William C. Small, Nashua Building and Loan Association's first secretary, sits in the company's one-room office in 1890. Still secretary 18 years later, Small was authorized by the association's directors to buy a $25 bicycle for use in the business.

ened it to Nashua Cooperative Bank two years later. Continued growth brought about another move in 1956 to the Noyes Block on Main Street, the bank's first street-level location.

Nashua Cooperative Bank received a

federal charter in 1964 and changed to its present name in that same year. A period of strong growth then ensued, the bank's assets rising from $51.5 million in 1969 to $206.4 million a decade later.

In 1977 association president Charles Rutter chose historic preservation over new construction for the opening of a new branch on 101A, one of the busiest highways in New Hampshire. Nashua Federal purchased a brick dwelling, a late Federal-period home, renovated it, and used it for offices. A new barn added on to house banking operations sports a weathervane that had come down through the family of Jason T. Bickford, chairman of the association's board.

Nashua Federal Savings and Loan's assets now stand at $275 million, and it remains the dominant real estate lender in the fast-growing southern New Hampshire area. It has been a good citizen in Nashua, too, having donated land for playgrounds and thousands of dollars to the building funds for the city's Arts and Science Center, the YMCA/YWCA, and numerous other organizations.

_____

Situated on one of New Hampshire's busiest highways, this branch office of Nashua Federal Savings and Loan is housed in an 1835 brick dwelling that association president Charles Rutter wanted to preserve. The barn and silo were added during the mid-1970s.

The Concord Group Insurance Companies _____

The original agents for Farm Bureau Mutual automobile insurance were either New Hampshire farmers or people who worked with them regularly. The man in the center is Shelby O. Walker, who came from Ohio to run the firm and trained the agents individually. Clyde B. Foss, of Moultonborough (in suit), is still on Concord General's board of directors.

Long before the Great Depression, New Hampshire farmers had seen the decline of prosperity and the rise of large corporate farms to the west. Recognizing that the road to their salvation was cooperation and more technical expertise, a group of New Hampshire farmers organized the New Hampshire Farm Bureau Federation in 1916.

Twelve years later one of those farmers—George M. Putnam of Contoocook, whom former Governor John G. Winant often called "New Hampshire's First Citizen"—saw the need for another organization, one that could write fire insurance policies that farmers could afford. Many of the state's farmers had no fire insurance at all, rural property rates being so high that coverage from existing companies was beyond their financial grasp.

Farm Bureau Mutual Insurance Company (now Concord General Mutual, parent organization of The Concord Group Insurance Companies) began with $25,000 of capital pooled by federation members, who signed a master note loaning their credit for the purpose. In the same year, 1928, Farm Bureau Mutual Insurance Company of Ohio began writing automobile insurance in New Hampshire, and in 1930 it was spun off as a New Hampshire company.

Originally, both the fire and auto insurance were available only to federation members, and eligibility was strict. At first, a car could be covered if the owner either owned or operated a farm, but it could not be covered if it was used for commercial purposes of any kind. Cars carrying mail were not eligible, but if schoolteachers, ministers, and doctors lived in the country or a village with not more than 250 people, their cars could be covered by Farm Bureau Mutual.

Even as late as 1944 Farm Bureau policies were low, about $11 for basic liability limits compared to a $30 premium from other New Hampshire companies. But as more farmers began to work off the farm—nearly half of the ones in New Hampshire were doing so by 1933—federation membership ceased to be a requirement, and insurance was made available to people in rural and residential areas.

Today what was Farm Bureau Mutual insures more people who don't own farms than people who do. As the ratio of farm to non-farm families has declined generally, the firm has branched into a more general entity, and its name change in 1966 reflects that fact as well as the need for a more all-embracing title to cover five acquisitions of companies in New Hampshire, Maine, and Vermont over the years.

From its original policy limit of $2,500 on single risks, The Concord Group was able through reinsurance to increase those limits to more than one million dollars today. The group now has a net written premium of $24 million in property and casualty insurance and $54 million of life insurance, first written in 1965, in force today.

The Concord Group Insurance Companies now employ 185 people and have their headquarters at 4 Bouton Street.

Benson's Animal Park

Once billed as the "strangest farm on Earth," Benson's Wild Animal Farm became a tourist attraction almost inadvertently, its wild animals having piqued much curiosity in the area.

They used to call it "the strangest farm on Earth." Over the past 60 years, it has grown from a health farm where retired circus performers could rest and relax to a large "theme park" carrying on serious zoological work and research while entertaining well over one-half million people each year.

Benson's Animal Park in Hudson, formerly Benson's Wild Animal Farm, sits on 250 acres of what was, in the 19th century, the Interstate Fruit Farm. Benson's brought tourists and notoriety to Hudson, which for years had lived in the shadow of its larger and more prosperous neighbor to the west, Nashua.

Benson's was started in 1922 by John T. Benson, who had run away from his Yorkshire, England, home at the age of eight to join the Bostock and Wombell Circus. His first trip to the United States was in 1890, to exhibit a wrestling lion.

Just before the turn of the century, Benson became a wild animal scout for zoos and circuses. Traveling the globe in search of exotic breeds, Benson provided the Ringling Brothers Circus with John Daniel, the first gorilla ever exhibited in captivity. Ringling Brothers paid a staggering $32,000 for John Daniel, but the gorilla lived only three weeks longer.

After becoming a United States citizen, Benson helped organize and run Norumbega Park and the Franklin Park Zoo in Boston, as well as zoos in Rhode Island, Cuba, and Jamaica. And, under the direction of the New York State Fish and Game Commissioner, he stocked the Adirondack Mountains with elk, moose, and bears.

In the teens of this century, John T. Benson became the wild animal salesman and United States manager for Hagenbeck of Germany, the largest wild animal training organization in the world. It was this work that led him to Hudson.

When German boats began making their first U.S. stop at Boston, Benson moved his headquarters from New Jersey to New Hampshire. He set up the Interstate Animal Farm in 1922 as a quarantine base for wild animals. For many animals on their way to American zoos, circuses, movie studios, and laboratories, Benson's was the first stop. The staff would condition and train animals, and the farm also offered brush-up courses for animal acts.

Whether to encourage attendance by the public or discourage area residents curious about what was happening at the farm, Benson began opening his enterprise and charging admission to the public in the afternoons in the spring of 1924. Originally, the farm had a four-acre pasture where visitors could see camels, antelopes, yaks, and other unfamiliar breeds.

Benson's Wild Animal Farm provided the first chimpanzees ever used in motion pictures, in the early *Our Gang* comedies. In addition, the first shipment of North American wild animals was transported from Benson's to European zoos, circuses, and carnivals.

The farm brought a lot of color to the little town of Hudson. When the railroad siding in town was closed, farm employees would parade animals from Benson's to Nashua's Union Station. And, in 1950, when one of the elephants at the Atlanta Zoo died, Coca-Cola heir Asa Candler, Jr., sent six children to Benson's in his private plane to pick out a new elephant. Atlanta schoolchildren raised $1,200 toward the purchase; Candler paid the balance. Nashua staged a ceremony when the elephant was trucked south, and the city's school-

Vera Lovejoy, who managed the park from 1944 to 1952, oversees a medical examination of two of the farm's chimps.

children presented their Atlanta counterparts with a 100-pound sack of peanuts as a going-away gift.

Benson died in 1943, at which point the farm was bought by Raymond Lapham and Walter Brown, whose fathers built and operated Boston Arena, and, later, Boston Garden. Closed during World War II, Benson's reopened as a park, no longer trading in animals nor training them.

In the early 1970s Benson's Wild Animal Farm began to show signs of neglect. Only one animal act was staged each day, and the park was in dangerously poor physical condition and attendance

was declining rapidly.

Then a Nashua native who, like John T. Benson, had childhood dreams of running away to join the circus, bought Benson's early in 1979 and began the slow process of bringing the site back.

Arthur J. Provencher lived in nearby Nashua and, because of his love of animals, had developed part of the land around his Merrimack office into "My World of Pets." More than 15,000 people came, each year, free of charge, to Provencher's small park and were allowed to pet his giraffe, elephant, and various farm animals.

Then running a truck rental business,

Before he bought Benson's in 1979, Nashua native Arthur J. Provencher kept wild and domesticated animals on land outside his office in nearby Merrimack. Here, Tom Trow, animal keeper, watches as Provencher, his associate Connie Zanoni, and his daughter Jodie pet Jackie, Provencher's Asian elephant, who died at the age of 11 in 1979.

Provencher had hired a consultant to determine the feasibility of turning his animal hobby into a full-time occupation when Benson's was put up for sale. Pro-

When Arthur J. Provencher purchased Benson's Wild Animal Farm, only 70 of the site's 250 acres were developed as a park. Provencher's 10-year plan sees expansion of the park to 400 acres, much of it revised "open" habitats for the animals.

vencher seized the opportunity, having wanted to own the farm for many years, and added his own animals to the 389 animals already at the farm.

Provencher used his consultants, a widely known recreation area design firm, to develop a master plan for the farm's redesign and eventual expansion to a 400-acre family park. He also hired a full-time zoologist, Pat Quinn, to start rebuilding the species and to develop educational programs.

Provencher's aim is to make Benson's New England's major zoological institution and dominant theme park. Quinn notes the growing importance of zoos as living museums, as gene pools, and as survival centers for endangered species. They also play a vital role in zoological research. Aside from teaching workshops and seminars, Quinn also does work and research on animal reproduction and on redeveloping habitats for dwindling species at Benson's Animal Park.

Benson's does cooperative research with such institutions as the new Tufts University School of Veterinary Medicine in the areas of artificial insemination and species survival. It works with the U.S. Department of the Interior on wildlife conservation, and, also with Tufts, the park has plans to act as a rehabilitation center for injured wild animals.

Along with the research program, Benson's has moved toward making the park a more comprehensive educational experience for visitors. Those animals that thrive in open habitats will have areas newly designed for them. Graphics have been installed to tell visitors more about the animals and their original habitats. Benson's has concertedly built its stock up to the point that it features more animals than Stone and Franklin Park zoos—the only two in New England—combined. The park also exhibits rare birds, reptiles, and mammals that are not often seen in captivity.

In the three years of Provencher's ownership, park attendance has increased over '78 levels by more than 70 percent. The park is open every day from April to mid-September, on weekends through the end of October, and from mid-November through New Year's Day with a nighttime Christmas display from 4:00 to 9:00 p.m. New "theme centers," such as Circus City, Bavaria and Dutch Country, entertainment, and other attractions will add variety to the park over the coming years. Benson's Animal Park now features 15 shows each day, as well as parades and rides. Attendance figures, Provencher says, show that the public is responding favorably to his management of this Hudson landmark.

John T. Benson, the creator and owner of Benson's Wild Animal Farm, was taught to handle animals in England's Bostock and Wombell Circus. Here Benson handles Betsy, Benson's famous elephant. Rides on her back were the highlight of the park for many children.

Blue Cross and Blue Shield of New Hampshire

In the early days of the Plan, service employees would travel to New Hampshire town halls and community centers to sign up subscribers. This photograph shows one such community enrollment day at the Claremont Community Center, around 1944.

In the fall of 1938 a group of prominent New Hampshire industrialists and professional people met in a Pembroke home to discuss the future of the state's private hospitals, many of which had barely weathered a difficult storm providing health care to a Depression-stricken population.

The incorporation of New Hampshire Hospitalization Service in 1942, four years after that meeting, provided a double guarantee: It gave the state's hospitals the assurance of payment, and it gave New Hampshire health care consumers the assurance that, by paying a small sum each month, hospital care would be available and affordable when they needed it.

New Hampshire Hospitalization Service's first president, James M. Langley, was a planner by predilection, publisher of the local newspaper, and first chairman of the Concord Planning Board, its zoning board, and the State Planning and Development Commission. While the new service would strive to provide "the maximum hospitalization service at the lowest possible cost," Langley also envisioned that it would avert a consequence many feared in the New Deal years— "the constant threat," he said, "of federally socialized medicine and health insurance."

The New Hampshire service's first plan was a single hospital benefit that paid the average cost of a semiprivate room for 21 days and 75 percent of that cost for the next 60 days. In 1943 a semi-private room cost $5 a day (about 40 years later it costs, on the average, $140 a day), and the first subscribers were asked to pay $7.50 a month. The service paid its first claim in February 1943 to a member of one of its first groups, Laconia knitting machinery manufacturer Scott & Williams and Company, for the delivery of a child.

By the end of that year the service had signed up more than 31,000 persons. In 1982 it had about 500,000, only 20 percent of them not covered under group plans. Two years after the founding of the hospital service, the New Hampshire Physicians Service was incorporated and began doing business as the New Hampshire Blue Shield Plan. By 1946 both Plans had been extended to Vermont, which ultimately formed its own Plans in 1980.

After the first year of the New Hampshire plan, president Langley wrote, "A far-seeing service will tend in time to adopt every feasible measure to encourage preventive medicine in an effort to reduce the need for its services." The next year the New Hampshire Blue Shield program became one of the first in the country to cover office visits in pursuit of the prevention goal. The institution of the deductible was another means toward that end. Blue Cross of New Hampshire outpatient benefits (begun in 1968) and Blue Shield home health benefits (begun in 1978) helped shorten the average hospital stay from 10 to five days over the next 15 years.

The prevention philosophy penetrates the walls of the Concord headquarters, too; Blue Cross and Blue Shield of New Hampshire began a Healthier Employees Lifestyle Program (HELP) in 1977 among its own employees. The combination of diet workshops, no-smoking clinics, and various exercise programs has become a model for other states' Blue Cross and Blue Shield Plans. In 1982 the Plan began selling this program to other businesses and institutions.

Housing functions that once had been in 11 different locations in the city of Concord, this 1970 building now is headquarters to some 860 persons working for Blue Cross and Blue Shield of New Hampshire.

International Packings Corporation

The former Dodge-Davis woolen mill complex, on the banks of the Newfound River, was International Packings Corporation's original quarters in Bristol, New Hampshire. The main three-story mill housed rubber molding facilities, and adjacent smaller buildings served mechanical leather packings operations, purchasing, personnel, and other departments.

The story of International Packings Corporation begins with Graton & Knight, a company that became the world's largest producer of leather belting and other industrial products made of leather. Founded in 1851 in Worcester, Massachusetts, Graton & Knight also made leather packings, to seal lubricants and gases inside mechanisms and to keep dirt and debris out.

But when synthetic rubber was first compounded in the United States, in the early years of the 1930s, the future of Graton & Knight changed. The large company established a tiny division that began to explore uses of synthetic rubber when it became commercially available; by 1942 G&K was manufacturing and selling synthetic rubber automobile O-rings and seals and became excited about the potential and versatility of the new substance.

Labor problems at Graton & Knight by 1949 prompted company officials to relocate this division in Bristol, New Hampshire, and called it International

Packings Corporation because it was exporting gas pump leather packings to France and Germany. In 1949 Bristol was and today remains far north of the major concentrations of industry in the Granite State. But David S. Williams, soon to become IPC's president, chose this small town near Newfound Lake because of his family's long acquaintance with the Newfound area.

Although Bristol held the promise of a better quality of life for IPC employees, it was a mill town without an industry in 1949. Textile manufacturer Dodge-Davis Manufacturing Company recently had vacated a mill in the center of town that had been continuously occupied since 1857, making at various times white paper, the once-famous "Cardigan jacket," and baseball uniform flannels.

Keen on maintaining this tradition of productivity, IPC brought nine management and technical people up from Worcester to begin the company in New Hampshire and to start hiring personnel.

Within a few months of taking up the

old mill space, 70 people had been employed by IPC. By 1951 employment had climbed to 200, mostly devoted to making custom-designed shaft seals, gaskets, and packings for the automotive industry.

IPC strained at the walls of the Dodge-Davis mill by 1963 and built a new facility about a mile south of Bristol on the Ragged Mountain Highway. Troubling signs in the U.S. automotive industry began to signal the need for changes, both in traditional products and in the market mix, to Williams. Even though the company's sales had increased by more than 200 percent throughout the 1970s, a major program to maintain this profitability and growth was launched in 1979.

Williams' program was two-pronged. First, nearly 700 employees were invited to participate in a product quality improvement drive, the result of which was an employee-designed product awareness program that eventually was implemented in all IPC facilities in the United States. IPC employees were instructed in statistical control and analysis techniques and formed "SCAT" teams to deal with interdepartmental and statistical analysis problems related to product quality. "Quality Circles" were set up to handle intradepartmental problems.

Second, Williams set out to diversify the IPC product line. A Health Care Products Division was started in Bristol in 1980 to design and manufacture rubber syringe plungers, bottle closures, and other disposable medical grade parts. In 1982 a new wing was added to the Bristol plant for mixing compound from a raw gum base for silicone rubber, thereby allowing the company to satisfy its own requirements for the material at a lower cost.

As early as 1966, IPC needed satellite manufacturing facilities. The first sprouted among the Indiana corn fields in that year. By 1983 IPC had five production plants in Indiana and New Hampshire. In addition to the Bristol corporate headquarters, IPC owns two tool-manufacturing facilities in New Hampshire: one in Ashland and the A.E. Esty Machine Tool Division, adjacent to the Ragged Mountain Highway facility in Bristol. Another tool-making unit is located in Rushville, Indiana. The company also established TransTec Industries, a transmission rebuilding kit facility in Ohio. And two Canadian subsidiaries, ARMET Industries in Ontario and TYTON Seal in Quebec manufacture related products.

International Packings Corporation is New Hampshire's largest employer north of Concord, the state capital, and south of Berlin with its pulp and paper industry.

Each year it produces millions of custom-designed and -manufactured rubber parts for automobiles, washing machines, outboard motors, chain saws, aircraft, hydroelectric turbines, and products familiar in any home, such as pulsating shower sprays. One of IPC's plants in Indiana supplies more lip seals for new passenger car automatic transmissions than all other manufacturers combined.

The firm has also become a major benefactor in all of its communities. In the Newfound Lake area, IPC supports the Bristol Community Center, an area recreation program, with funds and volunteers. It also provides scholarships for underprivileged boys who wish to attend an area camp, and its employees contributed the funds necessary to revitalize a local health care center in 1982.

IPC molded rubber parts range from tiny shaft seals less than one-inch in diameter to enormous hydroelectric turbine seals measuring more than six feet across. Oil seals, bellows, mechanical face seals, diaphragms, packings, and scores of other precision-molded parts are produced by the millions for American industry.

IPC now occupies over 160,000 square feet at its Bristol corporate headquarters just south of the original plant. This largest production facility manufactures shaft seals and other rubber-bonded-to-metal parts, *and also contains administration, marketing, design and materials engineering, and financial staffs. A.E. Esty Machine Tool Division is in the lower left foreground.*

Foster's Daily Democrat

In the 1850s New Hampshire was a hotbed of political activity. The state's Democratic party had begun to fragment the decade before. One faction, led by New Hampshire's only U.S. President, Franklin Pierce, opposed railroad and bank expansion in the state, supported the annexation of Texas, and aligned itself with southern slaveholders with an eye to keeping the Union intact.

The other faction, led by abolitionist John Parker Hale, opposed allowing Texas into the Union for fear of abetting the spread of slavery. Hale lived in Dover, and the three weekly newspapers in that town engaged in lively debate about political philosophy. The one pro-Hale weekly, *The Dover Enquirer,* became *Foster's Weekly Democrat* on January 20, 1872.

An architect by training, Joshua Lane Foster had always shown a bent for journalism. Architect of many public buildings in New Hampshire until the Panic of 1857 stifled the construction trade, Foster bought the *Dover Gazette* in 1858 and then started the first Democratic newspaper in Portsmouth, the *States & Union,* in 1863.

Foster started other papers in New Hampshire and Connecticut and even returned to architecture for a time, but ultimately he returned to Dover, where he began his career in journalism, to turn the *Enquirer* into the *Foster's Weekly Democrat. Foster's Daily Democrat* was started on June 18, 1873. Today it is the only newspaper in the nation that carries a family name on the masthead, and is the only daily newspaper in the United States that has passed from father to son through four generations with members of the fifth generation now employed.

Continuing in the tradition of the crusading editor, Foster actively opposed the 1884 inauguration of Grover Cleveland to the presidency. He called the state and national Democratic party organization "false and un-American . . . cowardly and perfidious," and immediately threw his paper's support behind the Republican party—a change that, despite its Democrat name, was permanent.

Foster's son and grandson succeeded him at the helm of the *Daily Democrat* after his death in 1900. But it was not until his great-grandson, Robert Harding Foster, became publisher in 1956 that the paper began to grow significantly. A World War II veteran and author of his battalion's history, Foster brought the paper from its 1947 circulation of 1,000 to more than 23,000. Staff has grown from less than 20 employees in 1956 to more than 100 today.

Foster's Daily Democrat began as a four-page sheet selling for 1.5 cents to 150 people on its first day of issue. For most of its history it has served the three contiguous cities of Dover, Somersworth, and Rochester. But today it is a truly regional paper and the largest in southeastern New Hampshire. With bureaus in four cities, it is the second largest daily evening newspaper in the state.

Foster's Weekly Democrat is gone, but the daily still follows the original philosophy set forth by Joshua Lane Foster—to serve "the material and vital interests of Dover and vicinity . . . whatever may tend to benefit this people and enhance their prosperity will receive warm and enthusiastic support."

Left: Joshua L. Foster, an architect by training, founded Foster's Daily Democrat *and became a crusading editor in the finest tradition.*

*Right: Robert Harding Foster, great-grandson of the founder and today's publisher of the only daily newspaper in the United States to carry a family name on the masthead—*Foster's Daily Democrat.

In the early 1900s Foster's Daily Democrat *occupied the building on the left. Today it is on the same site and in the same building but with extensive renovation and acquisition of adjoining properties. Inside and out, the plant is in keeping with its New England locale.*

Edgcomb Steel of New England, Inc.

When Nashua textile giants left the city late in the 1940s, Edgcomb Steel of New England, Inc., was one of several firms convinced of Nashua's promise as a location for a metal warehouse for northern New England. Originally in part of Textron's old downtown plant, Edgcomb built the first section of its much-expanded West Hollis Street facility in 1952 and moved near the highway.

When textile giant Textron swept out of Nashua after World War II, it left more than two million square feet of mill space vacant and thousands of workers newly unemployed in its wake.

Edgcomb Steel of New England, Inc., was one of several business ventures persuaded to set up shop in Nashua by a local committee. The company certainly does not seem to have any regrets about what may not have been a very hard sell in the first place: Founder Arthur W. Moody, in search of a northern New England location for his enterprise, had vacationed often in New Hampshire and even spent his honeymoon in the state.

The firm is an outgrowth of a "metal service center" begun in Philadelphia in 1923 by Leslie Edgcomb. It acts as a middleman between the metal producer (such as a steel mill) and the metal user; the firm buys carbon, stainless and alloy steel, and aluminum in large quantities, warehouses it, processes it to a specified size, and ships it to the customer.

Edgcomb, his brother Harry, and J.H. Roberts set up another service center in Milford, Connecticut, three years later. And by 1950 the growing New England market bespoke the need for a northern New England location, and corporate vice-president Arthur Moody was sent to find one.

Edgcomb Steel of New England, Inc., is among some 150 metal service centers in the New England region. But it is the largest such operation based and located in New England and now has branches in six other cities along the Eastern Seaboard. Edgcomb started out in Nashua in April 1951, with seven employees in part of Textron's old plant. The following year it moved to the West Hollis Street location where it remains today, at least seven expansions later.

The warehouse originally stocked steel, brass, copper, and aluminum sheets, plates, bars, and shapes as well as fasteners and other construction materials. For metal users who formerly had to rely on Massachusetts sources of supply, Edgcomb would perform "pre-production processing," which in those days meant cutting to size with a band or hack saw and shearing on a machine considered primitive in 1983.

Edgcomb shipped about 7,400 tons of metal in its first year of operation for $974,000 in sales. In 1982 it shipped more than 105,000 tons to practically every major metal user in New Hampshire and the other New England states, New York, Pennsylvania, Maryland, Delaware, West Virginia, and North Carolina. Sales in 1982 exceeded $88 million.

Where less than 50 percent of its shipments were processed in 1951, more than 85 percent of it is today, much of it on very sophisticated equipment. It is flame-cut, sheared, leveled, cut, slit, sawed, and precision ground to customers' specifications.

Edgcomb Steel of New England, Inc., employs 500 people throughout its entire operation; about 250 of those work in the New Hampshire facilities in Nashua and Concord. It is run today by Arthur Moody's nephew, Charles C. Moody, Jr., who began working there on the third shift late in the 1950s, loading trucks during his high school summer vacations.

Originally stocking metals and simply cutting them to customers' specified sizes, the company now uses a variety of computer-controlled equipment to tailor orders more accurately to needs.

BankEast

When Manchester, the first city in New Hampshire, was incorporated in 1845, Manchester Savings Bank—which would later become BankEast—was chartered right along with it. It was a good time to begin a bank, for in the 1840s alone, Manchester's population increased from 3,235 to almost 14,000.

Manchester Savings was brought to life chiefly by Nathan Parker who, with his brother James, raised the initial capital of $50,000 in their native town of Litchfield, a farming village just south of Manchester. Parker was treasurer of the bank from its incorporation until shortly before his death in 1894. A major stockholder in three of the railroads active in New Hampshire and a state representative, Parker was also president of Manchester National Bank; when he died he was said to be the oldest bank president in the United States.

From 1860 to 1949 Manchester Savings Bank (now BankEast) stood at the corner of Elm and Market streets in the growing city of Manchester and for part of that time shared its lobby with Manchester Savings Bank. This view was taken in 1894, the year longtime bank treasurer Nathan Parker died.

The bank experienced steady growth in deposits from $30,000 in 1852, to $7 million in the 1890s, to in excess of $100 million in the 1960s. The bulk of this growth came during the 1950s and 1960s under the leadership of Charles S. Nims.

The bank has occupied a number of locations over the years, settling into its present Elm Street address in 1958 and expanding it significantly in 1973.

Ezekiel A. Straw, descendant of the original agent of Manchester's huge Amoskeag Manufacturing Company,

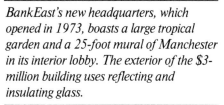

BankEast's new headquarters, which opened in 1973, boasts a large tropical garden and a 25-foot mural of Manchester in its interior lobby. The exterior of the $3-million building uses reflecting and insulating glass.

became president of the bank during the late 1960s. He perceived the need for a progressive commercial bank in the state and, in 1968, converted the bank from a mutually owned institution to a stock-owned commercial bank known as The Manchester Bank. In the process, a bank holding company was formed, its equity owned by 23,000 Manchester Savings depositors.

After Straw's death in 1972, First Financial Group of New Hampshire, the holding company of The Manchester Bank, undertook a major expansion and acquisition program. Under the leadership of Walter N. DeWitt, its new chief executive officer, and a board of directors, the company has become the third largest commercial banking organization in New Hampshire, with offices in 18 communities and total assets approaching $500 million.

In 1981 the name was changed to BankEast, reflecting the statewide orientation of the organization.

Citizen Publishing Company

Laconia Evening Citizen *owner Edward J. Gallagher also acted as reporter and editor for his daily Lakes Region newspaper. Here, he takes Associated Press wire news over the "pony wire."*

When he was in his teens, the nurses at Concord's Margaret Pillsbury Hospital used to think of him as "a delicate boy." But by the age of 20, Edward J. Gallagher had overcome a four-year struggle with tuberculosis and had become sole owner and publisher of the Concord *Daily Patriot.*

Gallagher's life was bound up heart and soul with journalism. He started his own news service covering the state legislature at the age of 14 and sold two articles—one of them "How to Care for an Invalid"—to national magazines before becoming the *Patriot's* city editor.

Eager to be on his own, Gallagher left the *Patriot* after 13 years, traveled the country for *Billboard Magazine* for a time, and returned to New Hampshire to start a daily newspaper in Laconia.

He bought a press from the Portsmouth *Herald,* upon agreeing that his newspaper would be "at least 12 miles distant from Portsmouth." He bought a linotype in New York City, and one day in 1926 the Concord *Monitor-Patriot's* new editor and publisher, James M. Langley, drove to Laconia with a carload

of type for the new venture.

The first Laconia *Evening Citizens* were four-page dailies, since there was only enough type for a paper that size. The first paper, issued on January 4, 1926, cost two cents and sold 500 copies in the city alone.

Gallagher published the *Citizen* until his death in 1978. Its circulation is now greater than 10,000 and the area it covers embraces nearly all of central New Hampshire.

Despite its growth, the Laconia *Evening Citizen* has remained a strongly local newspaper. Gallagher used to tell his cub reporters to look for the "Bronx angle" in every story—state, national, or international. Gallagher believed, like the Bronx newspaper from which the term arose, that there was a local angle in any story, and it was the job of the *Citizen* to find it and make the event meaningful on that level. He called the paper the *Citizen* because he felt the name implied "public rather than political interests. It's a mistake to have a newspaper," he said, "that keeps the town all riled up."

The *Citizen* always has been a public-spirited paper, reflecting Gallagher's

intense involvement in local affairs. In the Depression, during his two terms as mayor of Laconia, Gallagher had the newspaper sponsor a "model home" program to put unemployed Laconians back to work building 10 new houses in the city. The *Citizen* also was the only New Hampshire daily that ranked among the 100 newspapers in the nation carrying the largest volume of war bond advertising in 1944.

Gallagher's wife Etta was president of Citizen Publishing Company, begun in 1933. The firm published Gallagher's three biographies of New Hampshire people and now publishes the weekly *Lakes Region Trader.* The couple's only child, Alma Gallagher Smith, now is publisher of the *Citizen,* having come to the paper after college and a wartime stint as a flight instructor for Dartmouth students entering the Navy.

The Citizen's *newsroom acted as a guinea pig for Compugraphic's computer typesetting system in the 1970s. The staff includes 10 reporters covering a vast central New Hampshire region with 35,000 people.*

The Kingston-Warren Corporation

The year was 1945. World War II had ended and "suburbia," with its baby boom, had begun.

The new homes that the postwar period promised seemed like a golden opportunity to Lester Gibson, who, with his associates Herbert Grant and Elmer Clement, worked in an Amesbury, Massachusetts, company that roll-formed metal strips primarily for use in automobiles.

What was a sideline to that Massachusetts firm—custom roll-forming of metal strips into decorative trim molding for kitchen counters, sinks, and wallboards—became the chief business of a new New Hampshire enterprise, Kingston Manufacturing Company.

Lester Gibson already was a resident of New Hampshire, and in the postwar period the state had low taxes and a great deal of available land in its southern reaches. The three men left Amesbury, went straight north about 15 miles, and ended up on the first floor of what was once Mill Number Five of the sprawling cotton textile manufacturer, Newmarket Manufacturing Company.

In business for more than a century, Newmarket Manufacturing closed up shop in the early years of the Great Depression, but by the late 1930s shoe manufacturers began to fill up some of the mill space it had left behind. When Gibson, Grant, and Clement moved in in 1945, one shoe company occupied the mill's third floor, and silk weaving machines clattered away on the second floor.

Mill Number Five housed the old and new in New Hampshire industry until 1955, when steel handling and storage needs demanded more space. By that time the three founders of Kingston Manufacturing had been joined by Oliver Merrill and his Warren Manufacturing Company, which made metal channels lined with felt for car door windows.

By the time of the move to nearby Newfields, custom roll-formed metal for the automotive industry was the major product: The firm made enough window channels for 10,000 to 12,000

The Kingston-Warren Corporation's first facility in Newfields was situated beside the Exeter River.

In 1978 the firm was moved to this 88-acre site. The Kingston-Warren Corporation has become one of the larger employers in the New Hampshire seacoast area.

Chevrolets, Pontiacs, Oldsmobiles, and Buicks each week.

But the manufacturers had been on the lookout for a product of their own, and in the early 1960s they found it. Kingston made parts for the products of many other companies, but one such company's product was an industrial storage system that needed to be improved.

Kingston and Warren innovated with a gravity flow storage system made of steel frames that can be mounted on top of one another and that sit at an incline. The shelves of these racks are equipped with plastic rollers. Goods move from the back, where they are stocked, to the front, where they are picked, so that the whole system works on a first-in, first-out basis. The gravity flow storage system is especially useful for batteries and other perishable goods.

The storage system has been matched with a computer system called CAPS (computer-assisted picking system). After the computer receives information on orders to be picked, it will activate a light and a display on the rack where the item to be picked is stocked. After picking, the picker pushes a button on the rack, so that the data on the act just completed is reported to the computer for inventory.

In 1980 Kingston-Warren was one of the principal roll-forming companies in the United States. Here an employee operates the electronically controlled roll-forming equipment.

inventory.

The Kingston-Warren Corporation—the product of a merger between the two companies in 1971—had captured 80 percent of the marketplace in gravity flow storage by the late 1970s. But the founding of the new product did not dull the potential of existing and new markets for parts the firm routinely manufactured. Although it has long ceased to make

In the past this "chain-bending" equipment was part of the manufacturing process at The Kingston-Warren Corporation.

the decorative trim molding, Kingston-Warren now manufactures 50 percent of all the weatherseals for General Motors cars. And in 1980 it was one of the largest custom roll-forming companies in the United States.

In 1975 Herbert Grant, Jr., assumed management of the two companies, which then had 300 employees and annual sales of $10 million. The flourishing business necessitated a final move in 1978, to an 88-acre site only 1.5 miles away from the existing Newfields plant. It took 10 weeks to move 1,000 pieces of equipment and 600 employees to the new building, which sits back from the road behind a late 1800s farmhouse and barn that will be restored for possible use as a conference center.

The Kingston-Warren Corporation now employs more than 700 persons, making it one of the larger employers in the New Hampshire seacoast area and one of the larger privately owned companies in the state. Now emerging as a growth-oriented marketing (as well as manufacturing) company, K-W has licensees in six countries around the world.

Indian Head Banks Inc.

| Portsmouth | Claremont | Concord | Nashua | Laconia | Keene | Littleton |

In 1933, when newly elected President Franklin Delano Roosevelt first met the crisis of the Great Depression by declaring a Bank Holiday, it was clear to the directors of Indian Head National Bank of Nashua that the small-town and country banks of New Hampshire needed help.

Indian Head, one of the largest and healthiest national banks in the state, wanted to initiate branch banking to support its sound financial and management expertise on a broader base. But New Hampshire had no laws on the books allowing branch banking, and the state's attorney general ruled that the absence of such legislation meant branches were illegal.

So began the first bank holding company in the state of New Hampshire—New Hampshire Bankshares, Inc., which started in 1934 with the combined assets of four southeastern area banks: Indian Head National Bank of Nashua, Wilton National Bank, First National Bank of Derry, and Rockingham National Bank of Exeter.

Of the four banks, Indian Head National Bank of Nashua had come through the Depression banking crisis in a strong financial position, largely due to the able leadership of Harry A. Gregg, the second Gregg generation of four who have been involved in Indian Head's management since 1889. In fact, Indian Head was considered healthy enough to

be one of the few banks President Roosevelt allowed to reopen in 1933, immediately after the opening of the Federal Reserve Banks in large metropolitan areas.

Indian Head, named for the head of an Indian carved in a tree, is the oldest bank in Nashua, founded in 1851 even before the area of Nashua was merged into one city.

In 1889 David Almus Gregg became vice-president of Indian Head. Three years later he was made president, a position he held for 36 years until his death in 1928. Gregg's son Harry became a director of the bank in 1927 and the first president of New Hampshire Bankshares in 1934.

The holding company was designed to acquire shares in other New Hampshire banks and to furnish those banks with management services and advice. The arrangement was immediately beneficial to all of the banks in the original group. Beginning with combined assets of $8.3 million in 1934, the capital structures of the four banks increased from 18 to 42 percent by the end of 1938, and deposits increased from 22 to 96 percent in that time.

The Gregg family has remained active in its leadership of the holding company. Hugh Gregg, son of Harry, was named a director in 1964. He also was mayor of Nashua when Textron vacated its huge mill complex and left much of the city's

industrial work force without jobs. The Nashua Foundation, in which the Greggs, with the cooperation of Royal Little, president of Textron, were centrally involved, spearheaded the diversification of Nashua's industry and the relocation of numerous businesses in the city. Hugh Gregg went from his mayor's job to become the youngest governor in New Hampshire's history. His son Judd also was a director of Indian Head Banks, Inc., before being elected to the United States Congress in 1980.

New Hampshire native James Chandler was brought to the helm of the Nashua bank and the holding company in 1957. Son of the former president of Keene National Bank, Chandler began a series of acquisitions that, ironically, included his father's bank, which joined the holding company in 1973. Since 1958, 12 banks had become members of Indian Head Banks, Inc., the largest commercial banking group in New Hampshire with combined resources, by mid-1982, of $641.7 million.

The name of the holding company changed to Indian Head Banks, Inc., in 1972, and member banks also assumed the Indian Head name. The corporation now has 39 offices across the state and seven affiliated banks covering communities that hold 76 percent of New Hampshire's population.

General Electric

General Electric's Meter Business Department occupies both the 1843 Mill Number Three and this addition, built in 1920, to the Great Falls Manufacturing Company in Somersworth.

General Electric, the company that Thomas Edison helped found in 1892, has grown into a vast international concern of 402,000 employees and 335 manufacturing facilities. Two of its plants are in New Hampshire. Both were spawned by the sprawling Lynn, Massachusetts, plant following World War II, and both feature some of the most advanced automation to be found in any American factory.

As production expanded for GE after World War II, the firm sought a place to house the growing manufacture of time switches for kitchen ranges, hotel and restaurant radios, and other devices. It settled on the Collea Building in Somersworth, vacant since the Depression and owned by the father of one of GE's Lynn employees.

Within two years, the Somersworth arm of the company turned to the production of the I-50 watt-hour meter and had moved down the street to what was known as Building A. Most recently occupied by the Navy Department as an adjunct to the Portsmouth Naval Ship-

yard, Building A was built in 1920 as part of Great Falls Manufacturing Company, a cotton sheeting maker. At that time Building A was part of a grand plan to build the largest mill in the world under one roof. By 1952 half of all GE's residential meter business had moved to Somersworth, and in 1954 the plant became GE's Meter Business Department. Every watt-hour meter General Electric makes to measure the use of electricity in the United States is made in Somersworth.

With nearly 2,000 people on the payroll in 1983, GE's plant in Somersworth is one of New Hampshire's five largest employers. It is now the world headquarters for GE's meter business. It is also one of few plants in the state to use robots. The machines are used in the hot, dirty, and generally undesirable job of die-casting, and they've been there since 1966.

New Hampshire's other GE facility is in Hooksett, having taken over a facility vacated by Raytheon in 1966. A satellite of the West Lynn military engine business, the Hooksett plant is chiefly involved in the manufacture of parts for engines made at Lynn, primarily for the T700, a high-technology, lightweight, fuel-efficient engine for helicopters, small precision planes, and fighter planes.

While the original General Electric jet engine—the A1—weighed 400 pounds and generated 2,500 pounds of thrust, the T700 weighs only a little more than 100 pounds and generates 4,500 pounds of thrust. The compressor rotor for this engine is made in Hooksett's Plant Number Two, leased by GE in 1970.

To make parts for this rotor—parts whose geometry is so precise that man and machine could not duplicate them without a computer program to mediate—the Hooksett plant uses some of the most advanced "direct numerical control" equipment in the United States. Plant Number Two is 90-percent computer reliant, but the assembly of the rotor takes one person 26 hours to accomplish.

GE at Hooksett has grown from employing 184 people in 1966 to employing 587 in 1982. That growth has shown no signs of abating: Plant Number Two added 10,000 square feet in 1983.

General Electric's facility in Hooksett was one of the earliest in New Hampshire to plunge full-steam into automation. Here an employee operates a "direct numerical control" lathe, which turns parts automatically from a computer program.

GTE Lighting Products

Frank A. Poor went from grammar school to a leather tannery to a grain store to a company that rejuvenated blackened carbon incandescent lamps.

In 1901, when he was 21, Poor bought out this Middleton, Massachusetts, enterprise. Eight years later he began making his own incandescent lamps, later added radio tubes to his line, and then merged with a firm making the same two products in Pennsylvania to establish what eventually became Sylvania Electric Products.

Poor used to summer in Wolfeboro and died in that Lakes Region resort town. But it is probably coincidental that the company he founded chose to expand in New Hampshire, beginning in 1956.

Working with the state, Sylvania (now GTE Lighting Products) chose the town

After struggling in a business that sold hay, hominy, and cracked corn to Massachusetts farmers, Frank A. Poor borrowed $3,500 to buy a half-interest in this Middleton, Massachusetts, company that renewed burned-out incandescent lamps. The firm became one of the largest manufacturers of electric light bulbs in the country.

of Hillsborough, whose Parkhill Shoe Company had begun an unfortunate slide just as it had finished erecting a new plant on the town's West Main Street. Sylvania moved its semiconductor operation to Hillsborough, bringing 15 people up from Massachusetts and hiring 100 from the area of its new plant.

The Hillsborough plant stopped making transistors and diodes in 1970 and turned to the production of miniature lamps, called "miniature" mostly for their low voltage. These incandescent lamps are used in cars, telephone equipment, elevators, airplanes, flashlights, electronic games, and toys. The Hillsborough plant, which began in the miniature lighting field with a work force of 60 that has since grown to 450, also makes the capsules for GTE's new halogen sealed-beam automotive headlights.

The firm's second New Hampshire facility was begun in 1960 in Manchester, in the former Arrow Needle Company facility on South Willow Street. As Hillsborough is GTE's only miniature lighting plant, Manchester is the company's only plant that manufactures high-intensity discharge lamps.

These "HID" lamps are used in

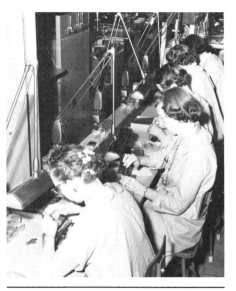

Women at the Hillsborough plant involve themselves in intricate assembly work three years after the facility opened in 1956.

industrial lighting for parking lots, streets, and highways, and for high-intensity store lighting. Mercury, Metalarc (a combination of several iodized metals in the lamp's arc tube), high-pressure sodium, and special-purpose lamps are manufactured by some 650 employees in Manchester, in a facility that has grown from 24,000 to 180,000 square feet since 1960.

GTE has three other New Hampshire plants. One, in Greenland, had manufactured glass for fluorescent tubing since 1970. In 1983 manufacturing stopped and it became staff headquarters for the company's U.S. glass operations, employing 35. Another, in Exeter, opened in 1963 to make "emissive products," the pressed ceramic components used in lamps, filament coils, and quartz crucibles. It employs 300 people.

GTE's newest New Hampshire operation is in Nashua, a small satellite of its Ipswich, Massachusetts, plant designing and making machines used in the manufacture of light bulbs and other products. The 30 employees of GTE in Nashua work in the former Poulin Machine and Tool Company, once a supplier of the Massachusetts company that eventually came to occupy its building.

The Suncook Bank

Suncook, the shopping village on the Suncook River that lies in both Allenstown and Pembroke, was created in the late 1800s to satisfy the needs of the growing number of people working in the Suncook Mills.

The cotton textile manufacturer had three mills in these two towns, and at one point there had been a savings bank named for one of them, the China Mill. But in 1916 there was no bank in Suncook, which by then had become the shopping center for five largely rural towns between Concord and Manchester.

The Suncook Board of Trade undertook to fill this gap in April 1916 by authorizing the creation of The Suncook Bank, to be located in the building formerly occupied by a jewelry store at the corner of Main and Glass streets in the village. Begun with $60,000 in capital stock and surplus, the bank opened in September and had $100,000 in savings deposits after its first year in business.

The Suncook Bank's main headquarters is located on Glass Street, Suncook, New Hampshire.

Its first president was Edwin Leighton Child, a farmer and dairyman born in Cornish, New Hampshire, in 1867. By the time the bank opened, Child had resigned his presidency. Judging by his record of accomplishments, it seems likely that Child found dairying more rewarding than banking: In 1900 and 1901 the butter he produced at his Cornish Creamery won New Hampshire its only gold medals at the Paris Exposition and the Pan-American Exposition in Buffalo.

But Child's short-lived career at The Suncook Bank did not affect George

In 1916 The Suncook Bank was opened at Main and Glass streets in Suncook. This photo was taken after a 1941 renovation.

THE SUNCOOK BANK

Winthrop Fowler, who was its first treasurer and remained so until his death in 1937. A native of Pembroke, Fowler was a Dartmouth graduate who spent most of his life in journalism. Attracted by the western frontier, Fowler lived in Bismarck, North Dakota, for four years, where he taught school and helped edit the local newspaper. Returning to his native state, Fowler entered the wholesale and retail grain business with his brother Edward, who later became one of the first directors of The Suncook Bank, and became director of the Suncook Valley Railroad. He was also editor of the *Nashua Gazette* and the *Manchester Union.*

The Suncook Bank always has been a small and independent bank. It was one of the first in New Hampshire allowed to reopen after the 1933 Bank Holiday; its 1938 assets of $850,000 have grown to $68 million today.

The bank moved to a new facility on Suncook's Glass Street in 1955, three years before its current president, K. Donald Woodbury, became a director. Formerly counsel to the bank, Woodbury became its vice-president in 1967 and its president in 1970. Under his direction The Suncook Bank has opened two branches, one in Hooksett in 1972 and another in Epsom in 1975.

Public Service of New Hampshire

It may be hard to imagine that the small state of New Hampshire had some 54 companies competing with each other to supply electricity at the turn of the 20th century.

Many of these small enterprises had, by 1926, been integrated into five utility corporations that formed Public Service of New Hampshire in that year. The oldest of the corporations, serving the city of Manchester, had begun operating in 1883, only four months after electricity was first produced at New York's famous Pearl Street Station.

The first general manager of Public Service was J. Brodie Smith. An electricity enthusiast, Smith wired a telephone system between the new Public Service's generating plants, and had all of the headquarter's electric clocks corrected periodically by radio signals.

Three years before the Depression may not seem like a good time to start a public utility. But Public Service of New Hampshire managed to weather the storm, continuing to buy utilities around the state and to install new electric line right up to and past 1929.

Public Service's first annual report notes the encouraging increase in the amount of electricity being used by residential customers, brought about in large part by their growing use of appliances in the home. In 1929 Public Service set up its Home Service Department, only a few years after every housewife in the town of Swanzey who was asked refused to take a three-dollar Hotpoint electric iron into her home, even on trial.

The Home Service Department helped customers select appliances and taught them how to use them correctly, even going so far as to conduct cooking

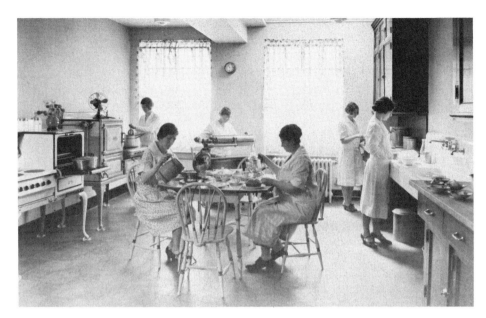

schools around the state. From 1928 to 1931 the average residential use of electricity jumped 45 percent, and people dauntlessly continued to buy appliances right through the Depression.

After selling 153 electric ranges in 1933, Public Service sold 910 the next year; sales of refrigerators climbed 133 percent over that year. Even then, as

In 1932 Public Service worked with appliance dealers to encourage people to use electric appliances, despite how fearsome they still seemed to many people. The cooking classes, like the one shown here (probably in Nashua), taught women how to use the appliances. Public Service sold 197 of the irons, at the rear, in 1934.

During a January snowstorm in 1979, a line worker clears line from branches weighed down with snow in Hillsborough. Even with rapid population growth in New Hampshire, there is one Public Service employee for every 127 residents, a ratio that has remained fairly constant since 1975.

Interior of the Amoskeag hydroelectric station in Manchester. Amoskeag began operation in 1922 and remains the company's largest hydro plant, producing 16 megawatts of electricity.

Public Service president Avery Schiller said in 1950, "The average home now is an institution of one wife and many motors."

Originally, Public Service sold appliances on a retail basis and was in the gas, steam, and electric railway business as well. By the late 1940s, however, the profitability of all of these ventures paled vastly compared to the ever-growing application of electricity. Most steam railways had been abandoned by 1940, the company's gas business was sold in 1945, and steam sales ended in 1949. And, where only 19 homes on Public Service's lines were heated with electricity in 1959, nearly 20,000 were by 1970.

The Manchester-based corporation not only survived the devastating floods and hurricanes of the 1930s, but it also figured critically in the city's comeback after the 1936 shutdown of Amoskeag Manufacturing Company, once the largest cotton textile plant in the world.

Public Service bought all the bankrupt firm's electrical and power installations, which helped a new corporation (formed to keep the mill buildings from being auctioned off piecemeal) leverage more money to buy the property. President

Schiller also arranged for Public Service to buy 18 percent of the new corporation's stock and saw the mills nearly half-filled with new businesses by the end of 1937.

Just as electricity became preeminent over gas, other power sources changed in

Ground was broken for the two-reactor Seabrook nuclear plant, located on New Hampshire's 15-mile Atlantic coastline, in 1970. Public Service anticipates that the plant will produce enough electricity each year to replace 23 million barrels of oil or 5 million tons of coal.

prominence. Through 1951, New Hampshire's hydroelectric facilities were supplying more than half of the state's electrical needs. However, erratic water flow from year to year made hydropower less reliable than fossil fuels. Also, new technology made large fossil plants more economical than hydro plants. As a result, the organization began retiring some of its hydroelectric facilities. By 1973, 41 small facilities had been taken out of service.

Today, Public Service of New Hampshire operates nine hydroelectric facilities, four (Merrimack, Schiller, Newington, Daniel Street) fossil-fueled plants, several combustion turbines, and has shares of four New England nuclear plants. Presently, oil fuels 51 percent of the company's electrical generation, coal provides 31 percent, and hydropower 7 percent.

Oil will only fuel 4 percent of the firm's generation by 1988, as more effort is spent converting to coal, refurbishing hydroelectric facilities, conserving energy generally, and developing nuclear power, the last of which will provide 67 percent of the state's electricity needs. Public Service is the major owner and prime builder of Seabrook Station, a two-reactor, 2,300-megawatt nuclear plant. The Seabrook plant, which would be the state's first nuclear facility, has been in construction since 1976. The first unit is scheduled to begin operating in 1984.

Public Service of New Hampshire supplies power to 75 percent of New Hampshire's population—291,600 people living in 200 cities and towns. More than 2,000 Public Service employees work in a service area of 5,445 square miles, crisscrossed by nearly 11,000 miles of electrical distribution and transmission line. Public Service's efforts in that last endeavor are historically noteworthy: It put up more than 300 miles of rural line in the years after its founding so that, by 1935, New Hampshire had one of the highest rural electrification rates in the country—well before the New Deal's Rural Electrification Administration ever got under way.

Laconia Savings Bank

The fourth oldest savings bank in New Hampshire traces its humble beginning back to July 2, 1831, when the state of New Hampshire approved a charter for the incorporation of "a Provident Institution for Savings at Meredith Bridge Village, to be called the Meredith Bridge Savings Bank." The Speaker of the New Hampshire House of Representatives who signed the charter was the Honorable Franklin Pierce, who later became the only United States President from New Hampshire, and, incidentally, had as his U.S. Secretary of War a gentleman named Jefferson Davis, the future President of the Confederacy.

It was not until nine months later that the Meredith Bridge Savings Bank received its first deposit in the amount of $10.50 (which, in 150 years, would have grown to $5,438.71). This mutual savings bank, in a community of about 300 persons, offered an opportunity for people with meager incomes to safely set aside a few cents or dollars and earn interest on their savings; and the pooling of many small deposits eventually made a new investment capital available in the community. The bank issued its first real estate loan (for $1,200) in 1833; by 1841

its deposits had grown to over $31,000, and the deposits more than doubled in the next decade. That same decade the institution set up its oldest continuous account—that of the Odd Fellows Winnipeseogee Lodge No. 7, in July 1845.

Also during the 1840s, the bank

Beginning with its founding in 1831 and for the next 16 years, Meredith Bridge Savings Bank occupied a building at 588 Main Street and shared it with Belknap Savings Bank and a hotel.

moved from its original location at 588 Main Street to 513 Main Street, where it stayed from 1847 to 1971. In 1971 it moved to its present quarters on Pleasant Street, a building specifically designed for the bank. Its three-lane drive-up facility, built in 1981, is one of the first such structures in the state to use solar energy to meet more than half of its heating requirements.

Meredith Bridge became part of Laconia in 1855, and the institution changed its name to Laconia Savings Bank in 1869. Since receiving its first deposit 150 years ago, the bank has continued to pay dividends to its depositors without fail.

Laconia Savings Bank serves the entire Lakes Region of the state, with deposits of more than $104 million in 1982, and it has over 3,600 real estate loans and more than 23,600 savings accounts.

Laconia Savings Bank's present location is the former site of the old city hall. Its drive-up window, heated by solar power, is connected to the bank building by a 90-foot underground security walkway.

D.D. Bean & Sons Co.

Delcie D. Bean (1833-1964), founder of D.D. Bean & Sons Co.

Founded in 1938 by Delcie D. Bean and his two sons, Vernon and D.D. Jr. (Jack), D.D. Bean & Sons Co. was a major supplier of the Armed Forces during World War II.

In 1944 a lonely soldier "somewhere in France" wrote a deeply touching letter to the firm, telling what it had meant to him to see a view of Mt. Monadnock on the bookmatch he was using. There were many other letters from young servicemen all over the world who recognized in the tree-shaded mountain something tangible from America. The mountain, which dominates the town of Jaffrey and the Monadnock region, was a natural for the company's house match.

Although the Monadnock house match was used for the servicemen, advertising on the bookmatches was important. Many familiar products use the bookmatch as an advertising medium. By 1952 the firm was making one of every eight bookmatches produced in the United States, and it is now the largest manufacturer in the field.

The bookmatch company was preceded by the New Hampshire Match Co., founded by D.D. Bean in the 1920s, to make wooden matches. With the onset of the Depression, the enterprise was sold to the "Swedish Match King," Ivar Kreuger, whose fraudulent effort to establish a match monopoly later collapsed.

Before that, Bean had been a supplier of white pine to the Diamond Match Co. His knowledge of wood led to the founding of a box shook company, Bean & Symonds, and later to the New Hampshire Match Co.

After the Depression, with the help of the Reconstruction Finance Corporation and private capital, D.D. Bean and his two sons were able to enter the bookmatch business. From a single factory in Jaffrey, the company grew to the point where five billion matches are manufactured each year, or 20 million books a day. There are about 170 people in the Jaffrey plant, a former 1827 textile mill. Another 300 work in the five other plants in the United States and Canada.

A number of D.D Bean's grandsons and two great-grandsons work in the company's different plants today.

Copy supplied by D.D. Bean & Sons Co.

Part of D.D. Bean & Sons Co.'s facilities are located in this 1827 textile mill in Jaffrey, New Hampshire.

Located in Jaffrey, New Hampshire, this is D.D. Bean & Sons Co.'s present mill and office.

Vernon J. Bean, president.

B. Leonard Krause, vice-president.

D.D. (Jack) Bean, Jr., treasurer.

Kendall Insurance, Inc.

Kendall began as the A.S. Parshley & Son Agency in the town of Strafford in 1867. In 1904 it was purchased by Frank L. Kendall, a native of St. Johnsbury, Vermont, who had begun working in insurance in Laconia in 1892. The agency has been in the Kendall family ever since and has insured New Hampshire industries as they come and go—the icehouses, shoe manufacturers, woolen mills, loggers, and furniture makers.

Kendall originally offered fire, life, accident, steam boiler, plate glass, and burglary insurance. In 1914 it was one of the few agencies asked by the Hartford Insurance Group to represent it in the new field of automobile insurance, for what one insurance agent that year described as "gasoline cans on wheels."

The Rochester company wrote its first group insurance policy in the late 1940s for about 1,500 persons employed by a textile manufacturer. Its efforts in that direction have grown considerably in volume and sophistication since that time. It is the only New Hampshire agency that provides technical assistance on all of the risk management services it

After 70 years in the Wentworth block on Rochester's Main Street, Kendall Insurance moved in 1970 to larger quarters on the same street and now occupies a modern, 23,000-square-foot office building. Kendall Real Estate, established in 1946, occupies an adjacent site.

offers.

Kendall Insurance has claims administrators and engineers who work on developing programs in self-insurance, self-funding, risk management, loss prevention, and training in worker safety. It has helped employers implement new cash-flow methods that help deal with the rapid rise in the cost of employee benefits. It even administers a self-funded group health plan for the city of Rochester, which saves the municipality the money it would ordinarily spend on taxes, commissions, reserves, and insurance company profits for a traditional policy.

Kendall Insurance is the nation's largest insurer of ski areas, insuring over half the country's ski areas. Its coverage

In 1942 Kendall Insurance celebrated its 75th year in business. The staff of 10 employees—including Kennett R. Kendall, president, standing in front of the vault—has grown to 115 today.

of 300 ski areas in 34 states, ranging from town-run rope tows to large areas such as Aspen and Squaw Valley, is a natural outgrowth of its century-old motto—"serving the New England business enterprises." The agency's ski area insurance comprises 25 to 30 percent of its total business. Kendall entered the business in 1975 by merging with Connecticut agency Barringer and Williams, for whom it had written New Hampshire ski areas policies since 1969. Kendall also writes insurance for other recreational facilities such as manufacturers of ski lifts, boots, and bindings, and for inns and marinas.

The company's growth through merger and acquisition is traditional. After its first purchase, a competing Rochester agency in 1925, it bought eight others, all in New Hampshire. Its merger with Manchester's Burpee, Griffin and Perkins in 1982 made it the largest insurance agency in northern New England. Its annual sales have kept pace, climbing from $60,000 in premiums in 1932 to over $25 million in 1982.

Catholic Medical Center

Significant developments in health care for Manchester residents were set in motion in 1858 with the arrival of Mother Mary Gonzaga, one of the original Sisters of Mercy of Dublin, Ireland. The zeal with which Mother Gonzaga worked to establish a hospital sponsored by a religious community was matched by Monsignor Pierre Hevey, who arrived in Manchester in 1880 from Lewiston, Maine.

Monsignor Hevey's wish to open a home that would minister to the needs of the poor and the sick was shared by the Sisters of Charity of St. Hyacinthe (also called the "Grey Nuns"). From these beginnings, Mother Gonzaga's dream was realized in 1892 when Sacred Heart Hospital was opened on Manchester's east side.

Similarly, the dedication of Monsignor Hevey and the Grey Nuns to minister to the needs of the poor was rewarded in 1888, when the Sisters of Charity opened an orphanage and home for chronically ill elderly women. This home became Notre Dame Hospital, located on Manchester's west side.

Following their founding, both hospitals experienced tremendous growth in services as a result of a growing population and the community's desire for

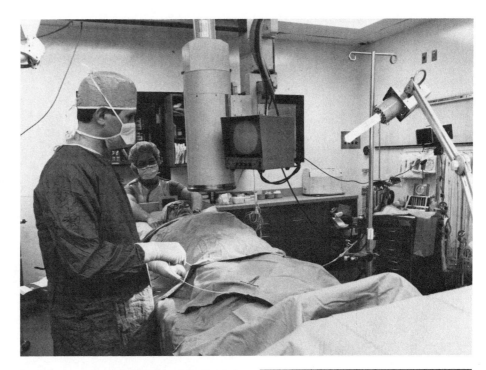

The original Notre Dame Hospital was an orphanage and home for chronically ill elderly women, built in 1888 on Manchester's west side. Today Catholic Medical Center is a progressive 330-bed health resource.

health care that fulfilled spiritual and emotional, as well as physical, needs.

In 1938 a five-story addition increased Sacred Heart Hospital's bed capacity to 125, followed in 1956 by yet another wing, increasing capacity to 150.

A three-story building containing 30 beds was added to Notre Dame Hospital in 1894 and, in 1912, its capacity was again increased to 55 beds. A new hospital was dedicated in 1956, bringing Notre Dame's capacity to 114 beds.

By this time, the need for patient services that ministered to a person's emotional and physical health was evident. To strengthen the religious community's ability to provide patient care in the spirit of Christ, Manchester's Bishop Ernest J. Primeau urged, in 1973, that Sacred Heart and Notre Dame hospitals merge. This merger was successful and, in 1974, Catholic Medical Center was founded.

Among the diagnostic procedures available at CMC is right and left heart catheterization. The procedure is used to determine the presence and extent of cardiovascular disease.

Growth in health care services continued, resulting in the 1978 dedication of Catholic Medical Center, located at the site of the former Notre Dame Hospital.

Today CMC is a major health resource that provides diagnostic, therapeutic, and preventive health care. The hospital's department of education actively promotes community outreach and health awareness through cardiac, respiratory, and diabetes education, emergency medical services, corporate fitness, natural family planning, and adolescent pregnancy and parenting programs.

Among CMC's specialty units are a hospital-based alcoholism treatment unit, a community-affiliated inpatient mental health unit, and the state's only inpatient rehabilitation medicine unit for patients requiring acute care.

In April 1983 the North Tower addition was completed, increasing CMC's capacity from 264 to 330 beds.

—Donna Gatnarek

Winebaum News, Inc.

It was the initiative 17-year-old Harry Winebaum showed as he led the 1915 newsboys' strike in Lawrence, Massachusetts, that led the Hearst Newspapers to offer him an agency in New Hampshire.

Winebaum, a Russian Jewish immigrant who had worked in the Lawrence mills with his sisters when he was not in school, accepted the offer to distribute Hearst's *Boston Record* in Portsmouth. In those days, a person had to change trains five times to get from Lawrence to Portsmouth, a distance of about 40 miles. Winebaum did so, met the Portland train at the Portsmouth depot the next morning, picked up his *Records* and sold them through the streets of the old seaport from a pushcart.

By the '20s Winebaum began distributing magazines, and by the '30s he had added paperback books to his line. In 1922 he also began, in Portsmouth, a retail operation called "Winebaum's Reading and Greeting Shop," which today is a seven-store chain throughout the New Hampshire seacoast region.

Harry Winebaum's son Sumner, who had left Portsmouth to work in television and advertising (he started the advertising firm of Young and Rubicam's offices in France and Italy), returned shortly after his father's 50th year in the distribu-

Aside from his growing wholesale distribution business, Harry Winebaum (standing at right, beneath the arch) began a chain of retail news stores in the New Hampshire seacoast region.

tion business.

Sumner Winebaum embarked on a series of acquisitions and improvements in distribution technology that has, in the past 15 years, made Winebaum News one of the two largest distributors of periodicals north of Boston, and the largest non-city newspaper distributor in New England.

Winebaum News now handles all of the major northeastern newspapers as well as 2,200 different magazine titles and 25,000 book titles through a com-

When the historic restoration Strawbery Banke was created in Portsmouth, Harry Winebaum donated his former offices, the 1760 Joshua Wentworth house, to the project. Too large to travel through Portsmouth's narrow streets, the house was put on a barge and floated down the Piscataqua River to its new site.

puter-controlled inventory system that the small agency pioneered. It was one of the first to use UPC computer codes on magazines and paperback books—and thus one of the first to use an optical scanner to accelerate the distribution process.

Winebaum agreed to have his agency help develop a software program for "financials" with a computer software company. The system includes a "perpetual" inventory, which keeps a real-time record of the 7,000 paperbacks the agency stocks, prints invoices and warehouse orders, automatically reorders books when inventory gets low, automatically records back orders for books not in stock, and sends them automatically once they arrive. The system virtually eliminates error and loss in inventory.

Winebaum News now covers part or all of eastern New Hampshire's counties and southern Maine. It distributes books to New Hampshire, Maine, and Vermont libraries and schools as well as bookstores throughout New England. It is one of the few wholesale distributors, too, that still delivers papers door-to-door, on one of its 50 routes.

J.A. Wright & Co.

One afternoon in 1872, John Artemus Wright was driving along a country road near his home in Keene, New Hampshire, when he spotted a cow mired in a bog. Although he was a city dweller and a successful hotel operator, Wright understood the value of a good cow; he stopped his buggy and helped the animal out.

As the mud dried on the cow's legs, Wright noticed that it turned an extraordinary white. Knowing something of chemistry and being an amateur geologist, Wright took a sample for analysis. As he suspected, it was diatomaceous earth, and of unusually fine quality.

Diatomaceous earth is made of tiny siliceous material of long-dead diatoms. When run back and forth over a piece of metal, the diatoms create just enough friction to remove tarnish but not enough to create scratches; because of that feature, it had been used for cleaning since ancient times. John A. Wright put this "secret ingredient" into a silver

At his Troy bog, John A. Wright had workers dig the diatomaceous earth, roll it into balls to dry, and then pulverize it. It was brought in barrels to Keene for sifting and packaging, and the first shipments were carried by wheelbarrow to the local railroad station.

cleaner that he first developed for use in his own hotel.

Wright soon started a business to manufacture and market a product sold in powder form under the trade name of Red Star Cleaning Powder in 1873. By the turn of the century the silver polish was in paste form under the trade name of Wright's. J.A. Wright & Co., incorporated in December 1893, also sold "infusorial earth" to other manufacturers.

By 1896 J.A Wright & Co. was producing nine different polishes, including one for bicycles. To Wright's sons falls the credit for the early use of advertising and promotional techniques to build visibility for this "elixir of life for silverware." The silver polish was the first silver cleaning agent to be advertised nationally, and, as early as 1896, the firm was taking space in such widely circulated periodicals as *Good Housekeeping.*

A liquid silver polish was introduced in 1958 and an anti-tarnish silver polish was developed in 1973 for which a patent was issued. In the mid-1970s brass and copper polishes were added to the Wright's line by the founder's great-grandsons.

Wright's silver polish is now sold in all 50 states and in many foreign countries, either directly or through food brokers in some 64 districts across the nation. The firm employs 22 people, only 10 of whom are involved in manufacturing the product, and has maintained its distinctive identity and character amid enormous changes in the world of business. Still a family concern, J.A. Wright & Co. is managed by the fifth generation of descendants from its founder, descendants who continue to exhibit Yankee confidence in the value of a good product first demonstrated when John A. Wright became "the right man in the right place at the right time."

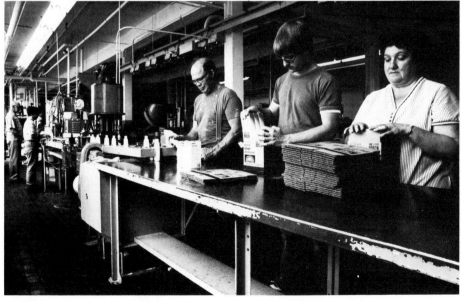

Wright's metal polishes are processed and packaged under close personal supervision. The company is the largest silver polish manufacturer in the United States.

Elektrisola

When manufacturers are planning to relocate, they seem to be attracted to New Hampshire for similar reasons—the availability of land, the presence of a skilled labor pool, the favorable tax climate, and the relatively low costs of transportation and construction.

When Dr. Gerd Schildbach wanted to open his first United States plant to produce Elektrisola's fine insulated copper magnet wire, he was looking for one additional thing—first-generation German-Americans.

Dr. Schildbach, a medical doctor in the German Army during World War II, went into his family's wire manufacturing business after the war. In 1948 he set up a copper wire factory in Eckenhagen, Germany, and by 1967 he had additional facilities in Italy and Switzerland.

Within four years after he first began to sell his copper magnet wire to U.S. companies for use in electromagnetic devices such as motors and transformers, Dr. Schildbach had built up a considerable business in this country. With the value of the dollar declining in the early 1970s, exporting wire became less desirable than the prospect of building a factory in the United States.

Elektrisola's insulation application machinery is company built. Because of this and the fact that non-English-speaking Germans had to do the initial

When Elektrisola decided on Boscawen as the site for its first United States facility, the town voted to rezone U.S. Route 4 land to industrial uses. The remodeled Cape on the property is used for offices.

training in New Hampshire, German-speaking Americans had to be found and hired to overcome communication barriers.

Dr. Schildbach and his two sons came to the United States many times in the early 1970s in search of a factory site. Two areas east of the Mississippi River were known to have significant German populations: Milwaukee, Wisconsin, and around Manchester, New Hampshire. Because a greater number of German-speaking Americans lived in the Manchester area, Dr. Schildbach settled on New Hampshire and bought acreage

The Elektrisola plant has undergone frequent expansion. In 1982 the company added 37,000 square feet, 33 more employees, and twice the wire-producing capacity.

and an old Cape Cod-style house in rural Boscawen for his new plant.

Then came the task to locate these German-speaking people. Herbert F. Margenau, the plant manager and first Elektrisola employee hired by Dr. Schildbach, quite coincidentally met a German-speaking waitress who gave him names of some German-speaking friends and relatives who might be interested in working at the Boscawen facility. Margenau made the contacts and ultimately found 15 to be employed by the company; they were trained in the summer of 1976 by four German supervisors. The plant opened in August with 28 employees and a monthly production capacity of 70,000 pounds of wire.

In seven years Elektrisola has seen three major expansions. Its employment has risen to 138 and its production to 650,000 pounds of wire a month. The high-speed work involved in drawing the wire to ultra-fine sizes creates other startling statistics: One drawing machine can literally produce a mile of wire a minute, and 60 of them can produce enough wire in an hour to stretch from Concord to Ireland.

Elektrisola is Boscawen's largest employer, and the Boscawen facility alone produces 25 percent of the international company's wire.

The O.K. Tool Company, Inc.

Late in the 1930s Thurston V. Williams was a young man looking for something that he and his father, a trained civil engineer, could do for work. At the time, Williams' father was farming. "He wasn't a farmer," Williams points out. "He was farming."

Williams convinced his father to buy land in Milford, New Hampshire, and

The Souhegan River and a field of corn formed the backdrop for The O.K. Tool Company after it moved to Milford in 1949 and helped add to the town's economy of making things out of wood and granite by making tools out of metal.

run a fruit stand, later turned into a fried clam roadside stand. Then the younger Williams struck out on his own in 1938 with Straightway Motors, an automobile dealership named for this stretch of unusually direct New Hampshire road.

But the war came along, and Williams saw a new opportunity—making machine tools. One of the suppliers of Straightway Motors had just repossessed four machines from a failing foundry; Williams bought them all for $100 and set them up in the back of his garage.

Both Williams and his new partner, Forrest A. Hussey, had worked in a machine tool business in Wilton when they began their venture. Initially, what became known as Williams and Hussey Machine Corporation subcontracted with larger companies to make parts for bombs, clips to hold submarine nets together, and other small machine-made parts for the war effort.

Even though Williams retained his automobile business until 1950, the machine tool enterprise grew quickly. After the war Williams and Hussey had 100 worn-out machines and turned toward the manufacture of parts for knit-

A Milford shop foreman sharpens an O.K. cutting tool on an O.K. tool and cutter grinder. The company builds 50 to 100 such machines each year and sells them worldwide.

ting machines, running gear for trailers, and locomotive rings for the 68,000 locomotives still crossing back and forth across the country.

But Williams was on the lookout for a product his company could make and market itself, and he found one in The O.K. Tool Company of Shelton, Connecticut, one of Williams' first in a long list of acquisitions. The O.K. Tool Company moved to Milford in 1949 and Williams and Hussey became its subsidiary.

Founded in 1901, when New England was a manufacturer's mecca and the center of the machine tool industry, The O.K. Tool Company was probably the first American manufacturer to develop an inserted blade planer tool, where the actual cutting edge is made of high-tungsten steel and the body of the tool is made of a less expensive steel. Formerly, planer tools had been forged of a single, and singularly expensive, steel.

By the middle 1950s the textile business that had fostered the growth of the New England machine tool industry had virtually disappeared, but, through numerous acquisitions, The O.K. Tool Company has greatly diversified its markets. It manufactures cutting tools, machine tools, woodworking machinery, and other tools that produce almost anything made of metal or wood on any market today.

Thomas Hollis, Jr., came to Milford in 1975 to become president of The O.K. Tool Company, and Williams became chairman of the board. Like Williams, Hollis had sold cars during the 1930s and began his own machine tool business during the war; before coming to Milford, he was president of the small-tool division of Connecticut's Pratt and Whitney, one of the founder companies of machine tool manufacturing in the United States. Today the Milford-based manufacturer employs 260 people in three plants and has annual sales of about $15 million. With 19 stockholders, The O.K. Tool Company is one of the largest privately held corporations in its industry.

Loon Mountain Recreation Corporation

When he was appointed Assistant to the President by Dwight D. Eisenhower in 1953, Sherman Adams had been a resident of the White Mountains logging town of Lincoln for 30 years and knew the surrounding woods probably as well as he knew the back of his hand.

He had been the woods superintendent and timberlands manager for the Parker-Young Company, a major logger in northern New England, from 1928 to 1945. After four years in the New Hampshire House of Representatives, he left the mountains in 1945 to become a member of the United States Congress.

He returned to New Hampshire and became its governor in 1949 and, when New Hampshire staged the first presidential preference primary in 1952, Sherman Adams was on board from the beginning to help maneuver Dwight Eisenhower into the presidency.

But even while he served as Eisenhower's assistant and confidante— "You are, you know, much, much more than my good right arm" Ike wrote Adams in 1957, "You are—in truth— the 'Rock' on which I lean"—Sherman Adams was a New Hampshire man who lived in a renovated stone barn while he served in Washington. In 1958 he resigned from the Eisenhower Administra-

With a magnificent view of the White Mountain National Forest in the background, skiers undertake one of the 28 Loon Mountain trails.

Built in Berlin, Germany, in 1934, this train operates on a quarter-mile route moving skiers from one Loon Mountain base area to another.

tion and returned to New Hampshire, and six years later he set off on snowshoes to find a good site for a ski resort.

By 1961 the Kancamagus Highway, a 34-mile scenic White Mountains National Forest route connecting Lincoln and Conway, was completed and Adams knew that Interstate 93 was being built north to Lincoln. Loon Mountain, a gently sloping and well-forested peak, was large enough to accommodate 5,000 skiers, long enough for two-mile trails, and only three miles from the path of the future interstate.

During eight months in 1967, 90 acres on Loon Mountain were cleared and graded into 10 trails. A German-made gondola, still the longest in New Hampshire, and two chair lifts were ready to begin operations two days after Christmas that year, but the 500 skiers who showed up the first day had to content themselves with eating from a small lunch cart and sharing a single washroom.

Loon Mountain attracted 30,000 skiers in its first year. Since its beginnings, when expert skier friends of Adams called his area "medicare mountain," Loon has added a more difficult choice of trails demanding far greater skill to negotiate. It now offers free shuttle service to neighboring villages and to Cannon Mountain, an advanced area north of Franconia Notch.

Loon Mountain now has 28 trails for skiers at all levels of skill, and six lifts. The area has helped an economy painfully winding down from the logging industry's heyday: Loon currently employs over 300 in the winter and 70 year-round. With snowmaking covering 75 percent of the area, the resort saw its business jump 50 percent last year: The 1981-82 season brought 223,000 skiers to Loon Mountain.

In 1981, aware of his advancing years, Adams turned the management reins over to Phil Gravink, now president and general manager of the corporation. With his experience in managing larger ski areas in his home state of New York, and two years' service as President of the NSAA, he has added strength and leadership to a thoroughly competent staff, thus assuring Loon a secure position as one of the best-managed recreation areas in the nation.

Copy supplied by Loon Mountain Recreation Corporation.

Elliot Hospital

For years, so little was known about Dr. John Seaver Elliot of Manchester that the hospital built in his memory was thought to have been constructed in the name of a totally different Elliot.

Even today, little is known about the man, a Vermont native who studied medicine with a doctor in tiny Boscawen, New Hampshire, went on to Dartmouth and Philadelphia's Jefferson Medical College, and began practicing in Manchester in 1844, two years before it became a city. Most of his wealth, left to his wife Mary at his death in 1876, was gained through intelligent real estate investments, it is said, and when his wife died four years later a large bequest in her will made the Elliot Hospital possible.

Twenty-seven acres of orchards, cattle pasture, and fields on the brow of a hill in southeastern Manchester were bought at auction for the new hospital, which was chartered in 1881 and the cornerstone laid in 1888. During the years before additional bequests made building the actual hospital possible, trustees spent much of their time dealing with canker worms in the orchards and selling hay and apples.

The first patient to use the new facility was a woman from Whitefield, in New Hampshire's northern climes, who traveled more than 100 miles to Manchester for an eye operation.

In 1892 the average length of stay at the Elliot Hospital was 40 days, and there was a great deal of bronchitis, pneumonia, rheumatism, and amputa-

In 1983 Elliot Hospital was steadily expanding its regional services, such as Level II nursery care and federally designated trauma and emergency care.

Chartered in 1881, Elliot Hospital opened in 1891. Built on the brow of a hill east of downtown Manchester, the hospital was clearly visible to the community it served.

tions. There was also an occasional case of senile dementia, nervous prostration, and, as it was then known, "La Grippe." Although growth was slow, Elliot Hospital treated 87 patients in 1891, 300 in 1903, and more than 1,600 in 1923.

Today the average length of stay at the Elliot Hospital is less than seven days and, with 291 beds at the end of 1982, it is the second largest hospital in the state.

From the start, people of Manchester were generous in their support. On annual Donation Days, the people gave to the hospital in great profusion—quarts of canned vegetables, barrels of flour and potatoes, kindling wood and tons of coal, barrels of apples and pecks of cranberries, and bottles of whiskey, rum, and brandy.

The ladies' auxiliary first met in 1890, which led to the Associates of Elliot Hospital in 1894, an organization active to this day. Initially gathering at the hospital to sew linens, the Associates endowed free beds for indigent patients and an indigent sick fund, found the Elliot its first dietitian and paid her salary for four years, helped pay the annual coal bill, and funded the 1904 operating room, the 1908 maternity ward, the 1909 nurses' home, and the 1918 children's ward. The Associates today number over 500 and continue to perform nearly 20 services voluntarily for Elliot Hospital.

Hanover Inn

In 1772 the town of Hanover had 20 families, one church, two taverns, and a three-year-old college named Dartmouth.

Six years later, to remove the burden of management from Dartmouth founder Eleazer Wheelock's shoulders, college officials convinced General Ebenezer Brewster to come up to the wilderness college from Connecticut to be college steward.

In those days, a college steward managed provisions and nearby crops that would feed college students. Most definitely, Dartmouth officials did not wish Brewster to apply his talents to the creation of yet another tavern to lure students away from their studies.

Yet create another tavern is precisely what Brewster did on the half-acre of land the college used to lure him to Hanover. He opened a tavern in the two-story wooden building he erected adjacent to the Dartmouth green in 1782. That building's subsequent history is a series of unusual arrangements to keep it growing until it became what it is today—

Back when the Hanover Inn was known as the Dartmouth Hotel, it was occupied by visitors to the college and by some college professors, who boarded there for $12 a week. The hotel, seen at far left and adorned with white columns, burned to the ground in 1887 and was rebuilt by Dartmouth College two years later.

one of the most successful and well-filled country hotels in the nation.

Eventually, Brewster's tavern passed to his son Amos, who managed to overcome his father's refusal to enlarge the operation by convincing the general to visit his niece in Haverhill, a town 25 miles north. Frontier travel being what it was in the early 19th century, Amos was able to move his father's tavern to another site and begin his new Dartmouth Hotel next to the green before the general returned.

The Dartmouth Hotel then went through the hands of numerous managers before 1857, one of them being Rosina Fuller, who had to marry her bookkeeper "as the shortest method of effectual settlement," one account has it, when his accounts became hopelessly complicated with those of the hotel. Then, in 1857, the enterprise fell to Horace Frary, who as manager over the next two decades put some $40,000 into enlarging and improving the facility.

Despite Frary's efforts, though, the life of the structure was no more stable than it had been before his tenure. On one January night in 1887 when the temperature dropped to 20 degrees below zero, the hotel burned to the ground in a seven-hour conflagration that left Dartmouth College with no place to board

Students and hotel guests pose in front of the building renamed the Hanover Inn in 1903. Always classed as an inn rather than as a resort hotel, the Hanover Inn still experiences a summer swell and takes on at least 100 more employees for the summer months.

alumni, guests, and even professors who lived there. Reluctantly, the college eventually bought the lot for $5,000 and built a hotel large enough for 100 people there in 1888.

The new hotel, the Wheelock, was remodeled greatly in 1901 and took on its present name, the Hanover Inn, in 1903. Another expansion in 1924 prepared the building for the birth of New Hampshire's ski industry in the late 1930s. The hotel ran a ski program and set up dorms for skiers until the advent of World War II in 1941.

The Hanover Inn's average visitor now stays two days instead of a month or a season as that average visitor did at the turn of the century. The regular visitor, one who would come year after year, also is a creature of the past. But the Hanover Inn's 101 rooms are all taken more than 75 percent of the time, a statistic boosted in part by the fact that Dartmouth is now a year-round institution.

Davidson Rubber Company
Subsidiary of Ex-Cell-O

Davidson, a pioneer in the development of front and rear urethane bumper parts and fascia products, was chosen to develop a flexible front end for Chrysler Corporation's research safety vehicle in 1978. This fascia is a urethane skin over a urethane energy absorber.

Fewer than 20 years after Charles Goodyear discovered the process of vulcanizing rubber, Charles Hamilton Davidson and his brother, Dr. Herman Elva Davidson, patented a rubber syringe "adopted by the Government for Army use," its post-Civil War advertisement read, "in preference to all other kinds of soft rubber syringes."

The company founded by the Davidsons in Charlestown, Massachusetts, moved to Dover in 1957. Today it is the world's second oldest rubber company and one of the largest employers in New Hampshire.

In the pioneering days of the United States rubber industry, Davidson Rubber fashioned more than 50 items—including a pocket atomizer for hay fever sufferers—from the vulcanized substance. But in 1905, when this diversification spelled financial trouble for the company, Alexander McAdam Paul assumed the reins and reduced the product line to six items, among them syringes and syringe tubing, no-colic baby bottle nipples, and hot water bot-

tles, which once comprised a full 60 percent of Davidson's production.

Paul was a member of one of the two families that have owned Davidson Rubber; his grandson, E. Paul Casey, would later become president of Ex-Cell-O Corporation, Davidson's current parent company.

The fact that 100 percent of Davidson's production today supplies the automotive industry tends to mask the firm's former versatility. During World War I, Davidson manufactured collapsible water bags for military use. During the 1930s the company made bathing caps, badminton cups, and orthopedic devices. By 1952 bathing caps alone constituted 35 percent of production, and Davidson offered them in Waikiki tan, Pacific blue, surf white, island green, coral red, and Hawaiian yellow.

Davidson first ventured into the transportation industry in the 1940s, initially making rubber pads for railroad cars and then, in 1948, filling its first order for the automotive industry—molded sponge pads for Ford and General Motors' Fisher Body.

Though half of Davidson's production was given over to walkie-talkie parts and jungle food bags during World War II, by 1954 half was devoted to the auto industry. Within three years work had expanded so greatly that new quarters were necessary, and Davidson president Virginia Paul Dee chose the recently vacated Sawyer Mills in downtown Dover for the new site.

Shortly after the move to New Hampshire in 1957, Davidson engineers developed and patented a one-piece molded urethane armrest that soon became a standard part on American cars. Its padded dashboards, seat cushions, head rests, consoles, and, most notably, its flexible bumpers, or "fascias," have made Davidson the world's largest supplier of both exterior and interior automotive trim. The two plants in New Hampshire at Dover and Farmington employ 1,800 people, and other North American plants employ another 1,000.

The feeding bottle advertised in American Druggist *in 1887 was one of Davidson's 50 products before the turn of the century.*

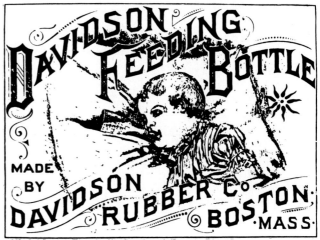

Buckbee-Mears Company/Nashua Division

When Harry Coronis was a student at Dartmouth during the early years of the Great Depression, he bought himself a shop and earned money by pressing the pants of his fellow students.

After his graduation in 1936, Coronis returned to his native Nashua and opened Coronis Cleaners. But even though he ran the shop for more than 25 years, he knew he didn't want to spend his entire life in dry cleaning. So in 1963 he started a company that has become one of the largest manufacturers of flexible electronic circuits in the nation.

The Nashua Division of St. Paul-based Buckbee-Mears Company began as Industrial Reproductions, Inc., based on Harry Coronis' hobby, photography. IRI's first product was a screen that Sprague Electric Company used to print hybrid microelectronic circuits. Coronis and his initial three employees would photograph the circuit by means of fine-

On the premise that modern competition requires continual improvement in product quality, Buckbee-Mears places unusual emphasis on quality control. Here, a technician inspects flexible circuits.

The Nashua Division of Buckbee-Mears Company grew out of Industrial Reproductions, Inc., a fine-line photography business that evolved from Harry Coronis' (seated, right) avocational interest in photography.

line photography, reduce it, and imprint it on a stainless-steel mesh.

Industrial Reproductions sold $60,000 worth of these "thick-film hybrid screens" in its first year of business, and the screens were the firm's only product. Today the screens comprise only 20 per-

cent of its volume; 80 percent of it is custom-design flexible circuits.

Flexible circuits are strips of copper embedded in mylar that replace wiring in electronic component connections. They are used primarily in peripheral equipment for computers, in test instruments, in communications industry equipment, in medical instruments, and in aerospace applications—in short, in any electronic application where limited space, weight constraints, or continual motion require a lightweight circuit that can fold to fit where a rigid circuit board can not.

IRI became involved in flexible circuit manufacture in 1976, six years after its merger with Buckbee-Mears Company. As part of Buckbee-Mears' Precision Components Group, the facilities in Nashua and in nearby Hudson are one of only 27 independent flexible circuit manufacturers in the United States, as compared to more than 400 manufacturers of rigid circuit boards.

The Nashua and Hudson facilities of Buckbee-Mears employ more than 150 people, all of whom participate in regular "quality circles" designed to maintain and improve the quality of products manufactured there. A $150-million corporation with 2,500 employees, Buckbee-Mears has facilities in New Hampshire, California, Illinois, Minnesota, New York, Georgia, Massachusetts, Pennsylvania, Florida, Nebraska, Singapore, and West Germany. The two New Hampshire plants underwent a major expansion in 1982.

Annalee Mobilitee Dolls, Inc.

Annalee Davis Thorndike, creator and designer of Annalee Dolls, is quick to credit the late puppeteer Tony Sarg for inspiring the young schoolgirl from Concord, New Hampshire. The impression he made during a stage show was enough to start her on a career of doll making.

That was 1936, about the same year that Roosevelt's New Deal programs were helping to build New Hampshire's downhill skiing industry. And it has been Annalee Thorndike's continuing attention to what occupies the state's residents both at work and play that has made her flexible-doll business a continuing success.

While she and her husband Charles Thorndike, who moved from Boston to Meredith, New Hampshire, to farm in 1938, tried to make a go of the family's hatching-egg business, Annalee continued to make dolls and sell them herself in Concord and Boston. And when the poultry business went the way New England's textile mills had slightly earlier

(south, that is) Annalee and her husband turned to doll making on a full-time basis.

Although New Hampshire was one of the first states in the country to support its cottage industry in arts and crafts, banks in the state remained reluctant to finance craft businesses. The Thorndikes scraped together what money they could from friends and relatives and squirreled away bits of cloth and thread for the dolls whenever possible. But when the State Planning and Development Commission chose to use a set of her skiing dolls, with minature chairlifts and other accessories, for a promotional display at Rockefeller Center in New York City, Annalee's dolls began to take off.

The first dolls weren't flexible, but they are today. The first puppets she made soon gave way to her own unique type of felt dolls with the whimsical painted faces; and wire framework was added for flexibility. They are made of felt, flannel, and cottons.

Originally sold to department stores and banks for window displays, they soon caught the eye of individual buyers. By 1954 Annalee incorporated the doll-making enterprise as a business, and in 1971 a retail operation was added to the barn-like complex of buildings where some 250 people make the dolls in

Meredith.

The collection of dolls, which includes mice, skunks, ducks, dragons, elves, Santa Clauses, butterflies, and snowflakes, changes annually, with about 175 different ones being offered each year. They are always engaged in various sports, in different positions, and they range in size from three inches to six feet high. They have been used to decorate Disneyworld displays, a window at Jordan Marsh Department Store in Boston when a new wing was being added (these dolls were poised on miniature scaffolding and I-beams), and a White House Christmas party for children during the Ford Administration.

Still a family business, Annalee is head of design, Charles Sr. is president and general manager, son Chuck is vice-president of manufacturing and design, and second son Townsend is vice-president of marketing and finance.

The newly opened Annalee Doll Museum houses a comprehensive collection of Annalee's creations over the past 50 years.

From her first accessory—a pair of miniature skis and boots—Annalee went on to create entire populated landscapes especially suited to window display, such as this one for a California swimwear manufacturer in the early '50s.

The array of expressions that are the dolls' trademark are reflections of the artist's own face and the result of many hours studying facial lines before a mirror.

Dartmouth-Hitchcock Medical Center

"There are men and there will always be men to whom the country service is the first choice," Dr. John P. Bowler wrote in the *New England Journal of Medicine* in 1929. "They will find in the country practice more opportunity, more usefulness, more appreciation, and more satisfaction than their city brethren who ... can never be so close to their patients."

Two years earlier Dr. Bowler and four other Hanover physicians had founded the Hitchcock Clinic, the first multi-specialty group practice in New England. These five physicians also formed the clinical staff of the Mary Hitchcock Memorial Hospital and the clinical faculty of the Dartmouth Medical School. Dr. Bowler served concurrently as dean of the medical school, president of the hospital's staff board of governors, and president of the clinic. He engaged in teaching, research, and patient care, three pursuits that define academic medicine and continued a distinguished tradition in medicine which had taken root in Hanover late in the 18th century with the establishment of this nation's fourth medical college.

Today the medical school, the hospital, and the clinic, in conjunction with the Veterans Administration Hospital in nearby White River Junction, Vermont, form the Dartmouth-Hitchcock Medical Center. This confederation, the only academic medical center in New Hampshire, is involved in service, education, and research programs which provide northern New England with comprehensive medical services as well as with the benefits of several outreach programs tailored specifically to the needs of the region.

The medical center began ambitiously, if simply, enough. In 1796 a Cornish, New Hampshire, doctor named Nathan Smith approached the trustees of young Dartmouth College with a proposal to create a professorship in the theory and practice of medicine. Dr. Smith was a Massachusetts native who apprenticed in Vermont to a Putney doctor, practiced in Cornish, traveled to Boston and became one of the earliest graduates of Harvard Medical School, and then returned to his Cornish practice. He built one of the largest practices in New England, and regularly traveled throughout New Hampshire and Vermont as a consultant.

The Dartmouth Medical School as it appeared around the turn of the century. Erected in 1811, it was the first building constructed solely for the purpose of medical education in this country.

Dr. Smith's proposal was greeted with hesitancy by the trustees, but nonetheless, he went to Edinburgh, Scotland, then the world capital of medical knowledge, to study the scientific basis of medicine in preparation for assuming the professorship. He returned in the fall of 1797 to begin his medical lectures at Dartmouth, and taught virtually the

The first diagnostic X-ray examination performed in America took place at Dartmouth on February 3, 1896. Professor Edwin B. Frost (left) and his brother, Dr. Gilman D. Frost, used the procedure to examine the fractured wrist of a youth who had fallen while skating on the Connecticut River.

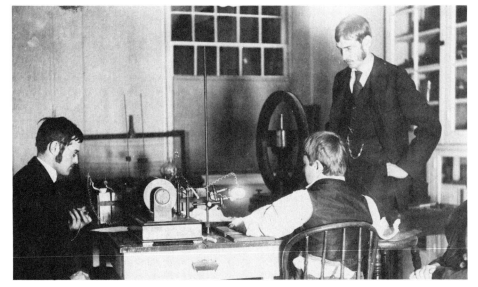

entire curriculum of the medical school for the next 12 years.

Dr. Smith's first students—64 graduated with bachelor degrees in medicine from 1797 until the doctor left Hanover in 1813—were schooled in his belief that a medical institute at remote Hanover would attract doctors to the area and would improve medical care for its inhabitants. One student's diary records how Dr. Smith taught his students on horseback as they traveled together to homes on the New England frontier; the kitchens and bedrooms of these rude houses became their clinical classrooms.

After leaving Dartmouth, Dr. Smith went on to participate in the founding of three other medical schools: one at Yale in 1813, one at Bowdoin in 1821, and one at the University of Vermont in 1822. However, he left the Dartmouth Medical School prepared for growth. He had persuaded the State of New Hampshire to buy $600 worth of medical equipment for the school and to provide $3,450 for the construction of its own building. This facility was the first to be constructed in the United States specifically for medical education.

For 150 years this building served as a center for medical education and research. Such noted physicians as Oliver Wendell Holmes, Dixi Crosby, and Frederic Lord lectured on portions of an ever-expanding medical curriculum in the classrooms of that facility and pursued their scientific interests in its laboratories. Despite the construction of the Nathan Smith Laboratory in 1908 to accommodate additional research space, the medical school outgrew the old building by the middle of this century. In 1961 the students and faculty moved to a new complex which had been built near the hospital and clinic.

While there always was space for education and research in the old medical school, clinical training often was less available. At first, medical students traveled with faculty members to the homes of their patients. Later, faculty members established small hospitals in Hanover. These hospitals, however, never sur-

Mary Hitchcock Memorial Hospital, circa 1893.

vived the departures of their founders. The school needed a permanent hospital and this need, combined with the foresight of the school's dean, Carleton Pennington Frost, led to the establishment of the Mary Hitchcock Memorial Hospital in 1893.

Dr. Frost had begun the Dartmouth Hospital Association in 1885 and bought

Dr. John P. Bowler, founder of the Hitchcock Clinic.

land for a hospital over the next five years. It was he who persuaded Hiram Hitchcock, a successful hotel proprietor who was born in Claremont and had lived in Hanover since 1871, to build a hospital in the memory of his late wife.

Hitchcock's life had taught him to appreciate the counsel of doctors. His eyesight deteriorated during his career as a teacher at Black River Academy in Ludlow, Vermont, and doctors felt a southern climate would help stem the decline. Hitchcock went into the hotel business in New Orleans and then created New York City's Fifth Avenue Hotel. Both of Hitchcock's children by his first wife, Mary, had died in early childhood, and then, in 1887, Mary died of pneumonia.

His wife's death and his excellent relationship with Hanover doctors persuaded Hitchcock to give a hospital to the community and to the medical school. Opened in May 1893, the hospital was one of the first completely fireproof hospitals in the United States.

Even though the hospital was felt to be far too large for the community when it was built, Mary Hitchcock served 108 patients in its first year. Although hospitals were built in Franklin, Claremont, Woodsville, Saint Johnsbury, Whitefield, and Plymouth shortly after 1900, admissions to the Hanover hospital continued to grow. Daily average occupancy rose from 5.5 patients in 1893 to 40.7 in 1913.

The reason for the growth was that Mary Hitchcock clearly never was exclusively a community hospital; it was from the start a regional hospital as well. Even in the first year, 48 patients hailed from different New Hampshire towns, 34 from various Vermont towns, and the rest from other states. By 1934 patients at the hospital came from 71 New Hampshire and 55 Vermont towns. In 1968 less than 10 percent of the 8,500 patients served at Hitchcock came from Hanover or from Norwich, the Vermont town directly across the Connecticut River.

Despite this growth and the existence of a large population in need of medical service, the medical community at Hanover was plagued by the trend toward urbanization of medicine and the view that rural medicine was somehow less challenging—indeed, stultifying.

Then, in 1914, the American Medical Association told Dartmouth Medical School that because of the area's inaccessibility, its small population, and the corresponding size of Mary Hitchcock Memorial Hospital, clinical opportunities were not sufficient in Hanover to permit the college to award doctor of medicine degrees. The medical school became a two-year program. By 1925 only five doctors were on the hospital's staff.

One of them was Dr. John Bowler who, with Dr. John Fowler Gile and three other doctors, reversed the drain of physicians from the Upper Valley by creating the Hitchcock Clinic in 1927. Though the AMA had once called group practices ''medical soviets''—clinic members' salaries are prorated, and none of them have private practices—Drs. Bowler and Gile realized that only by

The Dartmouth-Hitchcock Medical Center today.

forming such a multispecialty group could ''a medical atmosphere throughout the countryside'' be restored.

Because of the clinic, it was hoped, town doctors would be encouraged to remain in their towns due to the presence of a group of experts in a variety of medical specialties nearby. Experts could handle a wider variety of cases in the region than any number of individual doctors working in isolation, and their combined medical knowledge could be applied to individual problems in such a way that area medical care in general would be improved. Expenses would be kept down because clinic doctors would share equipment and administrative expenses. The clinic, Dr. Bowler said, would show men ''who prefer the country that there modern medicine can still be practiced and that there can be found the physical equipment and facilities and technical laboratories on which they may

A young patient turns the tables on a physician.

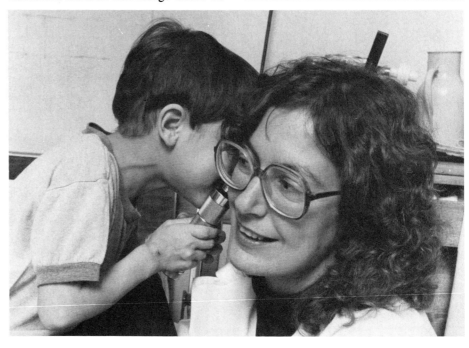

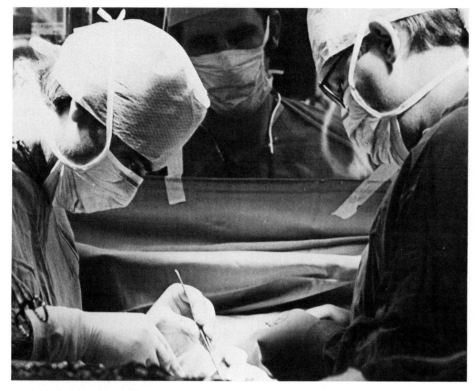

Dartmouth-Hitchcock Medical Center surgeons performed more than 9,600 operations in 1982.

Medical school personnel observe the operation of a fluorescence-activated cell sorter. One of the cell sorter's most important research uses is to detect the presence of a small number of cancer cells long before a recognizable tumor forms.

depend."

With the clinic's formation, seriously ill people in northern New England could now be treated closer to home. By 1943 the Hitchcock Clinic had 23 members and its own building, and it had begun to bring Hanover back to the medical community concept that Dr. Nathan Smith had originally foreseen. In 1955, 49 doctors were practicing at the clinic; today there are more than 125. In 1973, the same year that Dartmouth-Hitchcock

Medical Center was formed, Dartmouth Medical School awarded its first M.D. degrees since 1914.

The decision to reinstate the M.D. program stemmed from the hospital's growth and from the additional clinical opportunities at the White River Junction Veterans Administration Hospital, with which Dartmouth had begun a joint internal medicine residency program in 1946. By 1979 the VA Hospital was providing 27 teaching faculty and 37 staff to the medical school. Today 30 percent of all Dartmouth medical student clinical training takes place at the 224-bed VA.

Reaching out to the growing area it serves is still as strong a commitment as it was in 1797. The 411-bed Mary Hitchcock Memorial Hospital served patients from 228 New Hampshire towns, 172 Vermont towns, 33 other states, and nine foreign countries in 1982. In addition, its staff made more than 4,000 home health visits and serviced nearly 8,000 outpatient visits in outreach clinics in area communities that year. Dartmouth Medical School sponsors community programs for child neglect and abuse, cancer detection and control programs, alcohol treatment programs, well-child clinics, and senior citizen self-health care programs all over the region. There is a computerized network linking 35 primary care practitioners in New Hampshire, Vermont, and Maine to the medical school to provide continuing education. In addition, the school has developed a vigorous constellation of research programs in the basic and clinical sciences. These programs attracted $7.2 million in support from national sources in 1982.

As this history of New Hampshire goes to press, the state's academic medical center is entering a period of transition and modernization. The next 10 years will see the continuing development of the interdependence of the center's components and the growth of its facilities and its programs as it prepares to answer the medical needs of northern New England during the coming decade and the coming century.

M/A-COM Omni Spectra, Inc.

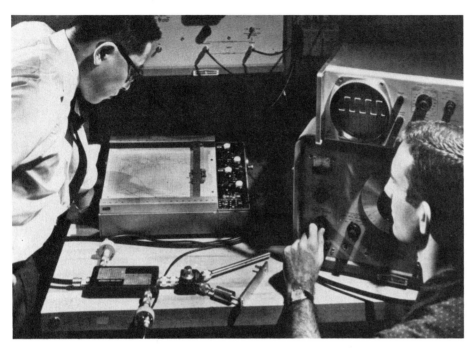

Two Omni Spectra employees test product performance on an X-Y recorder for microwave signal-carrying devices used in radar and navigation equipment. The man at left, James Kubota, is in charge of new-product development.

From World War II until the early 1960s, systems for transmitting and receiving the ultra-high-frequency radio waves we now know as microwaves had had little progress. Built in what the industry calls "wave guide," the systems were generally large, rectangular, and rigid.

Omni Spectra came into being in Ann Arbor, Michigan, in 1962 to build components for a new type of microwave system, one that used coaxial cable. Soon, however, it became clear to the original four founders of the new enterprise that even though the coaxial structure was simpler, cheaper, highly flexible, and smaller, the microwave market offered nothing that could connect these supple conduits to anything else in the system.

Within months of its creation, Omni Spectra offered 15 different miniature connectors and components and became the market leader in miniature radio fre-

quency connectors, a position it continues to hold. The firm has developed parts for every U.S. satellite and space vehicle launched. And, in its efforts to diversify, it has entered the TVRO (television receive only) field, where six or seven satellites are used to transmit up to 100 different channels to home television. Within years, Omni Spectra's current president Richard M. Hale predicts, it will take a computer to figure out *TV Guides* as TVRO systems penetrate the market.

In 1974, as labor and union problems made leaving Michigan imperative to the company's continuing success, Omni Spectra's then-president William P. Sharpe warmed to the efforts of the state of New Hampshire and the town of Merrimack and decided to relocate the company in the southern New Hampshire town. A series of acquisitions since that move has brought a total of six facilities under Omni Spectra's wing; the corporate headquarters remains in Merrimack.

Hale came to Omni Spectra from Addington Laboratories in 1977 and shares Sharpe's feelings about the state, having worked at a boys' camp in Peterborough in his teens. He has helped guide the diversification of the organization and its course while it was acquired

by M/A-COM of Burlington, Massachusetts, in 1980.

While 100 percent of Omni Spectra's sales originally were for military uses—connectors, couplers, power dividers, and wave guide components for radar and missiles—its activity in telecommunications and TVRO has gathered 40 percent of sales over the past few years. Omni Spectra manufactures components for 3,000 TVRO systems each month, systems that retail at anywhere from $3,800 to $8,000 each. One of the company's six facilities also makes components for "land mobile telephones," actually radios that permit communication between vehicles and stationary sources.

Omni Spectra is the third largest operating company of M/A-COM, a Fortune 500 corporation with 9,000 employees and more than $500 million in sales in 1982.

In front of Omni Spectra's corporate headquarters in Merrimack, a technician installs one of the firm's products, a polarizer, on a TVRO earth station antenna, one of its newest markets.

The Tamposi Company, Inc. _____

After Nasi Tamposi, 16 years old and alone, came to the United States in 1907 from a small Roumanian village in Macedonia, it took 13 years of work in Nashua's mill and shoe shops before he could afford to buy and work farmland on the edge of town.

Forty years later, when World War II had ended and Nashua's industrial future began to look grim, Nasi Tamposi's son Samuel began a career that took him far from the dairy farm to the virtual center of southern New Hampshire's economic rebirth.

Sam Tamposi's work, collected under the name of The Tamposi Company, Inc., has been credited with bringing to New Hampshire the majority of the new industries that have located here in the past two decades. Buying and selling seem to be in Tamposi's blood; his investments in property in his native city made him the biggest individual taxpayer in Nashua in the late 1970s.

But buying and selling began modestly enough for Sam Tamposi. As a boy, he sold salves and birdseed door to door and then turned to selling the *Ladies' Home Journal* and *Collier's*. At the nearby Nashua airfield, Tamposi sold airplane rides; then he learned to fly and began ferrying the city's business executives around; then he turned to buying and selling the airplanes themselves.

At his father's wish, Tamposi sublimated his love of flying and stayed home to help work the farm during the war. But in 1946, during the slow winters, he began selling Electrolux vacuum cleaners in New Hampshire and Vermont, earning such large commissions that he was whisked away to New York by the company and formally commended.

Tamposi then began selling insurance and buying and selling land, mostly among farmers in the Nashua area. He incorporated his residential real estate company, Tamposi Associates, in 1955, but after building his first industrial park before the end of the 1950s, Tamposi turned to commercial real estate.

The Tamposi Company has been a central figure in the negotiations that have brought about the expansion or relocation of many major corporations in New Hampshire. The firm has developed nine industrial parks and over 100 buildings in New Hampshire alone and recently has expanded its own operations

Sam Tamposi, a farmer for 27 years, is still working the land. Each harvest year he participates in farming operations at the Tamposi Farm.

to Florida.

After much haggling with local property owners, Tamposi built an automotive shopping center in Nashua in 1965, a place where different dealers could gather to do business. Built on wasteland, the shopping center was a pioneering concept that showed Tamposi's sensitivity to local needs and careful planning.

A major land owner in the region, The Tamposi Company has continued to demonstrate this concern in its civic efforts. Sam Tamposi subjected himself to a roast in 1979 which brought $15,000 to the coffers of the planned Nashua Arts and Science Center, and he has donated land in the city center for the center. He also has given more than 750 acres to conservation commissions in three area towns. Tamposi was Southern New Hampshire Citizen of the Year in 1975. The award was presented by President Gerald Ford.

Waterville Valley

Even the Indians didn't live in Waterville Valley: That's how remote it was. In 1819, when settlers finally followed the Mad River to its source and discovered this high mountain valley, only 25 miles square, the only ones who followed them were fishermen—and only then after the railroad had made its way north to Plymouth in 1853.

The railroad's coming also allowed the town to send a representative to the state legislature for the first time; even though Waterville Valley had been incorporated since 1829, the two-day stage ride to Concord discouraged even the most politically active of the town's residents.

Tiny Waterville Valley never grew larger than the 96 people who lived there, cleared the land, and tried to farm in 1830. In fact, as late as 1950, when only 11 people claimed to live there, it was a figurehead residence for some just

The largest of Waterville Valley's two ski areas is Mt. Tecumseh, with 34 trails, 9 lifts, and 130 acres of ski runs covered with machine-made snow. The Mt. Tecumseh ski area was the site of the first professional freestyle event ever held, and has hosted World Cup ski races in 1969, 1978, 1980, 1982, 1983, and 1984, attracting the best international ski racers.

so it could stay a township in the state of New Hampshire's eyes.

Yet the little town today contains the largest ski area in New Hampshire, both in terms of its facilities and in terms of the number of skiers who come each year. When former Olympic skier Tom Corcoran formed the Waterville Company, Inc., in 1965, Waterville Valley had no zoning, no building codes, no public utilities. It just had mountains, 4,000-foot ones, one of which Corcoran had climbed up and skied down when he was a freshman at Phillips Exeter Academy.

For an entire century before Corcoran returned to Waterville Valley in 1965, the town had been comprised of a single hotel, a group of cottages, and a small collection of devoted and regular visitors. Unlike other White Mountain resort towns, Waterville Valley was populated by a rather soft-spoken type of tourist, many of them Transcendentalists who came from Thoreau's and Emerson's Concord, Massachusetts.

"To those who wish to spend time on hotel piazzas displaying dry goods, engineering matrimonial alliances, or dawdling away time, if such are consider-

After the Waterville Inn burned during the 1967 ski season, new inns were built to house the thousands of skiers and summer vacationers who travel there each year. In 1969 Waterville Valley hosted the finals of the World Cup Circuit, the premier event in skiing that year, and it has since hosted more international ski competitions than any other resort in the United States.

ing coming to Waterville, let me say at once and emphatically, don't," one regular wrote in the *Newton Graphic* in 1887. "Altogether life at Waterville is wholly unlike that anywhere else, and is certainly a beautiful example of sweet Christian living during vacation months."

The guests at the Waterville Inn and in the cottages around it have always sought to keep it the way it was. Even though logging had not penetrated the valley until the 1890s, one paper company's desire to put a logging railroad into the valley made the guests band together to convince the United States Congress to put all but 500 of the Waterville Valley's 43,000 acres into the White Mountain National Forest, the first eastern national forest in the country. Today the many ski trails in Waterville Valley operate under a special-use permit issued by the United States Forest Service.

It was not until the 1930s, however, that the Waterville Inn opened for the winter. In 1937 the New Deal's Civilian Conservation Corps put the first ski trail on 4,004-foot Mt. Tecumseh, and the first rope tow was installed on a small ski slope behind the Waterville Inn in 1941. And, during the war years, when the inn was operating on a shoestring and could not afford much paid help, its guests doubled as staff, making the beds, manning the front desk, working in the kitchen, and scouring the north country for affordable beef cattle and chickens.

It was after the war that Tom Corcoran first skied Mt. Tecumseh. A graduate of Dartmouth and Harvard Business School, Corcoran was a member of both the 1956 and 1960 United States Olympic ski teams, and placed fourth in the 1960 Olympic Giant Slalom, the highest placing any American man has achieved to date in that event.

Later, as assistant to the president of the Aspen Skiing Corporation, Corcoran kept wanting to come back east and open a destination resort in New England. He flew over the White and Green Mountains and chose Waterville Valley.

When the Waterville Inn was probably still Greeley's Hotel—begun by one of the valley's first settlers who took fishermen into his farmhouse—guests came only during the summer. Much of the surrounding forest was virgin, not logged before the 1890s.

As these skiers prepared for a day on the slopes in 1940, skiing was a very new sport in New Hampshire. They probably walked up the mountain and skied down the Mt. Tecumseh ski trail cut by the Civilian Conservation Corps in 1937; Waterville Valley's first ski lift was a rope tow installed in 1941.

Corcoran applied for and received a Forest Service Use Permit in 1966 and commissioned Sel Hannah, the dean of ski trail design and a resident of nearby Franconia, to lay out the network of trails on Mt. Tecumseh. Corcoran had four chairlifts, one T-bar, 21 trails, and 30 acres of snowmaking installed that first year and brought in 76,000 visitors; in Waterville Valley's first season, 1966-67, it attracted more skiers than any other ski resort in New Hampshire, and has every year since.

The 100-year-old Waterville Inn, the valley's only accommodations, burned to the ground on the crucial Washington's Birthday weekend during the very first winter season. The planned village of Waterville Valley began to take shape the following summer with the building of the first two new inns and the Fourways restaurant. The first resort condominium complex in New England, the Village Condominium, was started in 1969. Over the next 10 years, the town of Waterville Valley built a municipal water system, an advanced wastewater treatment plant with connecting sewer lines, a public building with complete fire and police facilities, and an elementary school.

Today the destination resort of Waterville Valley has 37 ski runs on two mountains, 10 ski lifts of various kinds, 60 kilometers of groomed ski touring trails, and 60 instructors in its ski school. The valley also has five inns, three restaurants, the White Mountain Conference Center, 500 condominium units, 65 single-family homes, 18 clay tennis courts, a nine-hole golf course, a pond for swimming and boating, and a children's summer day camp.

Corcoran's master plan for Waterville Valley calls for building more facilities in the area, all in keeping with the architectural styles present in the valley to date. There are plans to build a pedestrian commercial center of shops and restaurants, more hotel and condominium accommodations, new sports facilities, and expanded alpine skiing and ski touring—all in the high mountain valley surrounded by the peaks of the White Mountain National Forest.

James River Corporation

Rising from wild Umbagog, the northern lake that straddles New Hampshire and Maine, the Androscoggin River tumbles 171 miles to the Atlantic Ocean by falls and rapids that have rendered it practically unnavigable, except to the most venturesome canoeists.

But a river that is doom for boats is a dream for hydropower, and where there is hydropower in New Hampshire, mills are not far away. Within the city limits of Berlin, the Androscoggin drops 300 feet in two miles, and it is along that stretch that the sawmill that later became Berlin Mills Company, then Brown Company, and ultimately James River Corporation, was first built in 1852.

Logs to make lumber were floated down the Androscoggin even before 1852, but the coming of the railroad to this northern city made it possible to place mills closer to the source of trees. By 1868 William Wentworth Brown, a Maine manufacturer of the curved joists called "knees" that were used in wooden ships, had come to Berlin to buy into this first sawmill, and by 1888 he was sole owner of Berlin Mills Company's sawmill and an undetermined amount of its acreage.

Before its 1980 acquisition by James River Corporation, the Brown Company owned 600,000 acres of timberland, areas that taken together contain more land that the state of Rhode Island. Buying land, though, was determined not as much by the quality of timber as by its proximity to rivers that would drain into the Androscoggin's headwaters at Umbagog.

Originally, lumber production demanded that the longest possible logs be floated downstream. The Berlin Mills Company also made hardwood flooring, door and window frames, and other building materials. But even though the

mills were making 2,000 window frames a day as late as 1904, the firm set its sights away from lumber and on the manufacture of paper as early as 1887. The first Berlin Mills groundwood pulp facility was built in 1887, its first paper mill in 1891, and its first sulphite-process pulp manufacturing plant in 1892.

Groundwood and pulp make newsprint, the product of both the 1891

The earliest known photograph of the facility that became the Brown Company dates from 1870, two years after William Wentworth Brown bought part of H. Winslow Company's 1852 sawmill.

Riverside and 1903 Cascade Mills, the latter for many years the largest newsprint mill in the world. But pulp and

In the tradition of other New England manufacturers, the Berlin Mills Company built its own store and boarding house, both in 1853; its first major office complex, shown here, was probably built after 1900.

During the snow melt each year, Brown Company employees went to the woods for the annual log drive. Improvements in cutting have increased yield more than sixfold since the late 1930s, and manpower needs have been drastically cut. The last log drive was in 1963.

paper manufacture increased the demand for wood so greatly that the company pushed farther into the northern wilderness, cutting logs into four-foot lengths to float them down small streams, to be captured during each year's high-water season, towed across Umbagog, and let loose down the Androscoggin to be channeled to the Berlin mills by man-made islands in the active river.

In 1910, four years after buying timberland, cutting rights, and a hydropower site in Canada, the Berlin Mills Company built North America's third mill for the

James River's Cascade Mill, two miles down the Androscoggin from the Berlin facilities at the top left of the picture, originally was the largest newsprint manufacturing facility in the world.

production of "kraft" paper, a term taken from the German word for "strength." Kraft paper manufacture is an alkali process that allows chemical recovery and produces a higher-quality paper used for wrapping and converted to myriad other uses. Foreseeing that

Canada could produce newsprint more inexpensively, the Berlin Mills turned to kraft paper production, and the high quality of its product made it the industry standard for 20 years. In 1921, after the firm's name had been changed to the Brown Company to skirt anti-German feeling about anything "Berlin" after World War I, a Brown engineer named Corbin invented a method to crimp kraft paper to give it absorbency, or "wet strength." Corbin's name was spelled backwards and given to this first paper towel, and all towel and tissue from the Berlin/Gorham group of James River today carries the "Nibroc" label.

It often has been said that without the Brown Company, there would have been no Berlin. Indeed, the company's precarious financial position nearly brought the city down, too, in the early years of the Depression. In 1931 New Hampshire Governor John Winant had the state endorse Berlin's notes so that Berlin could buy Brown Company stumpage, use unemployed people to log and transport it, and sell it to the papermaker. But while the action kept the city afloat, it only stemmed Brown's decline temporarily: The firm went bankrupt in 1935 and ultimately reorganized to open again in 1940.

James River Corporation, the largest independent producer of specialty papers in the United States and the largest single purchaser of pulp, bought the Brown Company in 1980 to add to its enterprises its first pulp-making facilities. Today the so-called Berlin/Gorham Group is the state of New Hampshire's largest paper company and the only one in the state to make both raw pulp and finished papers.

The Berlin and nearby Gorham plants produce nearly 200 different grades of paper. Twenty percent of its production is devoted to the Nibroc absorbent papers, 30 percent to flat offset printing and specialty papers, and 50 percent to the manufacture of pulp both for its own facilities and for sale to other paper makers. Employment at the Berlin mills alone stands at 1,700 in 1983.

Ashuelot National Bank

Back in 1833, when Ashuelot Bank was founded, the city of Keene was smaller than the town of Richmond to the south. The railroad had not yet made its way to Keene. But in 1848 Thomas M. Edwards, Ashuelot Bank's third president, brought the Cheshire Railroad into town, and men intimate with the prosperity that followed the railroad into Keene have been involved with the bank ever since.

In the beginning, Ashuelot Bank's founders were more political than commercial in orientation. The first president was Samuel Dinsmoor, who had been a member of the United States Congress in 1811 and 1812 and had just completed his third term as governor of New Hampshire. At his death in 1835, his son and namesake Samuel Jr. became the bank's president after having been its first cashier for two years.

A Dartmouth graduate and lawyer as his father was, Samuel Dinsmoor, Jr., also served three terms as the state's governor. And Edwards, president from Dinsmoor's death in 1853 until 1859,

Samuel Dinsmoor, three-time New Hampshire governor and United States congressman, was the first president of Ashuelot Bank.

also sat in the United States Congress.

Ashuelot Bank became a national bank in 1865, and it may have been the new federal charter that saved it from falling victim to the exploits of the infamous Mark Shinborn, born Maximillian Schoenbein in Germany and a notorious bank robber since his arrival in the United States in 1860.

In 1864 Shinborn stole $40,000 from the savings bank in nearby Walpole, New Hampshire. Though repeatedly arrested, Shinborn escaped twice and then set his sights on Keene's Ashuelot National Bank. From a wax impression of the bank's keys, Shinborn cast duplicates in New York and returned to accomplish his deed—only to find too little money for his robber's standards.

Shinborn even returned to the bank a second time, but was confounded by the opposite problem—too much currency to remove at once. He never succeeded in robbing Ashuelot National Bank and was

On November 23, 1933, when the directors of Ashuelot-Citizens National Bank met to celebrate the institution's centennial, Prohibition was only 12 days away from repeal, so ginger ale was the drink of the day. The dinner was held at the residence of bank president Windsor H. Goodnow on Summer Street in Keene.

finally arrested in 1895, at the age of 68, and jailed at the New Hampshire State Prison.

Ashuelot National Bank merged with Keene's Citizens National Bank in 1924, and its combined and contracted name was shortened to Ashuelot National once again when its new building on West Street was completed in 1962. Today Keene is a city of 22,000 people, while Richmond is a town of 500, and the bank's 224 shareholders are mostly local people or descendants of local people.

Steenbeke & Sons, Inc.

James Steenbeke had been running a restaurant with his wife Mary on Broadway in New York when he decided to scout New England for a less hectic place to raise his three sons, now all involved in the family business.

It was just two years before the federal government's interstate highway program came into being that James and Mary Steenbeke left their New York City restaurant business in search of a better place to raise their three sons.

In 1954 Boscawen, New Hampshire, the town they chose, was a crossroads north of Concord. It was there that state highways 3 and 4 forked away from each other, 3 going north to the White Mountains and 4 going west toward Vermont.

James Steenbeke purchased a general store and a house on Route 4. At that time Boscawen had three other stores, all of them fairly well restricted to groceries; with Concord a good 30 minutes away, Steenbeke's fulfilled a need for a store that would sell not only groceries but

gasoline, kerosene, some simple building supplies such as nuts and bolts, and clothing and shoes.

Steenbeke put his family to work planting corn and potatoes and taking care of 2,000 laying hens. Steenbeke's store sold eggs, homegrown vegetables, meat (even chicken from their own small farm), grain, salt licks, and medicine for cows.

Steenbeke's Grocery Store, as it was then called, did $50,000 in business in its first year, but, when Interstate 93 built past Boscawen in 1960, the days of the general store were numbered. It was sheer accident that, three years earlier, Steenbeke had become involved with lumber, the principal concern of the company today.

A local sawmill operator told Steenbeke that he knew of someone in need of a load of finished lumber. Arrangements were made to pick up the load at a wholesaler and it was delivered to the builder. Steenbeke saw that the potential for profit was greater in lumber than it had been in eggs, so he took lumber on as another line. Early in the 1960s Steenbeke even

became a contractor for a time, building summer homes that, in those blissful days of low inflation, sold for $6,000.

Steenbeke's three sons, who attended the University of New Hampshire (two of them worked with other corporations), all eventually came to work in the growing retail lumber business, and with them, the founder went into the "home center" concept, pulling all the separate functions—plumbing, electrical, paint, and other building supplies—together under one roof.

Steenbeke & Sons was one of the first enterprises in New Hampshire to develop the home center concept, and it now is one of the 300 largest building material dealers in the country. During the 1970s, the firm expanded into three other New Hampshire towns and today employs nearly 100 people. The original general store still stands across the street from the main building on Boscawen's Route 4, a complex that includes a retail store of 20,000 square feet and facilities to manufacture roof and floor trusses, doors, windows, and counter tops.

James and Mary Steenbeke brought three citified sons to rural Boscawen in 1954 and promptly put them to work gathering eggs and planting vegetables to sell in the general store. At one point, when Steenbeke was building houses, it was possible to buy seemingly everything—from a one-cent stick of gum to a $6,000 home—from the store.

HADCO Corporation

HADCO Corporation, the largest independent manufacturer of printed circuit boards in the United States, was founded in 1966 by Horace H. Irvine, a Princeton graduate. Working as a production control manager for a small printed circuit board manufacturer in Lawrence, Massachusetts, Irvine was acutely aware of the rapid increase in demand for printed circuit boards. He also was aware that many companies which needed printed circuit boards were having trouble obtaining prototypes of designs that could be tested prior to production. So he along with two coworkers from the Lawrence plant, Al Marshall and Dana Davis, formed a new company—HADCO (for Horace, Al, and Dana), which offered high-quality, quick-turnaround prototype production of printed circuit boards.

The company, located in Cambridge, Massachusetts, grew rapidly. As the computer and electronics industries continued to develop, the demand for printed circuit boards continued to expand. In response to this demand, HADCO began to manufacture production circuit boards from the prototypes it built. By 1968 HADCO had outgrown its Cambridge facility, and was searching for a new location. The search ended when Irvine found six acres of land in Derry, New Hampshire. Derry offered an excellent opportunity for continued growth. There was a pool of skilled workers, many of whom were left jobless by the decline in New Hampshire's shoe industry, and there was plenty of room for expansion.

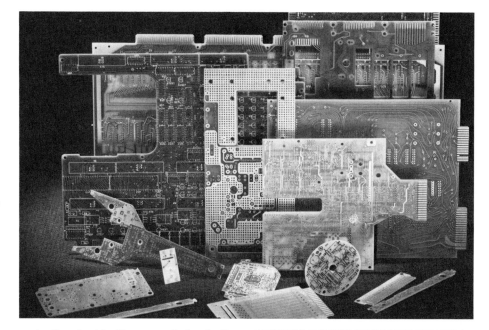

HADCO Corporation manufactures printed circuit boards for use in many diverse applications.

As the plant in Derry was being built, 30 newly hired workers commuted to the old location in Cambridge for training. By July 1969 HADCO employed 80 people. Five years later, in 1974, the Derry plant had undergone two expansions and 300 people were employed. The firm's growth was based on its commitment to develop new printed circuit technology, respond to customer needs for quick turnaround, and provide high-quality printed circuit board production.

As technology advanced, the market needed printed circuit boards capable of meeting increasingly demanding applications. Faster, smaller, and more efficient boards were required. In 1977, in response to these requirements, HADCO began the manufacture of multilayer printed circuit boards. These multilayer boards, substantially more complex than those previously produced, required a commitment to higher-technology production equipment. HADCO's commitment to higher technology paid off. The company continued to grow, and much of its growth was attributable to orders for multilayer printed circuit boards. In

1980 HADCO built its new corporate headquarters in Salem, New Hampshire, and also acquired a plant in Owego, New York, to help supply the demand for traditional two-sided printed circuit boards.

HADCO has since expanded its capabilities to include the production of backplanes, systems which facilitate the interconnection of multiple circuit boards. In addition, the firm acquired Lamination Technology, Inc., of Santa Ana, California, a supplier of laminate material for the production of printed circuit boards.

By 1982 HADCO had come full circle, opening a new technology center which offers state-of-the-art prototype production, the very concept that started the company in 1966. The firm, which began with only three employees, now employs more than 1,000 people, 700 of them in its New Hampshire facilities. HADCO's plan, its officials say, is to continue its history of innovation in printed circuit board technology and manufacture, and to explore new opportunities that offer growth for the company.

The firm continues to produce state-of-the-art prototype boards for printed circuits, as it has since its founding in 1966.

Northeast Electronics, Division of Northern Telecom

In the days when operators connected telephone calls and acted as troubleshooters for the growing telephone system, the products Northeast Electronics manufactures today had not even been conceived.

Once automatic switching took the operator's place, though, phone company technicians had to carry several cumbersome pieces of equipment either up the poles or down into manholes to diagnose problems—noise on the line, poor connections, or no connections. Better ways of testing communications equipment presented an opportunity for Dutch physicist and engineer Everhard Bartelink both to set up his own company and to leave the metropolitan New York area to be closer to the places where he hiked and skied.

Bartelink immigrated to the United States in 1937 after having worked for seven years as an engineer at the Netherlands Phone Company. After six years at General Electric, Bartelink was called to the Massachusetts Institute of Technology to assist in the development of radar technology during World War II, but six postwar years in the American communications industry made him eager to be on his own, developing his own products.

Bartelink began Northeast Electronics on the sunporch of his Bronxville, New York, home in 1952 and moved it and its three other employees to the basement of the Concord, New Hampshire, Municipal Airport in 1953. Originally, the company did research on a contract basis but by 1955 Bartelink and his engineers had invented the first in what would be a long line of precision telecommunication test devices.

In the trade, the invention was called the TTS-1, a telephone test system that fit in a case the size of a cigar box and weighed only six pounds, as against the combined weight of various earlier pieces of test equipment—40 pounds. The test equipment was made for Bell Telephone Laboratories to measure transmission performance of the longest overseas voice cable ever laid, and the first to be

Everhard Bartelink founded Northeast Electronics in 1952.

This is the first transmission test set produced by Northeast Electronics.

laid at mid-ocean depths. (The transcontinental cable was built in part by another New Hampshire company, Simplex Wire and Cable.)

Northeast Electronics was presented with a major opportunity in 1956, when a consent decree held that Western Electric Company could sell its test equipment only to Bell Telephone. Independent phone companies now needed a source of this equipment, and Bartelink's firm stepped into the void.

Today the company markets more

The latest technology is used in the design of today's sophisticated telecommunication test systems.

than 80 basic types of telecommunications test equipment, from compact, portable units for field use to computer-based systems. Sales have grown from $2.5 million in 1965 to $20 million in 1982, and the organization employs 350 people.

Northeast Electronics, which became a division of Northern Telecom Inc. in 1973, was Concord's first high-technology engineering/electronics firm and is known for the early application of transistors to replace vacuum tubes in telephone test equipment and of minicomputers in testing systems.

Barretto Granite Corporation

In New Hampshire, the Granite State, quarries are remembered for the structures fashioned from their stone. When John J. Barretto was young, he worked as a tool boy at the Chelmsford, Massachusetts, H.E. Fletcher quarries, granite from which came the pillars and pedestals of Boston's Quincy Market and the massive walls of that city's First National Bank.

By the age of 20 Barretto had worked his way from tool boy to stonecutter to foreman during the construction of the Boston Post Office; then he became a granite polisher and sawyer to foreman again. Finally, when he was production superintendent at the Fletcher quarries, he, his father, and his brother Dennis struck out on their own for Milford, once known as "the Granite Town of the Granite State." A few years later younger brother Gene joined the company as comptroller.

In 1908 reinforced concrete was yet unknown, and the granite business was booming. Milford had 15 quarries, and it

Barretto Granite Corporation offers design services for any scale and complexity of stonework. Quarrying and finishing facilities incorporate jet-piercing torches, wire saws, carbide-tipped tools, hydraulic splitting machines, and diamond wheels for final finishing.

has been said that the town's granite can be found in every city and town in the United States—in foundations, in buildings, in statues and monuments, in bridges, in curbing, and in paving blocks.

Milford's Kittredge Quarry, the "Kitledge" Quarry of Barretto Granite Corporation since 1952, probably was the first ever opened in the town. Started in 1810 by Peter Burns on a small corner of the eight-mile-wide Burns Hill south of town, Kittredge Quarry's first product was a set of steps, hauled to nearby Nashua by a team of oxen. Its stone created Boston's South Station, and was the material of paving stones for New York City streets.

By 1901 Kittredge Quarry had shipped 1,000 tons of granite a month by rail to numerous road and building projects throughout New England and the Eastern Seaboard. But the introduction of cheaper building materials, bituminous products, and the Great Depression stopped most of the Milford quarries short; Kittredge Quarry managed to hang on through the 1930s but closed in 1941.

The Barretto brothers' father had operated a shop that produced monuments from rough granite in Westford, Massachusetts, and it was his finishing skill that first brought the family to Milford. In 1951 they bought the Rossi stonecutting sheds and hired 10 local stoneworkers; one year later they purchased the idle Kittredge Quarry on Burns Hill.

John F. Barretto, son of John, joined the company at that time as a tool boy. He learned various trades and today is vice-president in charge of purchasing and personnel. John F. Jr. now is learning the business and his younger brother, Jayson, expects to follow him.

Today Kittredge Quarry is one of only two active quarries in a state that used to

Thousands of tons of Kitledge "Tapestry Grey," one of the largest volumes of granite employed on a single project, were supplied by Barretto for the Washington, MacArthur, and Eisenhower halls at West Point.

harbor scores of them, and is the larger of the two. "The granite lies under the surface in large, even sheets," the 1901 history of Milford says of the Kitledge Quarry, "and it is possible to quarry dimension stone, as it splits with remarkable evenness."

Barretto Granite quarries, cuts, engraves, carves, polishes, and ships granite of varying colors and configurations from two of the three quarries it owns. It also does finishing work on granites quarried in other states and foreign quarries. And it was the advent of improved technology, such as the substitution of jet-burners and silicon carbide-fed wire saws for dynamite, that has enabled the quarry to be viable when others have given themselves over to swimming holes.

At first, Barretto Granite produced memorials and later turned to building stone. But the passage of legislation creating the Interstate Highway System in 1956 made highway products a larger part of the company's market. Now 75 percent of its stone goes toward highway curbing and bridges, 20 percent goes into buildings, and five percent is used for memorials.

Four of the granites Barretto offers are quarried in New Hampshire: Grey, "Tapestry Grey," buff, and blue-grey stones are from Kitledge Quarry. The

blue-grey stone comes from a band 30 feet wide that cuts diagonally across the huge quarry, which covers from 60 to 70 acres. The fifth granite, a pink-hued stone with the trade name "Milford Pink," comes from a Hopkinton, Massachusetts, quarry.

Barretto Granite employs about 175 people, 25 in the quarrying operation and 75 in finishing work. The Milford quarry produced the stone for Concord's James C. Cleveland federal building and for Manchester's Hillsboro County Courthouse; its biggest job, a five-year undertaking, produced the granite for the United States Military Academy's Science and Academic Building and for three of its residence halls. The stone also makes a 120-foot wall and the semicircular granite platform at Robert F. Kennedy's gravesite in Arlington National Cemetery.

Barretto Granite's sales have risen from $85,000 to nearly $6 million over its 30-year existence in the "Granite Town."

Barretto supplied the granite for the Science and Academic Building at West Point.

The Balsams Grand Resort Hotel and The Tillotson Rubber Company

Neil Tillotson.

High in the White Mountains and just a few miles from the Maine, Vermont, and Canadian borders is the tiny community of Dixville Notch. Early in the 19th century Dr. Jackson, in his great work on the geology of New Hampshire, predicts of this notch "that its grandeur will yet make it a place of large resort."

And so it has. Since 1873 people from all over the world have traveled there to experience the charm and gracious hospitality of The Balsams Grand Resort Hotel. In this unincorporated township of only 26 voting residents, New England's premiere resort hotel and its neighbor, The Tillotson Rubber Company—producer of much of the world's supply of medical examination gloves and balloons—together employ some 650 people throughout the year.

Dixville Notch is a splendid example of New Hampshire in microcosm. A first-class enterprise in tourism is only a stone's throw from a creative enterprise in manufacturing harmoniously integrated in an unspoiled and spectacularly scenic natural environment. Such a bold

and striking combination could have been achieved only through the imagination and investment of one man: Neil Tillotson, a native son of the North Country whose ancestors settled there well over a century ago.

Tillotson's life is one continuous recognition of the value of enterprise and commitment. As a teenager in Beecher Falls, Vermont, he used to buy 1,000-mile railroad ticket books and sell single tickets for 2.5 cents. With railroad ticket offices selling single tickets for 3 cents, the young Tillotson saved his train passenger customers half a penny and made half a penny for himself. With the income from this and from selling coal and Baldwin apples, in 1913 at the age of 15 Tillotson left his home and enrolled in a community college in Lowell, Massachusetts.

At the age of 16, Tillotson secured a job at Hood Rubber Company in Boston and, returning there after a two-year stint in the Seventh Cavalry during World War I, he was the only one of 25 Hood chemists without a college degree. Yet his inventive talents earned him a place in new-product development with Hood; and when the first shipments of raw latex reached Boston Harbor during the 1920s, Tillotson began his lifelong association with the substance.

Hood's efforts with latex were unsuccessful at first, but Tillotson persevered on his own. At his Watertown home, he designed and produced a latex balloon with a cat's face and ears from a cardboard form which he cut by hand with a pair of scissors. He managed to make his first sale of these balloons with an order of 15 gross to be delivered for the annual Patriot's Day Parade on April 19, 1931. Tillotson put his family into production to meet the deadline while he continued his duties full-time at Hood Rubber and worked at home in the evenings on the balloons.

Tillotson incorporated his latex business in 1931 and left Hood the following year. As the Great Depression tightened

free money around Boston, he bought an unlimited bus ticket which took him across the country in search of novelty company buyers for his new balloons. The great majority of those initial customers still buy balloons from Tillotson Rubber Company today.

On trips home to his summer camp in Canaan, Vermont, Tillotson saw the continuing decline of The Balsams' reputation and business. Once an esteemed resort, it had fallen into a state of decay—a circumstance of the times characteristic of so many traditional American plan summer resorts. First built by the Parsons family from nearby Colebrook in 1873 as a three-story farm summer hotel with accommodations for 50 guests, by the turn of the century The Balsams was being developed into a major grand resort under the ownership of Henry Hale. By 1916 the "Switzerland of America" was one of the world's most elegant and inviting settings, with accommodations for 400 hotel guests.

In 1900 much of the land in Dixville Notch that comprised the 15,000 acres of this private estate was purchased from the Brown Paper Company to protect the magnificent view. Surrounding the hotel on all sides are rugged cliffs towering straight up some 600 to 1,000 feet above Lake Gloriette.

Tillotson, mindful of the financial havoc to be suffered by the entire community should The Balsams not operate and hopeful about an opportunity to try his hand in yet another business venture, bought the hotel in a federal foreclosure auction in 1954. The summer operation of The Balsams continued in uninterrupted seasons, and a previous owner, Frank Doudera, was enlisted to come back to the Notch and supervise. Many older guests of the previous successful era returned as well. Tillotson also initiated the first steps of moving to the Notch the finishing operations of his rubber company in Needham, Massachusetts. He located those operations in the facility that used to be The

Balsams' garage and part of the staff quarters. And in 1966, to allow the hotel to operate as a resort in the winter season, he built the Wilderness Ski Area—the 13th largest in the state but opened specifically for guests of The Balsams.

Winter business began to improve steadily, but faltering summer occupancy seemed an intractable problem. The successful manufacturing business helped Tillotson to keep the hotel operation in Dixville Notch on an even keel. While the hotel's fortunes fluctuated from season to season, the factory experienced continued growth and development. Finally, the original manufacturing plant in its entirety was moved from the Massachusetts location to Dixville Notch.

At The Balsams by 1970 the winter operation attracted more guests than the summer, and now the staffing of the hotel for both seasons was primarily done with local people. The professional brigades of employees traveling the circuit from Florida in the winter to New England in the summer would not consider working in the cold climate of a ski resort. So between the resort hotel and the manufacturing plant, Dixville Notch became a major employer in the region. The Balsams benefited immediately from the friendly folks who were now deliver-

The Balsams Grand Resort Hotel.

ing the service and hospitality of the hotel. To direct the operations of the resort Tillotson found a team of young, interested employees: Warren Pearson had been working there since 1966 when he came to direct the first Wilderness Ski School; Stephen Barba had come to The Balsams as a young boy in 1959, when he worked as a caddy at the caddy camp and continued working summer seasons thereafter in a great variety of hotel jobs; Phil Learned was the executive chef of the hotel since it had first opened for the winter. Through the combined attention of these three men and Raoul Jolin and the efforts of many of the valued employees, Tillotson was able to see a major turnabout in the hotel's business. Today The Balsams operates at near capacity in both seasons—offering classic American plan hospitality to social guests in both the summer and the winter and catering to dozens of large groups and conventions in the spring and fall.

And right next door, The Tillotson Rubber Company is operated by two of Neil Tillotson's sons and his partners in business, Tom and Rick Tillotson. The factory operates 24 hours a day, seven days a week, and employs 350 people. Millions of disposable latex medical examination gloves and over a million novelty balloons are produced here each

week. Unique to this plant is a creative system of work schedules which allows the plant employees to work three- and four-day work weeks.

In 1978 Tillotson built a new energy facility that burns 15,000 tons of wood waste per year. Since both the hotel and the manufacturing plant occupy a single complex of buildings, this facility produces electricity for both in addition to process steam for the rubber company and heat and hot water for the hotel. As much as 35,000 gallons of fuel each week is saved by this innovative facility. Also, The Balsams operates its own private telephone company and cable television system.

Dixville Notch is recognized throughout the country as the community that votes first in the nation for all national primaries and general elections. Every four years Neil Tillotson is put in the limelight for this curious distinction. A more appropriate tribute to this independent industrialist, this man of character and vision, this true Yankee entrepreneur, would cite his remarkable efforts in making Dixville Notch what has to be one of the world's most independent and productive communities.

—Stephen Barba

The Tillotson Rubber Company has been producing "Tilly's Cat Balloon" since 1931.

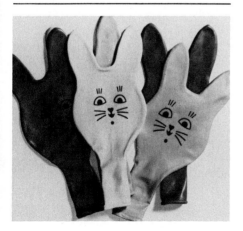

Fimbel Door Corporation

The automobile crept slowly, if not softly, into American life in the years around the turn of the 20th century. But by 1915 what had been a trickle began to turn into a deluge. In less than 10 years the number of registered cars in the United States jumped 300 percent, from 4.6 million in 1917 to 19.2 million in 1926.

More cars created an immediate need for more repair shops and more garages. By 1908 people could buy small, portable garages for $140, and some houses in large cities began to be seen with garages attached to them.

One day in 1923 Edward Fimbel, a building contractor from Irvington, New Jersey, went to an auto show and came out with a franchise agreement with the Overhead Door Corporation that made him the first person in the eastern United States to manufacture and install overhead garage doors. Overhead doors had a special appeal in the Northeast, because during the snow season people had to shovel the white stuff out of the way in order to open the predecessor swing

Through the years Fimbel Door Corporation has devised some unique solutions to different problems, such as this door within a door.

Fimbel Door Corporation's Nashua, New Hampshire, plant is located at 24 Fox Street.

doors and free their automobiles.

Originally, Edward Fimbel (doing business as Overhead Door Company) opened a small 1,200-square-foot factory in Irvington to manufacture wood overhead doors. In 1925 the operation was moved to Hillside, New Jersey, and shortly thereafter the first overhead door in New England was installed at Monson State Hospital in Palmer, Massachusetts.

By the 1950s the Overhead Door Company needed a plant in New England, near Boston and reasonably close to the three northern New England states. In Nashua, a manufacturer of prefabricated houses had just vacated a 40,000-square-foot facility; Edward Fimbel's son Paul, a professional engineer who had been supervising operations at the Hillside facility, came

north to run the New Hampshire plant, which has subsequently doubled its capacity.

By 1968 the company had changed its name to Fimbel Door Corporation and severed all ties with the Overhead Door Corporation. The following year a third plant, a 185,000-square-foot facility, was opened in Whitehouse, New Jersey. Today the corporate headquarters of Fimbel Door Corporation, it is run by the founder's son, Edward Fimbel, Jr. In 1970 the Better-Bilt Door Company of Egg Harbor, New Jersey, became a subsidiary of Fimbel Door Corporation.

Steel, aluminum, and fiberglass doors, as well as door operators and remote controls, gradually were added to the product line. In the late 1970s, keeping pace with demands for expanded energy conservation, Fimbel Door Corporation introduced its Iso-Dor, an energy-efficient door with steel, aluminum, or fiberglass components, available in both active and passive solar designs.

The firm has made overhead doors for every type of structure from a doghouse—this one radio-operated from the dog owner's home—to large industrial doors for airplane hangars. Fimbel Door Corporation is the original overhead door manufacturer in the eastern United States.

Tender Corporation

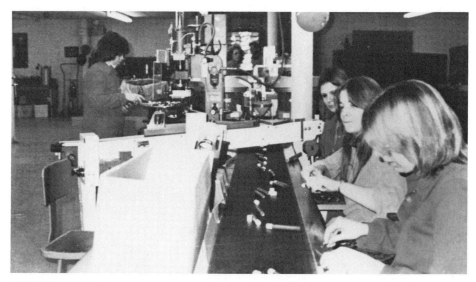

In 1982 Tender Corporation produced two million units of After Bite® in this assembly line. Its original building in Littleton had been a coin and stamp company and then the town's unemployment office.

Vacationing in Florida can be terrifying, as one Ohio woman wrote to a small manufacturer in Littleton, New Hampshire. While she was there, yellow jackets which she must have greatly aggrieved stung her—not once, but 30 times.

Such an attack can be fatal to certain people and certainly a painful catastrophe for anyone, but the woman used the Littleton company's product, and the swelling and pain of the stings stopped "immediately."

The product she used is called After Bite®, which comes in a plastic vial about the size of a magic marker and has been manufactured for only six years. After Bite® is the brainchild of Kenneth Martin Grout, who started a company appropriately named the Tender Corporation in Littleton to manufacture the product.

Grout had run his own business in Danvers, Massachusetts, before 1973, a successful concern named Kenics that manufactured another of his inventions, a mixer with no moving parts that is used to treat sewage wastes among other things. Though Grout received eight patents for his novel "Static Mixer" and

brought to life a field that is now peopled by at least 18 manufacturers, he was interested in leaving Massachusetts' highly populated and industrialized North Shore for a quieter, cleaner, prettier place.

After three years of touring his native northern New England, Grout and his sons settled on Littleton, one of the gateway communities to the White Mountains. Littleton in 1973 had a good hospital, was close to an interstate highway, and had a history of positive attitudes toward both work and light industry.

Grout originally proposed to help Littleton's existing industries design and conceive new products, but his wife's extreme irritation about New Hampshire's notoriously hungry black flies brought about the invention of his fourth new product. One of the Grouts' neighbors suggested the time-honored solution of ammonia, and Grout decided to package the stuff to make it easier to use and more clearly identifiable as relief for insect bites.

In 1975 Grout's Tender Corporation manufactured 50,000 vials of "After Bite®," a formulation combining ammonia with mink oil, an emollient to prevent drying the skin. Tender's first customers were several Littleton retailers, two campgrounds, and a dairy, which sold the little vials out of its milk trucks. Grout gave away thousands of vials that first year.

Tender Corporation now sells some 1.5 million units annually. Twenty-five people are employed to manufacture the product.

After Bite® has been clinically tested and proven effective for relief of the sting and itch of mosquito bites. Nonclinical testimonials from happy consumers—Tender gets three to five grateful letters each day—have established the product's effectiveness in treating black fly, man o'war, wasp, bee, fire ant, "no-see-um," or midge, moose fly, scorpion, and paraponara ant bites. Consumers also praise this wonder product for its effectiveness in relieving the itch of poison ivy, hives, coral scrapes, berry bush rashes, and even herpes simplex.

Late in 1982 Tender Corporation moved from downtown Littleton to the Littleton Industrial Park off Interstate 93, midway between Boston and Montreal.

Whitney Screw Corporation

In the early 1920s, when there were probably 20 companies that manufactured screws to fasten wood to wood or metal to wood, two men working for one of those companies in Worcester, Massachusetts, decided to strike out on their own.

Arthur L. Whitney and Rupert Jeffery chose Nashua, New Hampshire, in 1922 as the place to establish a new wood screw-manufacturing enterprise, having been attracted by the availability of space and the willingness of what was then the Second National Bank to assist a new industry.

Whitney and Jeffery rented space from Eaton D. Sargent, who soon would become Nashua's mayor for four years and would run twice, unsuccessfully, for governor of New Hampshire in 1926 and 1928. Sargent and his boyhood friend, Lester Thurber, were principals of the White Mountain Freezer Company, manufacturers of hand-cranked ice cream makers until 1963, and of the Second National Bank. With Sargent's and Thurber's help, Whitney and Jeffery established the Whitney Screw Corporation and opened up shop in 10,000 square feet of space rented from Sargent and then being vacated by Indian Head Table Company.

Perhaps the flight of the table manufacturer was an omen to Whitney Screw. In the early 1920s wood was still a major raw material for everything from furniture to houses to boats to automo-

Whitney Screw Corporation has 135 cut-threading wood screw machines, shown here, each of which can manufacture from eight to 30 screws a minute.

bile bodies. Whitney's major customers in its early years were furniture makers and the industries that manufactured auto bodies and rail cars.

Whitney Screw hired 25 people in its first year and made screws for furniture, vehicles, radio cabinets, caskets, boats, and buildings. But when steel began to replace wood in the transportation vehicle industry, Whitney Screw began to change the thrust of its marketing. Instead of selling directly to the user, the firm began to market its screws through wholesale hardware and mill supply companies. Today half of its business continues to be conducted through wholesalers.

Today Whitney Screw Corporation is a manufacturer and distributor of 18,000 different sizes and types of screws ranging from one-quarter inch to six inches long, from brass, silicon, steel, and stainless.

The Great Depression also influenced—providentially—the course of Whitney Screw Corporation. The economic strain made it wise to search for metals other than brass and steel, and the beginning of manufacturing silicon and stainless wood screws. That redirection put Whitney in a vital position during World War II, when its Nashua plant was given over totally to the war effort. Its nonmagnetic silicon-bronze and stainless wood screws, were particularly valuable to the U.S. Navy for use on mine sweepers, torpedo boats, landing craft, destroyers, and submarine chasers.

Whitney Screw now occupies 100,000 square feet of building space and produces 100 million screws a year, silicon-bronze ones for boats and ships, heat-resistant and stainless steel screws for food handling, textile, and papermaking equipment, and other steel and brass for a variety of industries and home uses. The company employs nearly 100 people and is the largest of only two cut-thread wood screw manufacturers still in operation in the United States. It is run today by Alan Jeffery and Richard Doyle, the grandsons of founders Arthur Whitney and Rupert Jeffery.

Hampshire Chemical Unit, W.R. Grace & Co.

From a modest beginning in 1958, Hampshire Chemical has become the world's largest manufacturer of amino acid chelating agents. It took a good idea and even more hard work. The original idea for a new process came from Dr. John J. Singer, the rest with the help of hundreds of others.

Chelating agents are chemical compounds whose molecular structure resembles a crab's claw—hence the term "chelate," from the Greek word for claw. Chelates literally grasp metallic elements in solution in their claws, either binding them so as to deactivate them, or "releasing" them in a form in which they can be used. Chelates can remove lead from the bloodstream in the event of poisoning, and they can bind with trace metals in the soil in such a way that plants can take up those metals as nutrients.

Chelates fascinated Dr. John J. Singer and, when new sources of raw materials became available, he used them to create the chelate EDTA at a higher level of purity and lower cost than previously available. With Mark Weisberg, principal in a chemical firm in Rhode Island, Singer perfected the chemical process. And with the aid of Bradley T. Dewey—in charge of U.S. gas defense in World War I, developer of the first water-based latex sealing compound, pioneer in the development of synthetic rubber manufacture and of hermetically sealed containers, and director of rubber production during World War II—Singer and Weisberg established Hampshire

On this site, formerly a field abutting the railroad tracks and the Merrimack River, Hampshire Chemical Corporation produced its first batch of the chelate EDTA in 1958. Although only one of many commercial producers of the compound, Hampshire excelled with a purer, less expensive version.

Chemical Corporation in Nashua, New Hampshire, to manufacture EDTA and other important chelates.

Chelates made by Hampshire are used to brighten and extend the life of paper products, to lengthen the shelf life and stability of foods, cosmetics, and pharmaceuticals, to treat boiler water, and to manufacture textiles and cleaning products.

By 1959 Hampshire was manufacturing NTA, a chelate that was designed to replace phosphates in household detergents because of its superior ability to soften water and its biodegradability. Another early market was the Florida

citrus groves, where chelated iron made this essential trace element available to iron-starved fruit trees.

By 1965, the year the young company was bought by W.R. Grace & Co., Hampshire employed 122 people. W.R. Grace & Co., which operates 260 plants and employs 88,000 people worldwide, made Hampshire part of its Organic Chemicals Division, headquartered in Lexington, Massachusetts. Grace's backing allowed Hampshire to construct a new plant to manufacture NTA and to build, in 1968, a new research center which brought Nashua employment to 200. The company developed a new compound, IDA, in 1976, as a crop protection chemical intermediate, and today it is the only commercial source of this compound.

Hampshire, the only chemical plant in New Hampshire that converts substances to new chemical molecules (as opposed to mixing and distributing chemicals), now manufactures more than 40 chelating agents and another dozen products for use in the areas of agricultural micronutrients, surfactants used in shampoos and other cleaners, and industrial intermediates. Employment at the Nashua facility stood at 300 in 1982.

Much-expanded since its early days in Nashua, Hampshire Chemical is now the largest unit of the Organic Chemicals Division of W.R. Grace & Co., which purchased the chelate manufacturer in 1965.

Jackson Jackson & Wagner

A new dimension of history in the 20th century is the creation of technologies to keep the democratic process working in a mass society. When most Americans were villagers or farmers, the decisions of self-governance were made in town meetings. It was easy to assure communication and participation. Today, with 225 million people living in a highly organized social structure, new ways have had to emerge if democracy is to survive.

Keeping the people informed, soliciting their opinions, and fostering public participation in all types of organizations is the role of the public relations profession. An example of its practitioners is Jackson Jackson & Wagner, an international counseling firm with headquarters in the colonial town of Epping.

Jackson Jackson & Wagner's work illustrates how public relations—often called applied psychology and sociology—has influenced New Hampshire. The firm helps clients bring issues into the court of public opinion so that informed decisions can be made. In this manner, JJ&W has been involved in topics like land use, health care, the environment, energy, education, tax policy, overseas self-help, and many others.

Since its founding in 1956, JJ&W has worked with every sort of organization. But early on the firm took a special interest in public interest groups.

In New Hampshire, its first client was Portsmouth's Theater by the Sea, which needed help with fund raising and the organization of its management and marketing. Another early client was the Society for the Protection of New Hampshire Forests, which needed to gain public support as a leader of the environmental movement.

The firm helped establish the New Hampshire Civil Liberties Union. It helped found SPACE (Statewide Program of Action to Conserve our Environment) and also the Environmental Coalition—an idea copied in many other states. Another nationally known public interest client is the League of New Hampshire Craftsmen.

Today's client list includes many public interest groups along with universities, corporations, hospitals, financial institutions, associations, and political candidates. Among these are many household names.

Speaking of names, one JJ&W specialty is creating them—for stores, brands, causes, and organizations. Another is providing trademarks and graphic symbols—as well as mottos or theme statements to epitomize a cause, a product, or a company.

A subsidiary, Dudley Research, performs formal and informal attitude, behavior, and marketing studies.

The firm and its principals help make New Hampshire known in other places. There are JJ&W offices in Grand Rapids and Albuquerque. Patrick Jackson, one of the founders, has conducted seminars or given speeches and lectures in all but four states. In 1980 he served as national president of the Public Relations Society of America. Isobel Parke and Peter Hollister serve as regional officers of PRSA.

Jackson edits *pr reporter,* an international newsletter now in its 25th year, and also *Channels,* a monthly newsletter for nonprofit organizations. He is co-editor of *Who's Who in Public Relations.* These publications are produced in Exeter, another New Hampshire contribution to this burgeoning profession that is adding a new dimension to the human interactions which make our history.

—Marcia Carroll

When Jackson Jackson & Wagner outgrew its headquarters in Epping (Tributary Farm, below, c. 1713), the firm opened another office in Exeter's historic Dudley House (bottom, c. 1810).

P·A·T·R·O·N·S

The following individuals, companies, and organizations have made a valuable commitment to the quality of this publication. Windsor Publications and The New Hampshire Historical Society gratefully acknowledge their participation in *New Hampshire: An Illustrated History of the Granite State.*

Annalee Mobilitee Dolls, Inc.*
Ashuelot National Bank*
The Balsams Grand Resort Hotel and The Tillotson Rubber Company*
BankEast*
Barretto Granite Corporation*
D.D. Bean & Sons*
Benson's Animal Park*
Blue Cross and Blue Shield of New Hampshire*
Buckbee-Mears Company/Nashua Division*
Catholic Medical Center*
Chubb LifeAmerica*
Citizen Publishing Company*
The Concord Group Insurance Companies*
Concord National Bank*
The Corrigan Company
Dartmouth-Hitchcock Medical Center*
Davidson Rubber Company Subsidiary of Ex-Cell-O*
Edgcomb Steel of New England, Inc.*

Elektrisola*
Elliot Hospital*
Fimbel Door Corporation*
The First National Bank of Portsmouth Portsmouth, New Hampshire
First NH Banks, Inc.
Foster's Daily Democrat*
General Electric*
GTE Lighting Products*
HADCO Corporation*
Hampshire Chemical Unit, W.R. Grace & Co.*
Hampton Historians, Inc.
Hanover Inn*
Ranald C. Hill Opticians, Inc.
Indian Head Banks Inc.*
International Packings Corporation*
Jackson Jackson & Wagner*
James River Corporation*
Kendall Insurance, Inc.*
Kingsbury Machine Tool Corporation*
The Kingston-Warren Corporation*
Laconia Savings Bank*
Maxwell H. Lacy
Loon Mountain Recreation Corporation*
Betsy & John McLane
M/A-COM Omni Spectra, Inc.*
Manufacturers and Merchants Mutual Insurance Company*
Richard P. & Joanne B. Millette
Monadnock Paper Mills, Inc.*

Nashua Corporation*
Nashua Federal Savings and Loan Association*
New England Ski Museum
New Hampshire Distributors, Inc.*
Northeast Community Development Group
Northeast Electronics, Division of Northern Telecom*
Norwood Realty, Inc.
The O.K. Tool Company, Inc.*
Pemigewasset National Bank, The
Public Service of New Hampshire*
Sanders Associates, Inc.*
Simplex Wire and Cable Company*
Steenbeke & Sons, Inc.*
Sugar Run—Fred and Mary Jane Rust
The Suncook Bank*
The Tamposi Company, Inc.*
Tender Corporation*
Waterville Valley*
Watson & Dunlap Realtors
Whitney Screw Corporation*
Winebaum News, Inc.*
J.A. Wright & Co.*
Yankee Publishing Incorporated

*Partners in Progress of *New Hampshire: An Illustrated History of the Granite State.* The histories of these companies and organizations appear in Part 5, beginning on page 169.

N·O·T·E·S

Page

Part I

16 "within eight . . ." Frederick W. Kilbourne, *Chronicles of the White Mountains* (Boston, 1916), pp. 7-8.

16 "the Country . . ." John Josselyn, *New England's Rarities* (Boston, 1865—facsimile of the 1672 ed.), p. 36.

17 "In great . . ." *Belknap's New Hampshire: An Account of the State in 1792*, ed. G.T. Lord (1973), Intro., p. ix.

17 "Nature . . ." Jeremy Belknap, *The History of New-Hampshire* (Dover, N.H., 1812), vol. III, p. 32.

19 "There is . . . kettle" Jere R. Daniell, *Colonial New Hampshire* (Milwood, N.Y., 1981), p. 25.

20- "all . . . thereof" David E. Van Deventer,
21 *The Emergence of Provincial New Hampshire, 1623-1741* (Baltimore, 1976), p. 72.

21 "live . . ." Daniell, *Colonial New Hampshire*, p. 135.

22 "Course . . ." *New Hampshire Provincial Papers*, vol. XIX, p. 478.

22 "full of . . ." Everett S. Stackpole, *History of New Hampshire* (New York, 1916), vol. I, p. 295.

24 "gives . . ." Jeremy Belknap, *The History of New Hampshire* (New York, 1970—reprint of the 1831 Dover edition), p. 392.

29 "The too . . ." Belknap, *History*, vol. III, p. 197.

29 "husbandry . . ." Belknap, *History*, vol. III, p. 156.

29 "Those who . . ." Thomas Jefferson, *Notes on the State of Virginia* (New York, 1964), p. 157.

30 "We have . . ." Harold Fisher Wilson, *The Hill Country of Northern New England, 1790-1930* (New York, 1936), p. 16.

30 "The almost . . ." Wilson, *Hill Country*, p. 19.

30- "Were I to form . . ." Belknap, *History*,
31 vol. III, p. 251.

Part II

38 "together . . ." *New Hampshire Provincial Papers*, vol. XVII, pp. 501-502.

40 "At great expense . . ." *Historical New Hampshire*, vol. XXVII (Fall 1972), p. 152.

41 "As late . . ." Belknap, *History*, vol. III, p. 192.

42 "They love . . ." Jere R. Daniell, "Lady Wentworth's Last Days in New Hampshire," *Historical New Hampshire*, vol. XXIII (Spring 1968), p. 19.

42 "infectious . . ." Jere R. Daniell, *Experiment in Republicanism: New Hampshire Politics and*

the American Revolution, 1741-1794 (Cambridge, 1970), p. 77.

42 "no jail . . ." Lawrence Shaw Mayo, *John Wentworth: Governor of New Hampshire, 1767-1775* (Cambridge, 1921), p. 145.

42 "All commissions . . ." Belknap, *History* (1970 reprint), p. 361.

43 "explicit . . ." *New Hampshire Provincial Papers*, vol. VII, p. 476.

43 "advice . . ." *Journal of the Continental Congress, 1774-1789*, ed. W.C. Ford (Washington, D.C., 1906), vol. III, p. 298.

43 "that it . . ." *Journal of the Continental Congress*, vol. III, p. 319.

44 "independence . . ." Belknap, *History*, vol. I, p. 367.

45 "We do . . ." Belknap, *History*, vol. I, p. 367.

45 "his hand . . ." Frank B. Sanborn, *New Hampshire: An Epitome of Popular Government* (Boston, 1904), p. 279.

45 "oppose . . ." *New Hampshire Provincial Papers*, vol. VIII, pp. 204-205.

46 "full and free . . ." *New Hampshire Provincial Papers*, vol. VIII, pp. 757-758.

46 "The love . . ." "A perfect . . ." *New Hampshire State Papers*, vol. IX, pp. 846, 845.

47 "When the . . ." *New Hampshire State Papers*, vol. IX, p. 846.

48 "at which . . ." Daniell, *Colonial New Hampshire*, p. 7.

48 "done by . . ." Nathaniel Bouton, *The History of Concord* (Concord, 1856), p. 22.

48 "purposed . . ." Bouton, *History of Concord*, p. 23.

48 "never to . . ." Bouton, *History of Concord*, p. 25.

49 "on a great . . ." *History of Concord*, ed. James O. Lyford (Concord, 1903), p. 74.

49 "and now . . ." Bouton, *History of Concord*, p. 28.

49 "chief sachem . . ." Bouton, *History of Concord*, p. 26.

51- "I have . . ." Lawrence Shaw Mayo, *John*
52 *Langdon of New Hampshire* (Port Washington, N.Y., 1937), p. 149.

53 "We obtained . . ." J. Duane Squires, "A Summary of the Events of 1777 . . .," *Historical New Hampshire*, vol. XXXII (Winter 1977), p. 170.

53 "The most active . . ." David L. Mann, "Bennington: A Clash between Patriot and Loyalist," *Historical New Hampshire*, vol. XXXII (Winter 1977), p. 187.

53 "This success . . ." Squires, "A Summary . . .," p. 170.

54- Quotations from Matthew Patten are from:

55 *The Diary of Matthew Patten of Bedford, N.H., 1754-1788* (Concord, 1903), pp. 342-393 passim.

59 "It is, sir . . ." Irving H. Bartlett, *Daniel Webster* (New York, 1978), p. 79.

60 "extension . . ." Stackpole, *History*, vol. III, pp. 72-73.

60 "at variance . . ." Stackpole, *History*, vol. III, p. 132.

61 "lacks fire . . ." Stackpole, *History*, vol. IV, p. 137.

61 "The true . . ." Frank Putnam, "What's the Matter with New England?" *New England Magazine*, vol. XXXVI (1907), p. 649.

61 "will rule . . ." Leon Burr Richardson, *William E. Chandler: Republican* (New York, 1940), p. 361.

62 "I say . . ." William E. Chandler, *New Hampshire a Slave State* (commonly known as *The Book of Bargains*,) (Concord, 1891), p. 69.

63 "Between 1910 . . ." Elizabeth F. Morison and Elting E. Morison. *New Hampshire* (New York, 1976), p. 181.

63 "always giving . . ." Bernard Bellush, *He Walked Alone: A Biography of John Gilbert Winant* (The Hague, 1968), p. 219.

67 "We spent . . ." *The Journals of Francis Parkman*, ed. Mason Wade (New York, 1947), vol. I, pp. 68-69.

67 "Sitting here . . ." Ronald Jager and Grace Jager, *Portrait of a Hill Town: The History of Washington, N.H., 1876-1976* (Washington, N.H., 1977), p. 487.

67 "Haying . . ." Kate Sanborn, *Abandoning an Adopted Farm* (New York, 1894).

67- "tied . . . farm" Ellen H. Rollins (E.H. Arr),
68 *Old-Time Child-Life* (Philadelphia, 1881), pp. 175-176.

68 "the progress . . ." *Washington & Marlow Times*, November 26, 1903.

68 "I was . . ." Tamara K. Hareven and Randolph Langenbach, *Amoskeag: Life and Work in an American Factory-City* (New York, 1978), pp. 152, 153.

71 "I came . . ." Hareven and Langenbach, *Amoskeag*, pp. 202, 203.

71 "I feel . . ." J. Duane Squires, *The Granite State of the United States: A History of New Hampshire from 1623 to the Present* (New York, 1956), vol. II, p. 674.

72 "given . . . valiant" Daniel Webster, *The Works of Daniel Webster* (Boston, 1881), vol. II, pp. 502, 504.

72- "another scow . . ." Henry David Thoreau,
73 *A Week on the Concord and Merrimack Rivers* (New York, 1966), p. 177.

Page

73 "more pleasing . . . banks" Thoreau, *A Week*, pp. 301-303 passim.

73 "we passed . . . sun" *Journals of Francis Parkman*, vol. I, p. 9.

74 "and asked . . . hospitable" *Journals of Francis Parkman*, vol. I, p. 68.

75 "apparently . . . conscience" Nathaniel Hawthorne, *Passages from the American Note-Books* (Boston, 1900), pp. 538, 542.

75 "Picking . . ." Horace Greeley, *Recollections of a Busy Life* (New York, 1868), p. 39.

75 "Yes . . ." Jager, *Portrait of a Hill Town*, p. 21.

75 "wending . . . again" Charles Carleton Coffin, *History of Bascawen and Webster* (Concord, 1878), p. 206.

76 "Any person . . ." *Laws of the State of New Hampshire*, June Session, 1878, Chap. 38, pp. 170-171.

76 about tramps Haydn Pearson, *That Darned Minister's Son* (Garden City, N.Y., 1950), pp. 194-195, 198.

77 "skimming . . ." Wilson, *Hill Country*, p. 280.

77- "All went . . ." Richardson, *Chandler*,
78 p. 645.

78 "To assemble . . ." Jager, *Portrait of a Hill Town*, p. 162.

79 "To see if . . ." Squires, *The Granite State*, vol. II, p. 755.

Part III

84 "It is . . ." Webster, *Works*, vol. II, pp. 418-419.

84 "I dread . . ." Mayo, *John Wentworth*, p. 93.

89 "endeavor . . ." Wilson, *Hill Country*, p. 35.

101 "If our old . . ." Hareven and Langenbach, *Amoskeag*, p. 11.

103 "a portable . . ." *Report of the Fish and Game Commissioners of New Hampshire*, June 1883 Session.

Part IV

118 "chiefe project . . ." *Annual Report of the Superintendent of Public Instruction*, June Session, 1876 (Concord, 1876), pp. 296-297.

118 "The promoting . . ." Squires, *Granite State*, vol. I, p. 96.

118 "Knowledge and learning . . ." Article 83, New Hampshire Constitution.

119 "physiology and hygiene . . ." *Annual Report of the New Hampshire Commissioner of Education*, 1884.

122 "were unable . . ." Squires, *The Granite State*, vol. II, p. 652.

125 "college where . . ." *History of the University of New Hampshire, 1866-1941*, ed. Fred

Page

Engelhardt (Durham, 1941), p. 8.

126 "agricultural school . . ." Engelhardt, *History*, p. 87.

126 " . . . all the agricultural . . ." Engelhardt, *History*, p. 92.

132 "under pretence . . ." Charles B. Kinney, Jr., *Church and State: The Struggle for Separation in New Hampshire, 1630-1900* (New York, 1955), p. 37.

134 "no person shall . . ." Kinney, *Church and State*, p. 108.

135 "Earthquake in . . ." Elizabeth C. Nordbeck, "Almost Awakened: The Great Revival in New Hampshire and Maine, 1727-1748," *Historical New Hampshire*, vol. XXXV (Spring 1980), p. 28.

135 "Impressions . . ." Nordbeck, "Almost Awakened," p. 43.

135 "one Vain Boaster . . ." Nordbeck, "Almost Awakened," p. 38.

135- "new settlements . . ." George H. Williams,
136 "The Seminary in the Wilderness," *Harvard Library Bulletin*, vol. XIII (Autumn 1959), p. 377.

137 "The wilderness . . ." Williams, *Harvard Library Bulletin*, vol. XIII, p. 400.

139 "A poetic fancy . . ." Belknap, *History*, vol. III, p. 39.

139 "the savage . . ." Thomas Cole, "Essay on American Scenery" (1835), reprinted in *American Art, 1700-1960*, ed. John McCoubrey (Englewood Cliffs, N.J., 1966).

142 "A stern . . ." Hawthorne, *American Note-Books*, p. 561.

142 "She could . . ." John Albee, "Memories of Celia Thaxter," in Celia Thaxter, *The Heavenly Guest with Other Unpublished Writings* (Andover, Mass., 1935), pp. 167-168.

143 "this solemn . . ." Celia Thaxter, *Among the Isles of Shoals* (Boston, 1873), pp. 140-141.

145 "In Cornish . . ." Hugh Mason Wade, *A Brief History of Cornish, 1763-1974* (Hanover, N.H., 1976), p. 45.

145- "called strongly . . ." Homer St. Gaudens,
146 "City Folks in Cornish" in William H. Child, *History of the Town of Cornish, New Hampshire, 1763-1910* (Concord, 1910), vol. I, pp. 220-221.

147 "My dream . . ." Lawrance Thompson and R.H. Winnick, *Robert Frost: A Biography* (New York, 1981), p. 192.

148 "Poetry is . . ." Robert Frost, "The Constant Symbol," in *The Poems of Robert Frost* (New York, 1946—Modern Library Edition), p. xvi.

S·U·G·G·E·S·T·E·D R·E·A·D·I·N·G

Adams, John P., *Drowned Valley: The Piscataqua River Valley* (Hanover, N.H., 1976).

Anderson, Leon W., *To This Day: The 300 Years of the New Hampshire Legislature* (Canaan, N.H., 1981).

Armstrong, John Borden, *Factory Under the Elms: A History of Harrisville, New Hampshire 1774-1969* (Cambridge, Mass., 1969).

Bartlett, Irving H., *Daniel Webster* (New York, 1978).

Belcher, C. Francis, *Logging Railroads of the White Mountains* (Boston, 1980).

Belknap, Jeremy, *The History of New Hampshire,* 3 vols. (Boston, 1791-92, reprinted in various editions).

Bellush, Bernard, *He Walked Alone: A Biography of John Gilbert Winant* (The Hague, 1968).

Benes, P., editor, *New Englsnd Prospects* [The Dublin Seminar, 1980] (Boston, 1980).

Brown, William Robinson, *Our Forest Heritage: A History of Forestry and Recreation in New Hampshire* (Concord, N.H., 1956).

Clark, Charles E., *The Eastern Frontier: The Settlement of Northern New England, 1610-1763* (New York, 1970).

Cole, Donald B., *Jacksonian Democracy in New Hampshire, 1800-1851* (Cambridge, Mass., 1970).

Daniell, Jere R., *Colonial New Hampshire: A History* (New York, 1982).

———, *Experiment in Republicanism: New Hampshire and the American Revolution, 1741-1794* (Cambridge, Mass., 1970).

Frost, Robert, *The Poetry of Robert Frost;* Edward Connery Latham, ed. (New York, 1970).

Garvin, James L., *Historic Portsmouth: Early Photographs from the Collections of Strawbery Banke, Inc.* (Somersworth, N.H., 1974).

Gilmore, Robert C., editor, *New Hampshire Literature: A Sampler* (Hanover, N.H., 1982).

Guyol, Philip N., *Democracy Fights: A History of New Hampshire in World War II* (Hanover, N.H., 1951).

Hareven, Tamara K., and Randolph Langenbach, *Amoskeag: Life and Work in an American Factory City* (New York, 1978).

Haskell, John D. Jr., and T.D. Seymour Bassett, editors, *New Hampshire: A Bibliography of Its History* (Boston, 1979).

Hunt, Elmer Munson, *New Hampshire Town Names and Whence They Came* (Peterborough, N.H., 1970).

Kilbourne, Frederick W., *Chronicles of the White Mountains* (Boston, 1916).

Kinney, Charles B., *Church and State, The Struggle for Separation in New Hampshire* (New York, 1955).

Kirkland, Edward Chase, *Men, Cities and Transportation: A Study in New England History, 1820-1900* (Cambridge, Mass., 1948).

Malone, Joseph J., *Pine Trees and Politics: The Naval Stores and Forest Policy in Colonial New England, 1691-1775* (Seattle, 1964).

Mayo, Lawrence Shaw, *John Langdon of New Hampshire* (Concord, N.H., 1937; reprinted 1970).

———, *John Wentworth, Governor of New Hampshire, 1767-1775* (Cambridge, Mass., 1921).

McLoughlin, William G., *New England Dissent,* 2 vols. (Providence, 1971).

Morison, Elizabeth Forbes and Elting E., *New Hampshire: A Bicentennial History* (New York, 1976).

Morse, Stearns, editor, *Lucy Crawford's History of the White Mountains* (Hanover, N.H., 1966).

Nichols, Roy Franklin, *Franklin Pierce: Young Hickory of the Granite Hills* (Philadelphia, 1958; reprinted 1969).

Page, Elwin L., *Judicial Beginnings in New Hampshire, 1640 to 1700* (Concord, N.H., 1959).

Pierce, Neal R., *The New England States: People, Politics and Power in the Six New England States* (New York, 1976).

Richardson, Leon Burr, *William E. Chandler, Republican* (New York, 1940).

Russell, Howard S., *A Long Deep Furrow: Three Centuries of Farming in New England* (Hanover, N.H., 1976).

Sanborn, Frank B., *New Hampshire: An Epitome of Popular Government* (Boston, 1904).

Stackpole, Everett S., *History of New Hampshire,* 4 vols. (New York, 1916).

Squires, James Duane, *The Granite State of the United States,* 4 vols. (New York, 1956).

A Stern and Lovely Scene: A Visual History of the Isles of Shoals (Durham, N.H., 1978).

Tolles, Bryant F. Jr., *New Hampshire Architecture: An Illustrated Guide* (Hanover, N.H., 1979).

Turner, Lynn W., *William Plumer of New Hampshire, 1759-1850* (Chapel Hill, N.C., 1962).

Upton, Richard F., *Revolutionary New Hampshire* (Hanover, N.H., 1936, reprinted 1971).

VanDeventer, David E., *The Emergence of Provincial New Hampshire, 1623-1741* (Baltimore, 1976).

Wallace, R. Stuart, editor, *Historical New Hampshire* (Concord N.H., quarterly, 1944-present).

The White Mountains: Place and Perceptions (Durham, N.H., 1980).

Wilson, Harold Fisher, *The Hill Country of Northern New England: Its Social and Economic History, 1790-1930* (New York, 1936).

Yates, Elizabeth, *Amos Fortune, Free Man* (New York, 1950).

A·C·K·N·O·W·L·E·D·G·M·E·N·T·S

During the two years that we lived and labored with this book many people .helped us in countless ways, and many others simply had to put up with our preoccupation. Our son, Colin Lovell Jager, did both of these in extraordinary degree—and he may now see his youth as thoroughly blighted or brightened by this book. R. Stuart Wallace of the New Hampshire Historical Society was a constant ally, counselor, and inexhaustible source of information. There is far more of him in this book than appears on the surface, and we are more indebted to him than to all others combined. We were also assisted in various ways by other staff members of the New Hampshire Historical Society: William Copeley, Kathryn Grover, Donna-Belle Garvin, James Garvin, John Page. Quentin Blaine helped shape some of our thinking by the photos he found and the comments he made on them. Well-deserved thanks go also to Frances Gates of the New Hampshire State Library, who was very understanding of our delinquencies. We had excellent and cheerful typing assistance from Karen Corey, Lauri Pendleton, and Valerie Mitchell. Certain friends were helpful and supportive in very special ways: Madeleine and Hubie Williams, and Annette B. and G.W. Cottrell.

R.J.
G.J.

Nearly four hundred photographs and captions were sent to Windsor Publications for their consideration. These photographs covered the entire spectrum of the state geographically and historically. The selection published in this book was made by the publisher. While most of the institutions and individuals providing these photographs are credited in the captions, some special recognition is due.

Photographers Ernest Gould of Hooksett and Bill Finney of Hopkinton spent long hours doing most of the copy work, while Bill Finney provided color transparencies of items in the collections of the Historical Society and the Currier Gallery of Art. Quentin Blaine and Mary Lyn Ray were of invaluable assistance in locating photographs and in contacting museums, photo archives, government agencies, and individuals. In recognition of the New Hampshire Historical Society's non-profit status, a number of institutions and individuals waived use fees. Particular thanks go to the Department of Media Services at the University of New Hampshire, the Dartmouth College Archives, and the Society for the Protection of New Hampshire Forests, for use of several photographs in their collections.

R.S.W.
R.J.
G.J.

New Hampshire's busiest newspaper publishing company in the 1930s, the Union-Leader Publishing Company is pictured getting out the paper's 75th-anniversary edition in 1938. MVHC

I·N·D·E·X